Public Economy and Urban Governance in China

Series Editor

Baijun Wu, East China University of Science and Technology, Shanghai, China

This book series aims to promote the research in innovation-driven development of public economy and urban governance in China, and ultimately the social governance model based on collaboration, participation, and common interests enhancing the foresight, precision, and efficiency of urban governance. Focusing on the urban governance of Chinese top megacities, this book series combines economics and sociology and explores a new way to solve problems of social governance concerning urban public goods supply mechanism, innovative models of social governance, as well as critical urban development issues like public safety, infrastructure and environmental pollution.

Liwen Hou

The Integrated Service in Urban Community Governance

Evidence from Shanghai

ECUST PRESS

Springer

Liwen Hou
East China University of Science
and Technology (ECUST)
Shanghai, China

ISSN 2948-1872 ISSN 2948-1880 (electronic)
Public Economy and Urban Governance in China
ISBN 978-981-96-6774-1 ISBN 978-981-96-6775-8 (eBook)
https://doi.org/10.1007/978-981-96-6775-8

Jointly published with East China University of Science and Technology Press Co., Ltd.
The print edition is not for sale in The Mainland of China. Customers from The Mainland of China please order the print book from: East China University of Science and Technology Press Co., Ltd
ISBN of the Co-Publisher's edition: 978-7-5628-6234-5

The original submitted manuscript has been translated into English. The translation was done using artificial intelligence. A subsequent revision was performed by the author(s) to further refine the work and to ensure that the translation is appropriate concerning content and scientific correctness. It may, however, read stylistically different from a conventional translation.

English translation of "城市社区治理中整合性服务模式建构研究" published by East China University of Science and Technology Press, 2021

This Springer imprint is published by the registered company Springer Nature Singapore Pte Ltd.
The registered company address is: 152 Beach Road, #21-01/04 Gateway East, Singapore 189721, Singapore

Series Editor's Preface

After more than 40 years of rapid development, China's economic and social landscape has shown some new characteristics in recent years. In terms of economic growth and structural changes, a notable feature is the continuously rising contribution rate of the public sector to the nation's economic growth, especially following the 2008 global financial crisis. To counter economic recession and maintain high-speed economic growth and social stability, the Chinese government has continuously invested a large amount of funds in public infrastructure construction. Meanwhile, in the context of urbanization and population system reform, to fulfill the growing welfare demands of the populace, the government has increased its investment in public service areas such as education, health, safety, and social security. This has made the supply of economic and social public products an important part of the total social supply, and in some years, public product investment and supply have even become the decisive factors for marginal economic growth.

Regarding economic expansion and structural shifts, although the overall social form and power structure have changed little, social forces such as the new immigrant class, middle-income class, and private capital class, which are generated based on modern economic activities, are continuously increasing, and their influence on economic and social development is also growing. These emerging social forces are subtly changing China's social structure and profoundly affecting the social interest pattern. At the same time, in the process of people's production and lifestyle becoming increasingly market-oriented and socialized, the thoughts, social needs, and demands of grassroots people have also undergone significant changes. This has added challenges to how to accurately grasp people's demand preferences and behavior dynamics in social governance and posed challenges to how to effectively implement public services. Moreover, with changes in production methods and the expansion of economic activity space, people's social mobility has continuously increased, far exceeding the scope that administrative regions can govern. This has posed a huge challenge to the traditional administrative management system and the government's top-down governance mechanism, and has put forward new requirements for how to reconstruct grassroots social governance structures and governance mechanisms in modern political and economic construction.

The current socio-economic transformation and transition have led us to form many uncertain judgments about future development. However, if we disregard the factors of political system changes, we might gain a clearer understanding of the laws governing socio-economic evolution. Looking at the history of human social development, changes in technology, transformations in production methods, and market expansion have provided economic security for people to break free from the constraints of the natural environment and pursue a prosperous life. However, the development of the private product sector cannot ensure a fair and safe development environment for social members. In contrast, the development of the public product sector, whether under a planned economy or a market economy, provides social welfare improvements that are commonly shared by social members through the supply of public goods and services. Therefore, the functional characteristics and social roles of these two sectors require that, during a country's economic development, resources must be reasonably allocated between the private product sector and the public product sector; otherwise, it will lead to an imbalance in economic and social relations. Meanwhile, in many countries, as the private product sector develops, the increase in social wealth is accompanied by worsening environmental damage, wealth disparity, and social injustice. On the other hand, the development of the public product sector, while enhancing social welfare levels and security, has also led to issues such as resource misallocation, low supply efficiency, bureaucratic privilege, and administrative monopoly. Thus, people are constantly seeking suitable systems to constrain excessive competition, negative externalities, and the widening wealth gap in the private product sector, while also attempting to improve supply efficiency and social benefits in the development of the public product sector through institutional arrangements.

From the perspective of economic development trends in various countries, as the economy develops and residents' income levels rise, the role and status of the public product sector in socio-economic development are gradually increasing, with its asset scale and proportion in the total social supply continuously growing. This reflects a state and trend of continuous socio-economic development. Referring to the development patterns of the public product sector in various countries, the rapid development of China's public product sector after the reform and opening-up is also a reflection of economic and social changes and a trend of regularity. However, we must be clearly aware that in the rapidly changing socio-economic development environment, not only will the growth of the private product sector encounter the impacts of technological, market, and institutional changes, but the development of the public product sector will also face many new challenges.

First, the issue of how to reasonably and effectively allocate socio-economic resources between the private product sector and the public product sector. This requires a comprehensive understanding of the objective needs of the economy and society, and the use of effective mechanisms for resource allocation to achieve a balanced state of supply between the two sectors and the needs of individuals and society, thereby achieving a balance between moderate economic growth and social welfare enhancement, and essentially realizing the dual goals of economic efficiency and social equity in development.

Second, the issue of effectively supplying public products, especially based on China's national conditions, to theoretically and practically solve the problem of truly reflecting the preferences of the people's needs, adopting appropriate public choice methods, and allowing the public to participate in the selection and decision-making system of public product projects. This issue involves a country's public product supply system and mechanism, as well as factors such as politics, technology, market, and social culture, but the core issue lies in the arrangement of the political and economic system and the design of mechanisms. How to break away from the old model of an "omnipotent government," truly centering on the people, with the government doing what it should and refraining from what it shouldn't, delegating power to the grassroots, and creating space for the development of social organizations and their role in social governance. At the same time, the government must reform the existing government-led public product supply mechanism through institutional arrangements and political procedures, exploring a multi-subject cooperative public product supply mechanism suitable for China's national conditions.

Third, how to create a social governance pattern of co-construction, co-governance, and sharing, establishing a social governance community where "everyone is responsible, everyone fulfills their responsibilities, and everyone enjoys," and how to establish a social governance system under the leadership of the Communist Party of China that integrates the government, social organizations, and the public, and how to stimulate the enthusiasm of the public to participate in community governance, improving the capabilities and levels of community workers and participants in community affairs.

Fourth, how to innovate grassroots governance methods. This requires grassroots social governance to become the cornerstone and focus of national governance, becoming a fundamental link in the modernization of the national governance system and governance capacity. At the same time, the government must eliminate the "idle operation" phenomenon in grassroots governance through institutional arrangements and legal means, establish governance methods that adapt to multiple governance subjects, break free from the administrative predicament of community institutions and their affairs, explore the de-administration reform path of community grassroots organizations, and construct the operational system and mechanism of community grassroots organizations in resource mobilization, public service provision, and public affairs decision-making.

Fifth, how to innovate public product production and supply methods based on new technologies such as the Internet, big data, and artificial intelligence, improve public service efficiency, and enhance the performance of community grassroots governance. This requires continuously improving laws and regulations, allowing public service departments to legally use information technology to obtain the real needs of social members for public products and services, providing sufficient information for public decision-making, and providing technical means for the supervision and performance evaluation of public services, to achieve the goals of effective resource allocation and effective supply.

Based on the above reflections and understanding of China's long-term socio-economic development and structural changes, East China. The Institute for

Advanced Studies in Social Sciences at the University of Technology has established a dedicated research team with the aim of exploring issues related to public economy and social governance in China's economic and social development. The goal is to conduct detailed observations and localized analyses of China's socio-economic development from the grassroots and microeconomic levels within the grand framework of social and economic transformation. Over the years, a group of young faculty members specializing in public economics, sociology, and public management at East China University of Science and Technology have focused on public economy and grassroots governance in urban communities, undertaking numerous international collaborations and national fund projects. Their research generally revolves around three main themes: first, the basic theories of public product sector development and China's practices, particularly through interdisciplinary research and the integration of multiple research paradigms, to explore the structural relationships and internal mechanisms of public economy and social governance during social development; second, the new methods and forms of public economy and social governance under new technological conditions such as the internet, big data, and artificial intelligence; third, conducting social surveys, field experiments, and empirical analyses in areas like public infrastructure, public services, and community grassroots governance, aiming to discover some beneficial practices with Chinese characteristics to review and revise classical theoretical viewpoints and expand the scope of theoretical research. This series is a preliminary summary of our previous research work, and each volume roughly reflects these research themes.

The content of this series mainly involves the fields of public economy, social governance, and social policy. Regardless of the discipline, the research is mostly based on the theories of public economics and public management, exploring scientific issues in public economy and social governance in an interdisciplinary manner; for policy issues, we also study them from different disciplinary perspectives. There are five books in the series that can be classified under the field of public economy. Among them, "Research on the Effective Supply Mechanism of Urban Public Products" reviews the theories and research literature on public product supply and explores the mechanisms and reform gains and losses of public product supply in China, with a focus on empirical analysis of investment, financing, production, and distribution in urban public infrastructure and public service fields. "Research on Urban Infrastructure and Economic Development" summarizes the achievements and challenges in infrastructure construction in China over the past 70 years, revealing the internal mechanisms of infrastructure affecting regional economic development from theoretical perspectives such as fiscal decentralization and comparative institutional analysis; it uses econometric analysis to explore the impact of China's infrastructure construction on market integration, open development, and livelihood improvement, proposing theories and implementation paths for innovation in infrastructure supply models from a political economy perspective. "Research on the Effective Supply Mechanism and Path of Environmental Public Goods" studies the supply mechanisms of various environmental public goods, focusing on the functions and behavior patterns of the less-attended household sector in environmental governance; it considers the household sector as the supply subject, incorporates intergenerational factors into the analytical framework, and constructs an effective supply theoretical model of environmental public goods based on three value assessment methods. "Research on the Spatial Layout Characteristics and Comprehensive Capability Evaluation of Urban Public Services" uses big data technology to comprehensively analyze the development process, resource scale, spatial layout, and service capability of urban public services, objectively analyzing the factors affecting urban public services, and proposing strategies to optimize urban public services. Interestingly, "Research on the Multi-Cooperative Governance of Urban Sharing Platforms" takes the sharing economy as the research object, exploring the widely existing issue of the public nature of private products. This book comprehensively reviews the development models, governance experiences, and mechanism roles of urban sharing platforms domestically and internationally, proposing the concept of multi-cooperative governance of sharing platforms with self-governance priority, government supervision, and social assistance. This research breaks through the traditional limitations of urban public product supply, conducting pioneering research on the revolutionary changes in the public consumption and production methods of private products in the new technological environment. Overall, these works take major urban public goods and public services such as infrastructure, environmental protection, and pollution governance as research objects, analyzing the characteristics and internal operational mechanisms of urban public product supply in China, and proposing institutional reform plans and policy recommendations for the effective supply of public products.

The series includes five books that study urban social governance issues. "Research on Urban Migration and Public Governance" examines urban governance in the context of urbanization, studying how to transform migration control into migration services to enhance migration governance levels and facilitate the integration of migrants into cities. "Research on Urban Public Safety Risk Prevention and Control System" addresses the frequent occurrence of urban public safety incidents. The sources and types of urban public safety issues were analyzed, and on the basis of a deep analysis of the causes of urban safety risks, the intrinsic mechanisms for effective safety risk prevention and control were explored, leading to the construction of an urban safety risk prevention and control system. "Research on the Social Mechanism of Resolving Urban Grassroots Conflicts and Disputes" takes the rapidly developing people's mediation organizations in recent years as an example, analyzing the real needs, functional positioning, organizational network, operational mechanisms, and development logic of social forces represented by them in resolving urban grassroots conflicts and disputes, to explore the social governance mechanism of a "Chinese-style risk society." "Research on the Construction of Integrated Service Models in Urban Community Governance" takes the grassroots governance practice in Shanghai communities as an example, examining the development status of grassroots social governance from various perspectives such as street system reform, government service procurement, community social organization development, and social forces' participation in social governance and community worker team building. It deeply reveals new problems in grassroots social governance, analyzes deep-seated social and structural reasons, and on this basis, explores the governance elements, innovative processes, and key links of modern grassroots social governance, proposing new ideas for constructing a grassroots social governance system and practical model in mega-cities. "Research on the Development and Operation of Urban Community Foundations in China" takes urban community foundations as the research object, conducting empirical analysis on the growth environment, localization characteristics, governance structure, and functional roles of community foundations under the administrative-driven logic, to explore the development path and operational mechanism of grassroots social organizations under China's political system.

At the time of the publication of this series, China is experiencing the novel coronavirus pneumonia epidemic. In less than 20 years since the "atypical" epidemic, the outbreak of this massive global public health disaster once again proves the importance of respecting the laws of nature, while also reminding us to constantly reflect on the effectiveness of public health system and mechanism reforms, the drawbacks of the current social governance system, and the deviations in public policy implementation. It is gratifying that the epidemic has been well controlled in our country, especially with anti-epidemic measures being strictly implemented nationwide, fully demonstrating the mobilization and response capabilities of community grassroots organizations in public events, indicating the importance of establishing a multi-supply mechanism based on social organizations and public participation in the reform of the social governance system, and once again proving the importance of establishing an effective public product supply system in the process of building a modernized strong country.

The publication of this series has been supported by the National Publishing Fund and the "University Service to National Major Strategy Publishing Project" of the Shanghai Municipal Education Commission. We are grateful for the generous support of the East China University of Science and Technology Press for making this high-quality publication possible! Some of the works in the series are the results of the major project "Research on the Urban Public Product Supply Mechanism" under the Shanghai Municipal Education Commission's Scientific Research Innovation Plan, hereby acknowledged, and we thank the funding departments!

May 2020 Baijun Wu

Preface

The spatial and temporal juxtaposition of the shift in the focus of social governance and community governance innovation is key to advancing and realizing the modernization of social governance. The practice of community governance in Shanghai is a practice in history. With the in-depth advancement of a new round of reforms, Shanghai's community governance and social construction have achieved positive results in some key areas and critical links, and have reached a broad consensus on corresponding methods and measures, forming some typical practices and experiences, accumulating certain universal experiences for exploring the governance of mega-city communities. At the same time, urban community governance also faces many problems, such as further streamlining of systems and mechanisms, linkage and coordination of multiple subjects, and further clarification of the functional roles of social organizations, as well as policy matching and implementation issues in the execution of the Shanghai Municipal Party Committee's "No. 1 Project"; unexpected consequences due to insufficient understanding of the development trends and laws of social governance; overemphasis on "innovation" leading to the replacement of innovation and service goals, the non-replicability and diffusion of innovative results and practices, and the production of a large number of "demonstrative governance" results and "growth without development" governance involution phenomena; etc. Particularly, the "fragmentation" logic inherent in refined governance has a deconstructive effect on the integrity and synergy of community governance, which needs to be given sufficient attention and fully researched.

In the new period, new stage, and new reform, there is an urgent need to review, sort out, and integrate the community governance experience in Shanghai since 2014, and on this basis, to observe, plan, and promote new development. Therefore, this book takes the new round of grassroots community governance reform in Shanghai since 2014 as an example, systematically analyzing the specific situation, main characteristics, and overall effects of the promotion and implementation of the "1 + 6" documents in Shanghai. On this basis, a comprehensive assessment of the "Shanghai Model" of community governance is conducted, focusing on key areas such as street system reform, government service procurement, community social organization development, grid management and block openness, social forces' participation in social governance, and the construction of community worker teams. This assessment deeply reveals the structural and social reasons behind these new situations and problems, and subsequently addresses grassroots issues. In the study of constructing an integrated service model for urban community governance, governance elements, innovative processes, key links, and diverse practices emerging in the social field are systematically and integratively reconstructed with a "community-centered, community-method" approach. This community-based integrated service model aims to explore and form a practical framework and operational model system for grassroots social governance in mega-cities, targeting the "Five Centers," global cities, and global science and innovation centers, thereby promoting the modernization of Shanghai's grassroots social governance system and governance capabilities.

In fact, the proposal of integrated services for urban community governance is based on correcting the previous fragmentation, individualization, and atomization phenomena in community governance. However, it is not a simple aggregation of multiple subjects, strategic logic, and experiential practices within the community field. Instead, it is a comprehensive architecture based on new service concepts, logic, and service processes, changing previous service strategies and methods. It is a governance reconstruction involving all elements, processes, and fields. Integrated services for urban community governance focus on the contextualization of community governance, advocating a cooperative governance relationship and an integrated team working method, promoting an empowerment service based on capability or community. This service model emphasizes the dynamic coupling and matching linkage of service supply, service integration, demand structure, and governance situations, effectively integrating governance subjects, strategies, and innovative elements in the process of serving the community.

Under the perspective of integrated governance, grassroots community governance mainly includes two dimensions. The first is the construction of a community-based integrated service model. Community-based is a value concept, as well as a methodology and ontology in a holistic sense. Community-based means that "community" should become the basic unit and starting point for grassroots social governance and services, where different subjects engage in multi-party interaction and consultation centered on public issues and public affairs of the community. Based on different practical explorations in various places, the theoretical paradigm, practical advancement, methodological techniques, service foundation, and action strategies of community governance should be integrated and connected in terms of subjects, mechanisms, resources, methods, logic, and effects, achieving unified model integration, process integration, and element integration. The second is the practical advancement of integrated community governance services. It is necessary to consolidate the party's organizational strength, integrate various theoretical paradigms, unite multiple subjects, adopt various methods, break professional boundaries, and reconstruct service processes to achieve effective integration of the party's grassroots social governance and the construction of a co-building, co-governing, and co-sharing grassroots social governance pattern.

In summary, the construction of an integrated service model for urban communities is key to achieving a social governance community. It is essential to examine grassroots social governance within the context of national governance modernization. The construction of a governance community is not a government action, nor is it purely a civil activity, but a process of joint participation and democratic consultation by various community subjects and social forces. The formation process of governance structures among different subjects, elements, and links in the community field requires a series of vertical and horizontal constructions and linkages of systems and mechanisms, enabling different subjects in community governance to collaborate and form a synergy, thereby advancing the construction of a community governance community.

Shanghai, China
February 2020

Liwen Hou

Contents

Chapter 1
Introduction

1.1 Research Background

With the establishment of the market economy system, the grassroots social management system, which was primarily based on the unit system and supplemented by the street-residence system, gradually disintegrated. A community-based grassroots social management system, compatible with the market economy system, emerged. To address the potential social atomization and national integration difficulties following the disintegration of the "total society," the state attempted to rebuild its "new channels" for connecting residents and linking the grassroots. This process is the process of building the state's penetration capacity and is also the process of the continuous downward shift of the focus of social governance. Consequently, communities gradually moved to the forefront of grassroots social governance, occupying a foundational position in social governance innovation, becoming the background field for the multi-subjects of grassroots governance to play their roles, and an important component of the "new channels," playing a significant role in social integration. At the same time, constrained by the inertia of the unit system, initial conditions, and the orientation of building control order, communities evolved into highly administrative organizations in grassroots social management practice, becoming the second unit or unit second after the unit, with the government developing communities into "self-management, self-education, The initial intention of a "self-service, self-supervision" community of life is contrary. To correct the trend of community administration and address the longstanding issues of "excessive administrative integration and insufficient community autonomy capacity" that trouble the construction of grassroots social order, various regions are actively exploring internal governance structure innovation and system mechanism reorganization under the large framework of innovative social governance. Therefore, "innovating social governance and strengthening grassroots construction" has opened a new phase of community governance and service innovation in Shanghai.

L. Hou, *The Integrated Service in Urban Community Governance*, Public Economy and Urban Governance in China, https://doi.org/10.1007/978-981-96-6775-8_1

In fact, the continuous shift of the focus of social governance downward is a historical legacy. The Sixth Plenary Session of the 16th Central Committee of the Communist Party of China proposed the goal of "building a harmonious society," marking the state's increasing emphasis on social order and stability, and the importance of creating a stable environment for social development. Since the 17th National Congress of the Communist Party of China, the concept of "innovating social management" has been proposed, emphasizing the transformation of management concepts and methods to achieve flexible social management. The Third Plenary Session of the 18th Central Committee of the Communist Party of China further proposed important concepts such as "innovating the social governance system" and "strengthening the separation of government and society." The Fourth, Fifth, and Sixth Plenary Sessions of the 18th Central Committee respectively emphasized major measures such as "governing the country according to law," "a social governance pattern of co-construction and sharing by all," and "comprehensively and strictly governing the Party." The 19th National Congress of the Communist Party of China clearly proposed the scientific judgment that "socialism with Chinese characteristics has entered a new era, and the principal contradiction in our society has evolved into the contradiction between unbalanced and inadequate development and the people's ever-growing needs for a better life," advocating for a transformation in development with "people-centered development thinking." Whether it is resolving the principal contradiction or "people-centered" development, the focus is on grassroots social governance and service innovation. Therefore, the 19th National Congress advocated continuing to "build a social governance pattern of co-construction, co-governance, and sharing," to "strengthen the construction of social governance systems, improve the social governance system led by the Party committee, with government responsibility, social coordination, public participation, and legal protection, and enhance the socialization, legalization, intelligence, and specialization of social governance," and to further "strengthen the construction of community governance systems, promote the shift of the focus of social governance to the grassroots, play the role of social organizations, and achieve positive interaction between government governance, social regulation, and residents' autonomy." Thus, grassroots community governance and service innovation, as the key to building a "new channel," will continue to be the convergence point for macro social system reform, mesosocial service delivery, and the integration of micro residents' sense of gain and happiness.

As the forefront of China's reform and opening up, Shanghai's enhancement of its grassroots governance system and the comprehensive modernization of its governance capabilities is a fundamental and overall task related to its future development. In recent years, in alignment with the central strategic deployment and Shanghai's social governance requirements, particularly under the vigorous promotion of the "No. 1 Project" of the Shanghai Municipal Committee of the Communist Party of China (hereinafter referred to as "Shanghai Municipal Committee") in 2014—"innovating social governance and strengthening grassroots construction," Shanghai has endeavored to establish a positive interactive pattern led by the Party committee, with government responsibility, social coordination, public participation, and legal protection, committed to serving the public, oriented by the needs of people's livelihoods, and establishing a multi-level community public service system to meet the diverse service needs of the masses. Shanghai adheres to reform and opening up, concept innovation, and to adapt to new trends in social governance and new requirements for government function transformation, continuously and actively exploring new models of grassroots community co-consultation and autonomy, cultivating and developing a large number of social autonomy organizations, continuously expanding the social worker team, and actively guiding various social forces to participate in social governance innovation in an orderly and standardized manner. Shanghai insists on the combination of focus sinking, resource sinking, and service sinking, further strengthening the grassroots and foundational role of streets, towns, and residential (village) areas in social governance, to better provide precise and effective services to the masses, continuously meeting the people's ever-growing needs for a better life. Following a new round of profound reforms, Shanghai's community governance and social construction have achieved positive results in some key areas and critical links, and have reached a broad consensus on corresponding methods and measures, forming some typical practices and experiences, accumulating certain universal experiences for exploring social governance in mega-cities. Shanghai's community governance practice has entered a new developmental stage—refinement of community governance. At the same time, Shanghai's community governance also faces further streamlining of systems and mechanisms, linkage and coordination of multiple subjects, and further clarification of the functional roles of social organizations, as part of the "No. 1 Project." Implementation issues in policy matching and execution; there are unforeseen consequences due to insufficient understanding of the trends and patterns in social governance development; there is an overemphasis on "innovation," leading to the substitution of innovation and service goals, the non-replicability and diffusion of innovative results and practices, resulting in a large amount of "demonstrative governance" outcomes and the phenomenon of "growth without development" governance involution. Particularly, the deconstructive effect of the "fragmentation" logic inherent in refined governance on the integrity and synergy of community governance requires sufficient attention and thorough research. In the new era, new stage, and new reforms, there is an urgent need to review, sort out, and integrate the community governance experiences in Shanghai since 2014, and on this basis, to observe, plan, and promote new developments. From this perspective, community governance is continuously constructed and reconstructed in the process of the social governance focus shifting downward. This construction and reconstruction inevitably carry the traces of "top-down" state power building and penetration; whereas community governance or community service itself is a process of community-based self-governance and service oriented by residents' needs, with a clear "bottom-up" and internal perspective as society continuously develops and grows. In the context of China, this process unfolds against the backdrop of the "downward shift of social governance focus," which means that community governance is a local narrative arising from this structural background. The structure of its narrative, governance discourse, development orientation, and interactive practices are all behavioral manifestations and representations shaped by this structure, which presupposes that the inherent tension in urban community governance will lead to a series of structural dilemmas in reform and innovation. Thus, ideally, good community governance should achieve the coordination and balance between the downward shift of governance focus and the development of social forces, i.e., the coordination of stock reform and incremental development. This is the ontological logical premise that needs to be clarified for the deep advancement and innovative exploration of urban grassroots social governance. In reality, community governance is a practical mapping and replicative performance of social governance in the community field. It is necessary to recognize and consider urban community governance within the process of social governance modernization. On one hand, the modernization of social governance is a complex and long-term process that encompasses the modernization of governance systems and governance capabilities. The modernization of community governance is also inevitably an integrative advancement process of continuously enhancing and coupling institutional mechanisms, main logic, carrier platforms, and capabilities modernization and specialization. Therefore, our understanding of urban community governance should adhere to a systematic and integrative thinking. This is the epistemological premise for the deep advancement and innovative exploration of urban grassroots social governance. On the other hand, the process of social construction is a continuous exploration and trial-and-error pilot process—an "exploratory" process of "crossing the river by feeling the stones." In this, different fields, diverse methods, and innovative practices coexist, couple, and converge in a practical process. Similarly, community governance innovation is also a process of exploration, experimentation, and replicative promotion. The practices and experiences from different times, spaces, regions, and stages constitute the "innovation points" in the process of urban community governance, and these "innovation points" unfold around different positions in the community governance chain and demand structure, eventually converging into "innovation lines," which, through replication, expansion, and promotion, can undoubtedly converge and link into the "innovation surface" and "innovation body" of community governance, thereby unfolding the "complete map" of urban social governance. This constitutes the methodological logic for the deep advancement and innovative exploration of urban grassroots social governance. Thus, this book, based on a systematic analysis of the specific situation, main characteristics, and overall effects of the implementation of the Shanghai "1 + 6" documents, comprehensively assesses the new situations and problems encountered in key areas such as street system reform, government service procurement, community social organization development, residents' committee (hereinafter referred to as "neighborhood committee") reform, social forces' participation in social governance, and community worker team building. It deeply reveals the structural and social reasons leading to these new situations and problems, and on this basis, conducts a systematic and integrative study of governance elements, innovation processes, key links, and diverse practices emerging in the grassroots social field, exploring the construction of a practical framework and operational model system for mega-city grassroots social governance oriented towards the "five centers," global city, and global science and technology innovation center, thereby promoting the modernization of Shanghai's grassroots social governance system and governance capabilities.

1.2 Research Significance

Firstly, forming the "Shanghai Model 3.0" of community governance. This helps to distill the new model of community governance in Shanghai since the new era. Through the experience and practical wisdom of community governance in Shanghai since the new era… Sort and summarize, place it within the context of national governance modernization for examination, and attempt to form a set of community governance and service innovation models with characteristics of the new era under the unified concept of "innovating social governance and strengthening grassroots construction." This will further endow the "Shanghai model" of community governance with new era connotations and innovative elements, providing a reference for refined governance in mega-city communities.

Second, reflect the Chinese characteristics of community governance—bring the political party into it. This helps summarize the service-oriented governance logic of grassroots party committees and governments. By collecting and analyzing a series of practical cases, one can extract the practical wisdom and action strategies of grassroots party committees and governments in innovating community governance and enhancing people's well-being. This will further reflect on how the party's leading and integrating functions can be feasible and actionable in the new era.

Third, it helps expand the new understanding of the new type of political-social and party-social relationships in residential (village) areas. Focusing on residents' bottom-up community autonomy and participation in community public affairs helps further analyze the correlation between residents' daily life (sense of participation, identity, gain, happiness, etc.) and current grassroots governance, and construct a greater connection between local governments and grassroots people. Fourth, it helps promote the development of refined grassroots social governance. Based on practical and comparative perspectives, combined with domestic and international community governance experiences and the practical experiences of Shanghai community governance, it is possible to further explore and optimize the structural dilemmas and emergent problems in the new round of grassroots social governance, deepen grassroots social governance innovation, and refine a new community-based integrated service model to promote the modernization process of grassroots social governance systems and capabilities.

1.3 Innovations

Firstly, this book focuses on "integration" and "comparison." Through systematic comparison and integration analysis of contextualized community governance practices and the innovation advancement paths and governance experiences of grassroots social governance, it helps overcome the simplification of existing perspectives, offering an innovative research perspective.

Secondly, based on empirical research on the practical experiences of Shanghai's new round of community governance, this book identifies and analyzes the differences in community governance innovation among different types of communities and the structural dilemmas they face. On this basis, it proposes constructing community-based integrated service practices, helping to compensate for the partiality of previous strategies, offering innovative research strategies. Research on the construction of integrated service models in urban community governance.

Thirdly, this book attempts to construct a theory and research methodology of community sociology by "centering on the community and using the community as a method." The book takes the community as the "center," focusing on the subject interactions, relational practices, and innovative approaches existing in the "community domain," and analyzes "process events" to clarify the expansion and changes of the "grassroots" connotation in the shift of social governance focus. Using the community as a "method" means using the "community" as a lens to observe and analyze political-social, party-social, and state-society relationships, aiming to construct the concept of the "community" as a "whole" from a local perspective and, on this basis, refine the "community-based integrated service model."

1.4 Research Approach and Structure

1.4.1 Research Approach

This book takes "integrated governance" as a theoretical perspective, reflecting on the current grassroots social governance's practical dilemmas and deep-rooted causes through historical tracing and current situation investigation of Shanghai's community governance and empirical research on the current state of grassroots community governance. On this basis, it constructs a community-based integrated service model to optimize and enhance grassroots social governance capabilities. The writing follows a research approach of "reflection—construction—empirical—reflection again" and a research method that unifies "history and logic."

Firstly, basic research. This book will systematically review and sort out relevant domestic and international literature, especially reflecting on representative cases and important research results on topics such as community party building, community governance, and community autonomy, providing a research foundation and possible directions for practical exploration.

Secondly, theoretical research. This book will sort out the theoretical system of grassroots governance innovation by combining existing theoretical orientations and construct a new theoretical framework and practical system with analytical and explanatory power, based on the specific historical, cultural, social, and economic foundations of Shanghai community governance.

Thirdly, empirical research. On one hand, longitudinal comb. Through in-depth sorting of typical daily governance practices in urban and rural communities in Shanghai, systematically examine the grassroots governance practices conducted in recent years. The historical review and empirical analysis depict the historical map of community governance and service innovation in Shanghai. On the other hand, a horizontal comparison is made. Taking the grassroots community autonomy of different community types in various districts of Shanghai as the main line, the study analyzes the conceptual foundation, practical motivation, action system, path differences, and social effects of community governance innovation in Shanghai, constructing a realistic map of community governance types. At the same time, it deeply analyzes a series of structural dilemmas faced in governance innovation. Finally, the study of countermeasures. Based on the empirical research of the new round of community governance innovation practice in Shanghai, it elevates and reflects theoretically. On one hand, it extracts the typicality of Shanghai's new round of community governance and service innovation from a theoretical perspective, providing experiential reference and policy inspiration for broader community governance innovation. On the other hand, it attempts to break through the structural dilemmas faced in grassroots community governance by integrating Shanghai's actual conditions, trying to construct an integrated community service promotion model to advance the modernization process of grassroots governance systems and capabilities.

1.4.2 Research Methods

This book mainly adopts qualitative research as the methodological foundation, specifically using participatory observation, case interviews, focus group interviews, related service project text materials, typical case collection and tracking, and other methods to collect first-hand empirical data, and analyzes the data using relevant qualitative research analysis methods. Firstly, through the collection of policy documents, methods, and opinions from the social work committees, civil affairs bureaus, street and town autonomy offices, and community party building, community autonomy, community service, community management, and community safety departments in various districts of Shanghai, as well as interviews with relevant responsible persons, it gathers experience cases, typical practices, and practical dilemmas of community governance and service innovation, to obtain an overall overview of community services. Secondly, focus group interviews are conducted with the diverse subjects, social organizations, brand projects, and their team members involved in the supply of social services in urban and rural communities in Shanghai's streets and towns, focusing on understanding the policy foundation, action practice, experience accumulation, and existing dilemmas of social organizations and community residents participating in community governance, to extract specific service innovation logic and action strategies. Thirdly, relying on and using projects such as Shanghai's "Doorstep" services, government-purchased services, and community autonomy funds as entry points, "thematic research" is conducted on government-purchased service projects in grassroots social governance, thereby achieving an integrated analysis of "structural systems" and "process events." Fourthly, it focuses on collecting some of the challenges encountered in urban and rural community governance, using multi-subject collaboration and consultation, and joint governance to solve related community public issues as typical cases, analyzing the interactive cooperation mechanism of grassroots multi-subjects.

1.4.3 Research Structure

The chapters of this book will unfold around the "point, line, surface" and "body" of community governance innovation, adhering to systematic and holistic thinking, focusing on the structural tensions existing in urban community governance innovation and their manifestations in different innovation points, and discussing based on the innovative practices of urban community governance in Shanghai. Chapter 1 Introduction. This chapter mainly explains the research background and writing logic. Chapter 2 Comparison of Concepts and Models Related to Grassroots Social Governance. It systematically sorts out the basic concepts of urban community governance, ideal types, and the relationship between the state and society, forming the literature foundation and starting point of this research. Chapter 3 Theoretical Foundation and Analytical Perspective. It focuses on the theoretical origins and evolution of "governance," social work and grassroots social governance, and cooperative governance, and constructs the content analysis framework of this book based on this. Chapter 4 Shanghai Model: Community-Based Service Integration. It reviews and deeply describes the logical starting point, phase division, in-depth exploration, and practical logic of the "Shanghai Model" of grassroots social governance through historical sociology. Chapter 5 The Downward Shift of Social Governance Focus and Service Integration Practice. Using the innovative practice of Shanghai's "Doorstep" services as an example, it analyzes the service integration exploration and existing governance tensions in the new round of reform of grassroots social governance in Shanghai. Chapter 6 Integration Practice of Social Organizations Participating in Grassroots Governance. It conducts a comprehensive analysis of how social organizations participate in grassroots social governance, focusing on the governance functions, innovative practices, new social organizations, and the participation of social organization systems in community governance. Chapter 7 Grid Management and Open Blocks: Two Paradigms of Governance Integration. It focuses on the grid management in grassroots social governance. Using the two practical models of grid management and the opening of closed communities as analytical approaches, this text examines the innovative logic, governance functions, and unintended outcomes of both. Chapter 8 focuses on project-based and technological governance: the integration challenges and structural dilemmas in grassroots social governance. It centers on the "structural dilemmas" in community governance reform, discussing issues such as the project-based system in grassroots social governance, the suspended development of social organizations, the identity tension of community workers, and the dual segmentation phenomenon in urban and rural governance. Chapter 9, Governance Community: Constructing a Community-Based Integrated Service Model, serves as the concluding chapter. It addresses the practical difficulties in grassroots social governance and the construction of a community-based integrated social governance service model, responding to the research questions posed at the beginning and providing a positive outlook and construction for the future development direction of urban community governance.

Chapter 2
Concepts and Model Comparisons Related to Grassroots Social Governance

This book centrally examines community governance and service innovation, necessitating a comprehension of the attributes of conventional community governance paradigms as identified through a literature review. What governance models have emerged in the community governance process? How is grassroots society unfolding and advancing governance innovation? What are the dominant analytical paradigms for grassroots social governance? This chapter will systematically review and organize the literature from the following aspects: first, sorting out core concepts and issues such as grassroots, grassroots construction, community, and community governance; second, systematically reviewing and reflecting on research on grassroots social governance from the perspectives of state and society analysis; third, reviewing the reform and improvement of community systems and the presentation and evolution of classic models of urban community grassroots social governance innovation; fourth, providing an overall review of research on social organization participation in community governance, "three-society linkage," and government procurement of services; fifth, providing an overall evaluation of recent research directions and the aforementioned research status to form a comprehensive and systematic literature framework for this book.

L. Hou, *The Integrated Service in Urban Community Governance*, Public Economy and Urban Governance in China, https://doi.org/10.1007/978-981-96-6775-8_2

2.1 Defining Core Concepts Related to Grassroots, Grassroots Construction, and Community

2.1.1 The Multiple Imaginations of "Grassroots" and the Connotations of Grassroots Construction[1]

In the past, the concept of "grassroots" has been constructed differently in discourse depending on different subjects or contexts. Grassroots, as an officially constructed institutional field, exists in official documents and political ecology, and as an academic concept, it is also concretized in people's minds as a series of entities. This can lead to confusion in policy texts and ambiguity in theoretical research, presenting multiple imaginations of "grassroots." First, the political imagination of grassroots, where grassroots = township government. Grassroots is seen as the location of township governments, and at the same time, residents' (village) committees are also seen as the lowest end of the administrative system, becoming the "entity" of grassroots in the political context. Second, the cultural imagination of grassroots, where grassroots = grassroots or civil society. As a spiritual pursuit and value belief, grassroots discourse practice is permeated with the breath of grassroots and the lower class, forming a conceptual category that may correspond to the state. Third, the social imagination of grassroots. This is the imagination of "grassroots" from the perspective of ordinary people, where grassroots has great elasticity and extensibility, becoming a category with great flexibility, opposite to the top level.

From the further extension of the above three grassroots imaginations, it is not difficult to see, first, in the political imagination of grassroots, grassroots equals township government, so from this perspective, grassroots construction is the construction of grassroots power, the continuous penetration and expansion of state power into society, and the micro-logical and action process of state power construction. Second, in the cultural imagination of grassroots, grassroots equals grassroots, so in this sense, grassroots construction is the process of protecting and constructing grassroots culture, focusing on recording and narrating local culture, reshaping people's collective memory of "rural society," and reflecting on the value of the "familiar society" community in an era of diverse values. Third, in the social imagination of grassroots, grassroots equals the imagined entity in people's minds, so in this sense, grassroots construction is the continuous reconstruction and construction of people's imagined space, the process of social production and reproduction. This indicates that "grassroots" itself is still a chaotic and ambiguous concept, making it difficult to clearly define what grassroots construction is and what it should be.

The "Modern Chinese Dictionary" defines "grassroots" as "the lowest level in various organizations, which has the most direct contact with the masses." This definition highlights the main characteristics of the grassroots, which is among the masses and at the lowest level of the social hierarchy. In other words, the grassroots is

[1] Some content has been published in the "Hebei Academic Journal," 2015, Issue 4.

not only at the "lower level" of the organizational hierarchy but also at the "foundation" of the entire society, existing as a tangible entity. In the current policy discourse system, there are expressions such as "grassroots society," "grassroots construction," and "grassroots government." This cluster of concepts reflects the grassroots society as the object of national governance, grassroots construction as the building and consolidation of national power, and grassroots government as an important executive body. This discourse construction clearly positions the "grassroots" as the core field for the state to manage or govern society.

How can we further enrich the connotation of "grassroots"? How can we move beyond the single administrative logic of the "grassroots" imagination? The author believes that the connotation of grassroots should be understood from two dimensions: relational and substantive. In the relational dimension, it reflects the non-governmental singularity in grassroots construction, involving the presence of the party, government, social organizations, and other diverse entities, which means that they inevitably engage in complex power interactions in the grassroots field. In the substantive dimension, besides reflecting the construction and consolidation of power, it is more important to promote the stability of grassroots social order. Therefore, the relational dimension is an important mechanism for achieving the substantive dimension.

In past grassroots construction, there often appeared phenomena of "putting the cart before the horse" in the aforementioned relationships. Despite the government's large-scale investment in financial, human, and material resources, the results in community construction were minimal. Fundamentally, this is because the traditional social system blurs the relationship between the government and society, often leading to government "overstepping," "misplacement," and social forces "absent" or "without position," further hindering the effectiveness of community construction. Therefore, future "grassroots construction" should further clarify the boundaries between the government, market, and society, incorporating social organizations into the main structure and target system of grassroots construction. At the same time, the legal attributes and social functions of community committees should be redefined, further enhancing the capabilities of community workers at the existing community committee level, and leading community workers and volunteer teams through professional social workers to cultivate the new force of grassroots community construction. In the author's view, the past habit of understanding "grassroots" as the party organization system at the levels of townships, sub-district offices, and community committees has led to "grassroots construction" simply becoming the strengthening of grassroots power construction and consolidating the integration ability and social foundation of party organizations at the grassroots level. This understanding has obvious shortcomings in the current context of service-oriented government and service party construction.

The author believes that the connotation and extension of "grassroots" need to be re-examined. In terms of connotation, "grassroots construction" is not only about strengthening grassroots power construction and maintaining social stability but more importantly, it is about enhancing people's well-being, taking the happiness level, quality of life, and other soft indicators of the community masses as the ultimate attribution of grassroots construction. In terms of extension, besides local governments (townships, streets) and community committees, social organizations that have been active and providing services in the community in recent years should also be included, forming a diverse subject for understanding "grassroots." Therefore, "grassroots construction" is essentially the construction process of the grassroots "society," a governance concept and practice based on people and the improvement of people's well-being. This expands people's imagination of "grassroots" and enriches the diversity of innovative practices in grassroots community governance. Research on the construction of integrated service models in urban community governance.

2.1.2 The Chinese-Style Application and Evolution of the "Community"

Connotation The concept of "community" entered the academic field starting with the publication of "Gemeinschaft und Gesellschaft" by the famous German sociologist Ferdinand Tönnies in 1887. Tönnies' "Gemeinschaft" aims to emphasize the intimate relationships and common spiritual consciousness formed between people, as well as the sense of belonging and identity to "Gemeinschaft." It is evident that Tönnies believed "Gemeinschaft" includes not only regional communities but also kinship and spiritual communities, with a shared cultural consciousness among people as its essence. This can be seen as the origin of the "community."

After World War I, American sociologist Parker applied Tönnies' concepts... The introduction of Tönnies' "Gemeinschaft und Gesellschaft" to the United States, translated as "Community and Society," facilitated the shift in the meaning of "Gemeinschaft" from a sense of community to that of a neighborhood. The concept of "community" was introduced to China from the United States in the 1930s, with scholars like Wu Wenzao and Fei Xiaotong making significant contributions to its introduction and definition. In his book "On the Sinicization of Sociology," Wu Wenzao translated "Community and Society" as "社区与社会" (Community and Society). In his view, society is an abstract concept describing collective life, encompassing all complex social relationships, while "community" is a concrete representation of people's actual lives within a region, characterized by observability and a specific material foundation. He defined the concept of "community" primarily through three elements: population, region, and people's lifestyle and culture. Influenced by Wu Wenzao and other scholars, Fei Xiaotong translated Park's "Community" as "社区" (community), thus beginning the spread of this academic concept in China, which developed into the core term of the "community school" in Chinese sociology. In fact, this "community" is a "holistic" concept.[2] Firstly, community is a research method, specifically referring to the research strategy and steps of conducting field

[2] The academic community's research and exploration of the "holistic" community during this period have been severely inadequate, directly leading to the decline and simplification of community research traditions.

research on a particular or a type of community through the anthropological "thick description" method; secondly, community is an ontological existence, a specific research object with distinct structural and functional elements; thirdly, community is also an academic community with a clear problem awareness, research tradition, academic team, and research achievements and positions based on this foundation. Subsequently, community research was interrupted for thirty years, and the revival of the community research tradition coincided with the dissolution of the unit system. Particularly since the 1990s, the state-driven top-down community construction and management initiated a journey of shifting and penetrating the focus of social management downward. Community, as the "basic unit of national governance" (Yang Min 2007), became an overly magnified perspective in research, transforming the holistic concept of "community" into a singular, entity-based "community system," analyzed within the tradition of state power construction. The research tradition of community governance was severely narrowed, with the holistic community research tradition being replaced by fragmented and singular research. Therefore, we need to place community governance within the historical tradition and the system of modernizing national governance capacity for "knowledge archaeology" and rediscovery, to promote the reconstruction of an integrated model of grassroots social governance, achieving a positive interaction between residents' autonomy, social regulation, and government governance. At the same time, through reflection on the practical governance of "community-based" reality and theoretical dialogue, a new "holistic community governance theory" can be formed.

2.2 "State and Society": the Dominant Analytical Paradigm in Grassroots Social Governance[3]

Regarding the dominant academic research territory of the "State and Society" paradigm[4]—urban grassroots communities—it is precisely because of the "encounter between state and society at the most realistic level of life" (Zhang Jing 1998) that the state attempts to integrate by sinking administrative power into grassroots society, while society hopes to express interest demands, seek self-service, and achieve self-governance. This "unconscious" historical coupling has produced extremely rich research results. In terms of existing research, it is mainly based on political science and sociology, with considerations from anthropology, history,[5] and philosophy, intersecting with each other; the research content is rich and diverse, deepening each

[3] A portion of the content has been published in the "Journal of East China University of Science and Technology (Social Science Edition)" in the 4th issue of 2016.

[4] Ding Huiping (2015) believes that the "sphere of influence" in "state and society" research mainly covers the fields of rural social research in China, urban community research, and research on social organizations. I basically agree with this viewpoint.

[5] The historical research on "state and society" is relatively limited, with representative studies such as — Zhu Ying. "Society and State in Modern China: A Review and Reflection" [J]. Jiangsu Social Sciences, 2006 (4): 176–185.

other; research methods complement each other in length, each with its strengths; research contexts have mutual inheritance and integration.

From the academic context, the development process of the "State and Society" paradigm has distinct stages. The 1980s to 1990s belong to the introduction stage of the paradigm, with related achievements mainly focusing on introduction and introduction, also including effective research by Western sinologists. After the mid-to-late 1990s... Research on the Construction of Integrated Service Models in Urban Community Governance Entered a period of paradigm flourishing and development, primarily based on the creative discourse of local scholars, with theoretical research and practical verification complementing each other progressively. Especially with the release and development of social space during the social transformation process, the state and society have also entered a new period of "mutual construction and game." Since the twenty-first century, the postmodern turn in the theoretical context of sociology and the dramatic changes in the social environment of the globalization era have catalyzed the "state and society" paradigm into a new stage of reflective dialogue. The research presents deconstruction and reflection at the theoretical level, and some studies have proposed ideas for reconstruction.

Accompanied by the decline of the urban grassroots social governance system dominated by the "unit system" and supplemented by the "street-residence system," the state and society have gradually unfolded complex, diverse, and dynamic relationship practices and game spaces. Most scholars believe that the existing grassroots community governance research using "state and society" as an analytical framework has three obvious orientations: state-centered theory, society-centered theory, and "state within society" (Zhang Jing 1998; He Haibing 2006; Ding Huiping 2014, 2015; Liu An 2015). Given the relatively systematic and comprehensive sorting of these three orientations in previous research, this book only provides a simple explanation, focusing on sorting and analyzing the enriched and deepened theoretical perspectives and analytical spaces of other alternative or complementary perspectives of "state and society" in grassroots community governance research. Following academic conventions, this chapter is also developed from the following dimensions.

2.2.1 State-Centered Theory

The state-centered theory views the state as the core force and key driving force of grassroots social governance, change, and reform, following the logic of state power construction. Although the traces of state power construction have weakened in the later stages, the state still maintains considerable control over society, appearing in some areas in specific, new forms, practicing state power penetration at the grassroots level in more "concealed" and "softened" ways. As a result, the state still has a strong influence on society, hence it is also called the "state power continuation theory."

From a chronological perspective, there are two successive stages. The first is the research on grassroots power construction since the 1980s, with researchers mostly being government officials or personnel from government departments, focusing mainly on policy orientation and practical application, primarily concentrating on the reform and exploration of the "street-residence system" in integrating grassroots society (Li Xueju 1994; Bai Yihua 1995; Shi Kai et al. 1997; Pu Xingzu 1998; He Haibing 2006). The second is the agenda of community construction that emerged in the mid-1990s, with researchers mostly being scholars in the fields of sociology and political science, focusing on theoretical research and academic analysis. Related research mainly focuses on the community system after the disintegration of the "unit system." Scholars in this field draw inspiration from the significant social changes during social transformation, further refining and emphasizing the important role of the state in grassroots social construction, the penetration of urban power into grassroots society, and the various forms in which the state reappears in neighborhoods, especially the core position and role of the party and government in community management (Gui Yong et al. 2000; Li Youmei 2002; Yang Min 2007; Xiao Lin 2013).

2.2.2 *Society-Centered Theory*

The core concept of society-centered theory is "civil society" (also known as "citizen society" or "folk society").[6] This approach believes that the driving force of social development exists within society, and the state is merely a restrictive force for society, being a "necessary evil," thus advocating for social self-governance, with as little state intervention as possible (Zhang Jing 1998). Since the 1970s, with the rise of social forces, the "civil society theory" has emerged in the West, especially after the dramatic changes in Eastern Europe, leading to an unprecedented surge in research on civil society in Western, particularly Eastern European, academia. Since the 1990s, with the rise of The disintegration of the work unit system and the advancement of community construction, especially the rise of non-state forces such as society and market in urban grassroots spaces, have led to increasing attention from the domestic academic community on civil society (citizen society) theory. Influenced by Western civil society theories, researchers believe that there is a clear distinction between the state and society, and the boundaries between them should be clarified and regularized. In the context of contemporary China, the state should gradually withdraw from the social sphere, which is a necessary condition for maintaining social vitality and enhancing state capacity.

Under the guidance of the "civil society theory," scholars believe that the ideal goal of current community construction in China should be the orderly and gradual withdrawal of the state from the community domain, gradually achieving community autonomy and democracy (Li Youmei et al. 2000; Xu Yongxiang 2001; Ma

[6] It should be noted that civil society, urban society, and grassroots society are different concepts with significant differences in their connotations and extensions. However, within the research scope of the state and society, these three have a considerable degree of interconnectedness. Therefore, this book does not make a clear distinction between the referents of these three concepts.

Zhongliang 2001; Fei Xiaotong 2002; Tang Yalin and Chen Xianshu 2003; Wei Na 2003; Chen Weidong 2004), and vigorously promoting community participation (Zhang Zhuo 1997; Li Tingyu 2001; Zhu Kongfang 2003). The ongoing community construction movement at this stage, which is the starting point of China's social reform, is an important measure to build Chinese civil society (Tong Shijun 1997; Zhao Chenxin 2001; Liu Jitong 2001; Li Jun 2003). Jing Yijia and Liu Chunrong (2007) found through research on the direct election process of neighborhood committees that government-led elections can empower community autonomous organizations, achieve the transfer and construction of community power, and quickly and effectively build a centralized grassroots democratic governance network centered on neighborhood committees, thereby stimulating community identity and promoting public participation. Additionally, some scholars have begun to notice a new type of community organization emerging in communities—homeowner committees—and have high hopes for them, believing they may be the precursor to Chinese urban civil society (Zhang Jing 2001; Xia Jianzhong 2003), nurturing the embryonic form of a true Chinese civil society, and have conducted multidimensional analyses of homeowner committees (Fei Meiping 2001; Chen Youhong 2005; Wang Ying 2006).

2.2.3 "The State in Society"

"The State in Society" refers to the theory of state-society interaction. This research approach mainly involves tracking and analyzing specific event processes, to some extent abandoning the previous binary opposition framework of state and society, representing a shift from structural research to relational research (Ding Huiping 2015), and also achieving a transition from "static theoretical analysis" to "dynamic process understanding." This approach posits that the state and society are not in a simple zero-sum game of binary opposition, but are in a dynamic process of continuous interaction and formation. Related research is mainly divided into two categories: early normative analysis focusing on how "state and society" should interact and the nature of the interaction, primarily theoretical research; and more recent empirical research focusing on the actual interaction processes and events of "state and society" in specific contexts. Since the 1990s, some scholars have been committed to the dynamic process research of state-society relations, correcting the previous "binary opposition theory." Scholars increasingly recognize the contradiction between urban grassroots government construction and social development in urban community construction (Sun Liping 2003), indicating that the relationship between state and society is not a simple zero-sum game. While emphasizing the independence of both (state-centered and society-centered theories), it is also necessary to discuss the interaction methods between the two, advocating for the establishment of a "state in society" to achieve the goal of "good governance" between the state and society (Zheng Hangsheng 2012).

The rise of governance theory has also expanded the analytical framework of the relationship between the state and civil society, highlighting the state. feasibility of achieving a positive-sum game relationship between the family and civil society, the integration of governance theory and the study of state-society relations in the community field has produced a wealth of research results (Zhao Mengying et al. 2001; Liu Ye 2003; Yu Jianxing et al. 2003; Chen Weidong et al. 2003; Ma Ling 2003; Liang Ping and Yao Yingyuan 2004; Liu Xianjing 2004; Gui Yong 2007). The study of state-society relations has thus entered a new era.

Since the relationship between the state and society is dynamic, the existing static perspectives on their relationship have insurmountable limitations, making it difficult to capture the dynamic nature of the relationship. Therefore, a series of new theories and observational perspectives have been introduced into urban community governance research. For example, first began to reflect on and critique the "state and society" perspective, proposing a potentially more effective "strategic action" perspective that is obscured by the "state and society." He believes that to overcome the "holistic" research tendency of "state" and "society," it is necessary to introduce the perspectives of "strategic action" and "event relations," and to reinterpret the relationship between the state and society from the process of interaction. Sun Liping (2002) also believes that since the relationship between the state and society is a dynamic process rather than a static structure, the research on it should be "event relations" analysis in methodology. He advocates introducing the analytical framework of "process events" to capture the practical logic that truly plays a role in real life during the practice process, to understand more deeply the substantive changes occurring in society during social transformation.

From an academic texture analysis, it can be found that the "state in society" approach often adopts "event relations" analysis in methodology, introducing analytical frameworks of "strategic action" and "process events," aiming to deeply describe the "micro-level of contemporary Chinese state-society relations." The former can avoid the "one-dimensional" institutional interpretation tendency easily made when using the state and society framework to study Chinese society, avoiding the "holistic" and "substantive" treatment of the two analytical units of "state" and "society," which obscures the differences, divergences, conflicts, and interactions occurring within "state" and "society" respectively. The latter can reveal the "hidden" parts of phenomena through the description of event processes, uncovering them dynamically (Yu Bing 2008).

2.2.4 *Attempts from Other Perspectives*

Previous assessments of state-society relations have generally presupposed the entirety of state and society, ignoring the diversity and hierarchy of state and society, thereby obscuring the dynamic and diverse, even fluid, nature of state-society relations. In fact, the relationship between the state and society changes with the changes in the activity fields of the state and social subjects, overall presenting a dynamic boundary relationship in mutual penetration. With the reflection on the application of the "state and society" perspective in grassroots community governance, the monistic tendency of this single perspective has been corrected. Some alternative or complementary perspectives with analytical validity have been proposed one after another. For example, Gui Yong (2005) liberated the state and society from binary opposition from the "actor" perspective, considering the state and society as a continuous system composed of various parameters with different values, where the relationships among these actor groups are intricate, with opposition, cooperation, conflict, and compromise coexisting simultaneously. Applied to community construction, community residents and community organizations are different actors, each with their own different interests and goals, and their interactions constitute the benign development of the community. Similarly, Ma Weihong et al. (2008), through empirical analysis of grassroots community governance in Shanghai, explained how the state and society are decomposed by actors with different purposes, thus presenting a fragmented state. They believe that "at the neighborhood level, the state and society are also ambiguous, and what is clearly visible are various actors with different interests and goals," thus advocating for assessing the real relationship forms of state and society at the grassroots from the "actor" perspective. Xu Bingkui (2012), through a review of community research literature since 1990, believes that existing research "lacks an integrative study of various research paradigms of state-society, spatial actors, power, and governance," calling for the integration of community governance paradigms. Xiao Ying (2014), based on a critical analysis of the previous "state and society" relationship, believes that "the application of this perspective in China is more normative and difficult to explain the complex mechanisms of social change in China." Therefore, he proposes to integrate "institution and life." The perspective, as an alternative viewpoint, uses the interaction between institutions and daily life as an entry point, "linking everyday practices with social structural changes to provide an explanatory framework for exploring the micro-dynamic mechanisms of social structural changes."

Regarding the three approaches to the study of the relationship between society and the state—"state-centered theory," "society-centered theory," and "the state within society"—the first two focus on seeking possible solutions for China's social construction amidst the binary opposition and tense game between state and social forces. Essentially, they are "structural" static interpretations, selecting empirical facts from different dimensions to complete a limited understanding of China's reality; they obviously overlook the "bargaining" between the state and society. In contrast, the latter analysis shifts the perspective to the mutual entanglement and interpenetration of "state and society," experimenting with the possibility of "positive interaction between state and society" within a mutually embedded vision. Essentially, it is a "practical" dynamic analysis, emphasizing an objective interpretation of social reality from a "process" perspective. However, the degree of interpenetration between state and society, the different original starting points of state and society, etc., as logical antecedents, shape the specific boundaries and scope of influence of "the state within society." Furthermore, once "the state within society" is proposed, it immediately transforms into a presupposition for the constructive interaction between state and society in China. As Deng Zhenglai (2008) stated, "This so-called positive interaction relationship is both a desired outcome and a means to achieve this outcome for Chinese civil society theorists." Thus, the positive interaction between state and society, as a theoretical and interpretative presupposition, begins its "self-verification" process in the field of grassroots community in China.

Reviewing existing research, it can be found that the core issues of state and society research cover two aspects. On one hand, following the tradition of "constructive realism," it treats the state and society as objects at the reality level, constructing them towards the vision of "positive interaction." This is manifested in specific research as using various pre-existing elements abstracted from Western social realities (such as mutual independence, clear boundaries, and mutual checks and balances between state and society) as references and criteria. They focus on empirically analyzing emerging extrainstitutional factors, spaces, organizations, and mechanisms in Chinese society, seeking evidence of their existence and conducting comparative research. From the actual effect, this category of research objectively plays a role in social mobilization, critiquing reality, and normative integration. Thus, theoretical knowledge shifts from understanding society to critiquing existing society and planning for future society. On the other hand, it adheres to the tradition of "interpretivism," treating "state and society" as a unique analytical framework and explanatory model for understanding and gaining insight into China's social transformation. This is manifested in specific research as providing imaginative interpretations of a series of empirical phenomena, especially the ebb and flow of "state" and "society" forces in grassroots communities. From the actual effect, it evokes people's imagination of "society," achieving a perspective switch in understanding China's social transformation to a certain extent.

In summary, "state and society," as a theoretical analysis paradigm, has shown great theoretical validity in the practice of urban grassroots governance. Scholars have discovered rich governance practices and theoretical innovations within this highly tensioned perspective. The paradigm of state and society has also achieved a transformation from "binary opposition" in entity construction to "mutual embedding and construction," realizing a shift from "static structural analysis" to "dynamic process evolution." It has also completed the unification from empirical research as an analytical paradigm to policy reference as a normative orientation and reflective dialogue as a scientific research object itself, becoming a dominant analytical paradigm in the field of social sciences. However, any paradigm has its analytical validity, applicable scope, and explanatory power. Ignoring research on the paradigm itself, lagging behind the actual social changes, or lacking reflective dialogue on the paradigm will inevitably encounter the "myth of the paradigm" and "solidification of the paradigm," leading to the "unconscious application" of the paradigm, which is not conducive to further updating and development of the paradigm. Therefore, we need to reflect and dialogue on the research of the "state and society" paradigm.

2.2.5 *Re-Reflection on the "State and Society" Paradigm in Grassroots Community Governance*

Although the "state and society" paradigm has provided an in-depth interpretation of transitional society, there is also a great possibility of misinterpretation during the interpretation. If there is insufficient sensitivity to misinterpretation, social facts... The presentation will experience significant distortion. On one hand, the misreading depends on the foreign nature of the "state and society" paradigm. From an academic convention perspective, as an external theoretical paradigm, it inevitably undergoes a complete process of introduction, application, reflection, and reconstruction. Without the advancement of subsequent stages, the theoretical paradigm can only be a "suspended" interpretation or directly a "reality of conceptual trimming," making misreading inevitable. On the other hand, the lack of "pre-reflective dialogue" and normative value orientation regarding this paradigm will lead to "short-termism" and "goal displacement" in actual reforms. The benign interaction between the state and society, as a reform vision, through the critique of the original unidirectional top-down "omnipotent state" dimension, pulls the "state" down from the "altar" and introduces the dimension of "society" into Chinese studies, to a certain extent, achieving the mission of transforming the research framework in the social sciences field. However, excess leads to the opposite extreme, as the "state" is abandoned and emasculated, continuously fermenting, leading to another extreme. As Liu An (2015) stated, "the lack of 'society' subjectivity in political practice leads to ruthless criticism of 'statism' in the knowledge domain," fostering unidirectional governance of "society," which, if continued, will undoubtedly result in catastrophic consequences (the Eastern European upheaval is a vivid example). In view of this, in this section, the author starts with scholars' reflective research, attempting to provide inspiration for the reconstruction of the paradigm through a reflection on the reflection in the "state and society" research.

Firstly, the starting point of reflection is the "myth" of the "state and society" paradigm in grassroots social governance. The so-called "myth" of "state and society" in grassroots social governance refers to the "monistic tendency" of the "state and society" paradigm currently existing in the field of grassroots social governance. Chapter 2: Comparison of Concepts and Models in Grassroots Social Governance 021 The "overconsumption" of the "state and society" paradigm. Simply put, as long as it is related research in the grassroots community field, the state and society are inevitably involved and utilized as a theoretical perspective. Deng Zhenglai (2002) believes that "any theoretical paradigm has its own limitations and cannot be used to explain all phenomena. Even within its applicable scope, it has its own various weaknesses." So why can everything that happens in grassroots society be analyzed using the "state and society" framework? This actually touches on the fundamental issue. As Ding Huiping (2015) stated, "no matter what topic, as long as it is placed within the 'state and society' analytical framework, it seems to naturally possess a certain legitimacy and rationality," and this monistic tendency "has the suspicion of overemphasizing and consuming 'state and society,' not only possibly obscuring the essence of the problem but also to some extent hindering the renewal of the research framework." However, Ding Huiping only raised the issue and did not explore the process of the "myth" of "monism." So, why has the "monistic" situation of the "state and society" paradigm in grassroots social governance formed? As analyzed above, the dominant position of the "state and society" paradigm in grassroots social governance is the result of the coupling of a highly tensioned and theoretically explanatory paradigm with the actual social transformation, and it is also the result of scholars' deep cultivation in grassroots communities (the best field for the state and society to engage in a game) over the past thirty years. At the same time, the involvement of different disciplines in research also highlights the interdisciplinary explanatory power of the "state and society" theoretical paradigm, providing "academic rationale" for its continuous expansion, thereby becoming a core research paradigm in the social sciences field. Coupled with the "symbolic significance" of academic hotspots and frontiers, "state and society" has achieved "symbolic significance" in theoretical paradigms, and through these processes of repetition, it has realized "mythification." Its manifestation is that, on one hand, as long as a study involves the application of the "state and society" paradigm, it seems to represent the forefront and level of research; on the other hand, the deep-seated forces behind grassroots social governance are the continuous intertwining, wrestling, and game of "state and society," and the absence of this paradigm's analysis means superficial and shallow research.

Secondly, the reflection on the systematic foundation of the "state and society" perspective. Xiao Ying (2014) represents this research, arguing that "'state and society,' as a basic perspective for understanding social composition and change under modernity conditions, is also formed under the dominance of social system theory." Its application in theory and practice has three basic assumptions. The first is holism. This perspective assumes the unity within the state and society, and their external independence and autonomy. This means that the state Both the state and society are imagined as entities with their own unique structures, clear boundaries, and operational logic. Research on the Construction of Integrated Service Models in Urban Community Governance Secondly, dualism. This mainly refers to the relationship between the state and society as a dualistic opposition in entity, a functional interdependence, and a balance of power. The common textual expressions are "strong and weak" and "big and small." Dualism is actually the logical result of holism. Thirdly, the duality of power. On one hand, the process of modernization is the process of suppression, control, and colonization of society by the nation-state; on the other hand, modernity also presupposes the institutional constraints and counter-control of a mature "society" over state power. In fact, as early as the introduction of this paradigm, Deng Zhenglai had already pointed out various risks that might exist or be caused by this paradigm from a methodological perspective. He believed that the state and society paradigm easily leads people into the trap of holism and reification, where in specific research, people tend to regard "state" and "society" as a homogeneous unified entity that truly exists, thus ignoring the infinite richness and complexity of "state and society" in the Chinese context (Deng Zhenglai 2002). Under the constraints of "holistic" thinking, what follows is the reduction of "state" and "society" to various corresponding subjects in grassroots communities, such as equating the state with "government or party organizations" and society with "community neighborhood committees," regardless of the credibility of this reduction (in fact, whether "neighborhood committees" are "society" or "state" is an unresolved issue, and there is also serious differentiation within the government at different levels). The process of reducing the macro-level state and society to corresponding subjects in micro-communities commits the "ecological fallacy," making it difficult to reach convincing conclusions.

Moreover, Ding Huiping (2014, 2015) and Liu An (2015) have recently conducted in-depth reflections on the systemic theoretical basis of the "state and society" perspective. Ding Huiping believes that in the analytical strategy of the "state and society" framework, "state and society are a priori regarded as two entities with clear demarcations, essentially adhering to a dualistic thinking of state and society, which, when projected into specific research, evolves into a structural analysis of comparing the influence of the two, even in state-society interaction orientations." Liu An (2015) conducted a systematic reflection on the subjectivity issue of "state" and "society." He believes that "whether from the perspective of conceptual form or theoretical logic, 'state' and 'society' in the 'state and society' paradigm are constructed as relatively independent and autonomous categories."

Thus, it can be seen that recent research has noticed the systemic theoretical assumptions of the "state and society" paradigm and has conducted imaginative reflections on these assumptions, to some extent avoiding the dualistic opposition of "state and society" and the "holistic homogeneity" assumption regarding "state" and "society." It also maintains sufficient sensitivity to the bidirectional mutual construction and constraint of "state and society," which is conducive to enhancing the validity of the "state and society" paradigm.

Thirdly, reflection on the "localization" issues triggered by the foreign nature of the "state and society" paradigm. The coordination problem between academic transplantation and local traditions has always been a difficult issue in Chinese social science research. As the introduction of a foreign academic paradigm, it inevitably faces the problem of "localization." Generally speaking, the introduction of a paradigm goes through three stages: introduction, localization, and universalization. Introduction is the initial stage, which needs to solve the issue of paradigm attention; localization is key, which needs to solve the issue of paradigm applicability; universalization is the goal, which needs to solve the issue of the paradigm's local contribution. These three stages progress step by step, forming the process of updating and replacing theoretical paradigms, that is, the process of knowledge production. Among them, localization is the difficulty, requiring breakthroughs in the paradigm's background, logical presuppositions, and integration issues. In this process, it is easy to encounter situations of "conceptual tailoring of reality" and "framework replacement and mixing." As for the former, researchers often directly apply this analytical framework to the study of Chinese experiential reality, using existing Western theoretical viewpoints for explanation. If the two do not match, it is attributed to local factors such as society and culture, causing the research to remain superficial and difficult to delve into; or they simply choose experiential phenomena that can verify the hypothesis under the guidance of theoretical presuppositions for interpretation, directly "confirming" the theory. As for the latter, as a Western-imported theoretical paradigm, "state and society" has dual functions of explanation and norm. Specifically, on one hand, this paradigm can serve as an explanatory analysis. Paradigm, on one hand, interprets existing social realities theoretically to form social knowledge; on the other hand, this paradigm can also serve as a standard and model for early modern states, to regulate and guide the adjustment of the relationship between the state and society in China, playing a role in evaluation and construction, and promoting social change. The interchange and mixed use of these two functions can easily lead to serious social consequences, causing the process of localization to evolve into a process of "Westernization."

Huang Zongzhi believes that "the binary opposition between state and society is an ideal type abstracted from the historical development experience of the modern West, and it is not suitable for China" (Huang 1993, 2003). He further proposed the concept of the "third domain" to indicate the "gray area" between the state and society, which involves the issue of the "localization" of the "state and society" paradigm in China. He Haibing (2006) also believes that "in discussions about the state and society, whether it is civil society theory or state-centered theory, they are based on Western concepts of civil society and the state to make normative judgments about Chinese society. These judgments only focus on the macro-historical perspective, lacking a micro-level description of the contemporary relationship between the state and society in China." Ding Huiping (2015) also reflected on the localization of the "state and society" paradigm, stating that "for Chinese research, the civil society theory derived from Western historical experience and Western values, and its derivative 'state and society' have neither historical traces to follow nor real experience to compare in China." Liu An (2015) believes that there is an insurmountable gap between the Western lineage of the "state and society" paradigm and its application in China, stating that "as social science concepts, 'state' and 'society' have significant differences between China and the West, both in knowledge and practice."

Therefore, as an imported theoretical paradigm, we must remain sufficiently vigilant about its potential "incompatibility" and stay sensitive to its ecological or growth process of transplantation. We should neither deny the theoretical explanatory power of the "state and society" paradigm for transitional societies nor simply apply Western theories and experiences. Instead, we should engage in equal dialogue and rational communication with Western theoretical paradigms within China's own historical heritage and development practice, timely guiding it towards "Sinicization."

Fourth, reflection on the complementarity and integration of multiple perspectives. Any theoretical paradigm is a product of its time, tending to improve in development, which means it has specific applicability and explanatory power, with strengths and weaknesses. Currently, on one hand, the theoretical explanatory power and methodological advantages of the "state and society" paradigm lead to a phenomenon of "overconsumption" in community governance research, which is not conducive to the renewal of paradigms. Indeed, the proposal of a theoretical perspective is the crystallization of collective wisdom in academia, and it will enter a period of prosperity, with many scholars using this perspective to study all the researchable issues within this theoretical framework. However, there will also be a phenomenon that is not conducive to academic progress, namely, due to the explanatory power and credibility of the theoretical paradigm, over time, research will become repetitive simple reproduction, difficult to break through. At this time, reflection on the paradigm is needed. On the other hand, the state and society perspective is overly macro, and the judgment in practice also ignores various premises derived from Western experience, making it difficult to accurately describe the grassroots governance practice in contemporary China; the state and society are adept at interpreting and analyzing macro phenomena, focusing on macro "structural system" analysis, lacking micro insights at the practice level, and there is a risk of oversimplifying the complex composition and interaction of the state and society, losing the rich content and complex dimensions of "state and society," making it difficult to explain the multidimensionality, entity extensibility, and practical complexity of the state and society during the transition period. Moreover, with the changes of the times, the evolution of paradigms, and the emergence of a series of theoretical perspectives, "state and society" gradually lost its hegemonic position in the grassroots community field, gradually becoming an "academic target" proposed and risen by other perspectives (undoubtedly, "academic target" also means the importance and far-reaching influence of the "state and society" paradigm). Among them, Huang Zongzhi, based on critical questioning of the embedding of "state and society" as a Western theoretical paradigm, proposed the concept of the "third domain," aiming to dissolve or alleviate the tension between the state and society, seeking the uniqueness of "state and society" in China. Additionally, Gui Yong (2005) introduced "actors" into "state and society," attempting to liberate the state and society from binary opposition, advocating for starting from specific community events. The process of life and the perspective of actors are used to understand the logic of community development. Based on a critical analysis of the past "state and society" relationship, Xiao Ying (2014) proposed that the perspective of studying social change in China should shift from "state and society" to "institution and life," achieving a certain degree of integration between macro institutional analysis and micro action research.

Thus, although the "state and society" perspective deepens the understanding of the relationship between the state and society at the macro level, the myth of its theoretical explanatory power has led to the exclusion and rejection of other perspectives, resulting in repetitive reproduction within the paradigm. The introduction and supplementation of other perspectives have broken the "monolithic myth" of the "state and society" paradigm in grassroots social governance research. However, it should be noted that this does not mean that the "state and society" perspective has lost its theoretical explanatory power for China's grassroots communities, nor does it imply that other perspectives have effectively "replaced" or "transformed" the "state and society" perspective. Instead, it has entered a new period of paradigm intersection and integration. Existing research shows that in the complex and diverse intertwining of "state and society" forces, the research on grassroots community governance has entered a post-"state and society" paradigm period. On one hand, there has been a linkage of perspectives, achieving mutual promotion and verification between "state and society" and "institution and life"; on the other hand, there has been a switch of perspectives, with macro issues receiving annotations at the micro level, becoming more enriched and comprehensive.

2.2.6 *Future Development: Moving Out of the Temple, Moving Towards Life*

Existing research has achieved some serious and earnest results. However, after systematic sorting, it is found that existing research mostly uses "state and society" in a methodological sense, treating it as an effective paradigm for analyzing grassroots community governance, with noticeable Western traces in its use. Chinese scholars are more inclined to find appropriate aspects from China's real experiences for research that amplifies meaning, and then conduct comparative studies with Western paradigms. In specific applications, this theoretical paradigm's premises are either "suspended" or "ambiguously handled" (neither confirmed nor denied). In other words, existing research has simplified the "state and society" as an analytical perspective, shielding the presuppositions of the state and society, and because of the "encounter" and "fit" of "state and society" at the grassroots level, it leads to "unquestioning" and "unwavering belief" in its application. However, the lack of reflection on implicit presuppositions and the use of the paradigm will lead to the continuous reproduction of low-level research, making it difficult to achieve academic progress and form a Chinese paradigm.

From the Chinese experience, as a normative concept, the "state and society" paradigm has shown a phenomenon of "overconsumption." However, from the perspective of entity construction and paradigm innovation, "state and society" still holds its constructive significance both in the West and in China. We need to further consider how to differentiate between theoretical paradigms and entity construction approaches, and then link these two levels through research on specific carriers, eliminating the "favoring one over the other" in existing research, which may achieve breakthroughs in "state and society" research.

Firstly, object inversion. Previous research often used "state and society" as a paradigm and perspective to analyze the interaction of subjects in the space of grassroots social governance. However, grassroots communities can also be used as a carrier of expression to explore the real performance of "state and society" on the platform of grassroots community organizations, thereby treating "state and society" as a specific research object, depicting, deconstructing, and reconstructing it in the Chinese context. This should become an important attempt to update the "state and society" paradigm and a theme that needs further deepening.

Secondly, paradigm shift. As analyzed above, since Migdal proposed the "state in society," "state and society" has gained new development space, and the process perspective of interaction has begun to be included in the "state and society" category. However, the "state in society" may be an illusory picture of the state-society relationship under Western discourse, inconsistent with China's historical practice and real experience. In China's grassroots society, perhaps "society in the state"[7] is a more realistic existence. On one hand, from the state's position, the state constantly maintains its "presence" and "appearance" at the grassroots level, and various "visible" and "invisible" state statuses exist in grassroots society. The state achieves this through diversified means and methods (albeit in forms different from previous rigid control). It reflects the "selective cultivation" and "indirect control" of grassroots society. On the other hand, from the perspective of social space, the real "society" is not an independently grown institutional space but a space ceded within the state, characterized by "dependent growth" and "parasitic existence" under the state's care, although society exhibits a certain "strategic game space." In this sense, the academic concept of "embeddedness" struggles to depict the origin of this relationship, revealing the validity and boundaries of the theory.

"Society within the State," from a methodological orientation, integrates the perspectives of "subject relations," "strategic actions," and "process events." Firstly, it can avoid the tendency of "unidimensional" institutional explanations when using the "state and society" analytical framework, preventing the "state" and "society" from being treated as "holistic" and "substantive" units, thereby unveiling the rich landscape of differences, disagreements, conflicts, and interactions occurring within the "state" and "society." Secondly, through the performance of specific practice processes and the realistic depiction of event processes in community fields, it reveals the "hidden" parts of things dynamically — the concretization of state-society relations, which can include behavioral patterns difficult to integrate in micro-action research, and factors previously overlooked in the macro-analysis framework of state-society relations may also be presented. These factors might significantly dominate the interactive practices between the state and society (taking "state governance transformation" as an independent variable to analyze its impact on the "state and society" relationship is also a good research entry point. Especially, the continuous advancement of state governance transformation impacts "society," and the changes occurring at the social level imply changes in the "state and society" relationship). In fact, "Society within the State" also bears the imprint of Giddens' attempt. For the research paradigm of "state and society," it aims to break the binary opposition between state and society, the holistic and integrated assumptions of state and society, neither "society-centered" nor "state-centered," and also different from the ontological domain of "state within society." Instead, it is the reality of China where "society" is embedded within the forces of the "state," with the state as a pluralistic component constantly "present" in community governance, reflecting the mutual interaction and penetration, interaction, and causal influence of the realistic state and sociality in China. Meanwhile, "Society within the State" is also a "relational practice" that continuously changes with the transformation of time, space, and fields, injecting concrete practice texts into originally macro-abstract theoretical speculations. This integration further injects Chinese elements into the theoretical proposition of "state and society," holding significant theoretical significance.

[7] Regarding "Society within the State," the author will elaborate in detail in a separate article. Due to space limitations and thematic considerations, the author will not expand on it here.

2.3 Ideal Types: Overview and Comparison of Urban Grassroots Governance Models[8]

2.3.1 Two Dimensions in Community Governance Research Community

Governance practices are generated in a certain historical time–space and environment, gradually advancing in real fields. The final result of community governance is inevitably shaped by various factors in specific fields (time–space), while the advancement of community governance also impacts the environment, being a product of environmental shaping itself. Therefore, the specific situation of the community, namely the community context, undoubtedly becomes an important dimension for examining its governance. In view of this, the analysis of community context mainly starts from the following two dimensions: one is the degree of organization of the community, that is, the degree of integration and interest differentiation of the community; the other is the degree of standardization of the community, mainly referring to the degree of state intervention and the development of social self-organization.

Firstly, the degree of organization of the community. The degree of organization, that is, the degree of integration and interest differentiation of the community, refers to the nature and degree of community integration. This dimension involves whether the community's organization is a "mechanical solidarity" or "organic solidarity," ultimately manifesting as whether the community is in a state of integration or differentiation. Organizations, residents, government, and local customs and regulations in the community environment inevitably constitute the "field" of community governance. Therefore, specific community contexts such as "homogeneity of residents" and "degree of community solidarity" will inevitably influence the choice of community governance models. The realization of community governance can only be achieved by fully considering these community context factors to achieve coupling with the environment, reaching the optimal governance state. Generally speaking, communities with a higher degree of organization, which are in a state of integration, can more easily achieve governance through effective bargaining among different governance entities. There are two different situations here: one is if the community achieves "organic integration" through the bargaining of multiple entities, it will more easily present a state of good governance; the other is if the community's integration is based on "mechanical integration" under a single dominant entity, then community governance will be the more suitable form of governance.

In contrast to the above situation, communities with a lower degree of organization, which are in a state of differentiation, present a decentralized and atomized state due to different interest entities acting independently within the community. Such communities face significant challenges in achieving effective governance.

---

[8] A portion of the content has been published in the "Social Science Journal" in the 4th issue of 2015.

Secondly, the degree of standardization of the community. The degree of standardization mainly refers to the relationship structure between "state and society," measuring the degree of division and cooperation between the state and social self-organization in the process of community governance. The degree of standardization of a community is essentially a continuum of the "state and society" relationship, with one end being the absolute control of state power, an omnipotent state; and the other end being the independent manifestation of social influence, with reasonable division of labor and orderly cooperation between government and society.

Community standardization mainly covers two situations. One is where the state is in a monopolistic position, with only state power and no social presence. The other is where social organizations are in an independent position, collaborating and orderly dividing labor with the state, playing an important role together in community governance. In the former, the state leads community management, with society being underdeveloped or absent, and the state advancing community governance according to its own will and logic, leading to community bureaucratization and involution. In the latter, the state and society form a reasonable division of labor, each performing its own duties, with various interest entities in the community engaging in equal consultation and bargaining within the community field, effectively achieving positive community governance.

2.3.2 Realistic Types of Community Governance

Based on the above comparative framework, through the rich and colorful governance practices and exploration processes carried out in the community field, empirical comparisons and typological contrasts can be made to conduct "typology" research on community governance practices. This allows for the examination of the characteristics and functional realization status of different types of community governance in different historical periods, verifying the effectiveness and explanatory power of the two-dimensional analysis framework of community governance, and further improving the relevant theories of community governance, achieving the integration of "process event" analysis and "structure system" research in community governance studies. The "ideal type" of urban community governance structure is shown in Table 2.1.

1. Traditional Government-Led Community

In traditional government-led communities, the government acts as an omnipotent "steward," and the relevant organizations in the community become its arbitrarily driven "servants," with the typical form being the unit system. The "unit" with a certain bureaucratic hierarchy acts as the sole entity in community governance, handling almost all affairs within the community. The neighborhood committee, as a grassroots community governance institution of the state, essentially plays an auxiliary role of "picking up the unit's leftovers and filling the unit's gaps." In such communities, there are basically no professionally meaningful property service companies

Table 2.1 The "ideal type" of urban community governance structure

	Traditional government-led community	Cooperative community	Modern self-governing community
Governance form	Unit system	Governance form	Governance form
Governance actors	Governance actors	Governance actors	Residents' committees + Homeowners' associations + Property management companies + Social organizations (diverse actors in equal negotiation)
Inter-actor relationships	Inter-actor relationships	Inter-actor relationships	Inter-actor relationships
Degree of interest integration	Mechanical integration	Differentiation, fragmentation	Organic integration
Governance effectiveness	Neutral operation	Governance effectiveness	Neutral operation
Typical cases	Typically found in communities with large administrative, public service, or state-owned enterprises within the jurisdiction	Typical cases	Typically found in communities with large administrative, public service, or state-owned enterprises within the jurisdiction

or homeowner committees and other community social organizations, as all these functional needs can be met through the unit itself. Some non-governmental organizations (NGOs) in the community are mostly interest or entertainment groups, and the community's political, economic, cultural, and social participation is dissolved by the unit's "omnipotence." This traditional community type still exists in small quantities in communities with large administrative, institutional, or state-owned enterprise units within their jurisdiction, such as "university family compounds" and "civil servant communities." In these communities, the resident units still play a leading role in various community affairs, serving as the modern continuation of the unit system.

In terms of power relations, the relationships between different entities in the community are more of a "domination-submission" relationship, with units (mainly referring to various state-owned enterprises and institutions in the post-unit era) in an absolutely advantageous position, able to issue orders on various community affairs. The community is in a highly, mechanically integrated state, not allowing any behavior that disrupts the community's commonality, representing a rigid governance state. The community often lacks vitality and creativity, being in a "highly stable" state, with slow development of community self-governance, as evidenced by the extremely low participation rate of residents in such communities.

2. Cooperative Community

A cooperative community is a transitional form during a period of social transformation. In this type of community, the work unit system has disintegrated or is merely nominal, and modern autonomous communities have not yet been established due to lack of conditions. Therefore, the governance form is characterized by the disappearance of the work unit, and the street-residence system cannot function as an effective governance system due to its alienation and blurred functions. The government's sole dominance in the community has been broken, and multiple governance entities with clear interests have emerged in the community field, attempting cooperative governance practices. However, the interests they represent are still highly fragmented, and their relationships with each other, as well as with the government and the market, have not been clarified. In this stage of community governance, the residents' committee, as an agent of state power in grassroots communities, inevitably seeks to achieve effective control and management of the community by the street government, which is seriously inconsistent with its statutory autonomous status, leading to an identity dilemma and governance predicament. Homeowners' committees and fragmented community resident teams or quasi-organizations, as "independent" entities, begin to appear in the space of community interest games, but their organizational attributes are still unclear, and their roles remain limited. Various types of community social organizations are also gradually entering the public's view, attempting to voice weak group discourses and claims, and a colorful picture of community governance is gradually unfolding. However, the power among the multiple entities in the community field is not balanced. The residents' committee, as an agent of the state, has strong "legitimacy," and due to the enormous inertia of cultural traditions, the public still has recognition and dependence on it, which presupposes its unique status and power as one of the community governance entities.

In a cooperative community, although multiple community entities have emerged, from the perspective of power relations, the status among the entities is severely unequal, making it difficult for them to engage in fair games on an equal basis. The relationship between the government and other diverse community entities is a "partner" relationship model, presenting a state of "collaborative competition," consistent with the nature of the transitional form. At this time, there is no consensus on which entity should play what role in the community. Different entities in the community are in a state of differentiation and fragmentation, with many voices but no "harmony," essentially leading the community into a state of "anomie," operating in an unbalanced and chaotic manner, making it difficult to form a consensus in community governance, and community self-governance is at an impasse.

3. Modern Autonomous Community

In a modern autonomous community, the community is in a highly integrated and organic state, with multiple community entities fully developed and playing their unique roles in community governance. The community governance form is the "community system." In the community field, community social organizations are fully developed, engaging in equal consultation and repeated games with other like-minded community governance entities around public community issues, jointly committed to good community governance. In such communities, residents' committees, homeowners' committees, property service companies, and community autonomous organizations are fully developed, each performing its duties. Community, social organizations, and social workers also achieve effective linkage and collaborative governance. Community residents' awareness of participation, participation ability, and participation carriers are continuously improved, actively contributing to the realization of community autonomy.

Regarding governance entities, residents' committees, homeowners' committees, property service companies, and community autonomous organizations form the core structure of governance institutions. The governance entities are diverse and independent, capable of interacting in different positions within the community governance field according to their respective action habits. From the perspective of power relations, the multiple entities in community governance form a "multi-composite" cooperative governance pattern around the goal of good community governance. The relationship between the multiple governance entities (including grassroots government organizations) is a "partner" style cooperative relationship. The interests of the multiple entities are highly and organically integrated based on full "bargaining," achieving positive operation and coordinated development under the norms of "public order and good law."

In summary, the above three types of communities coexist synchronously in the current community field in China, manifesting in various models and paths in practice. However, with the continuous development of multiple community entities, the gradual integration of community common interests, and the gradual advancement of national governance modernization, community governance will inevitably present such a picture: in terms of the degree of organization of the community, the degree of organization based on "organic integration" is continuously improving, community organizations are fully developed, and represent… The role in highlighting the interests of community residents is prominent; in terms of the standardization level of the community, the state and society have formed a reasonable division of labor, each performing its own duties. Various interest entities within the community use the community as a platform for negotiation, which is standardized and orderly, achieving the self-organization of the community. Therefore, the modern autonomous community is the ultimate effort direction and the legitimacy goal of grassroots social governance, while the traditional government-led community can only be regarded as historical and will eventually fade into the dust of history; cooperative communities only have "temporary" rationality in a transitional sense.

The different domestic and international community governance models mentioned above were formed in specific time-space contexts. From a historical perspective, community governance in our country has undergone historical evolution from the unit system to the street-residence system and the community system (He Haibing 2003). During the coexistence of the street-residence system and the community system, local governments exercised administrative power and provided public services through the community as a carrier. However, due to limitations in governance concepts, methods, and mechanisms, community governance during this period generally had a strong administrative orientation. Since the Third Plenary Session of the 18th Central Committee of the Communist Party of China and the release of the "No. 1 Project" by the Shanghai Municipal Party Committee, there has been an emphasis on the return of public management, public services, and public safety functions to the streets, emphasizing that the focus of governance is urban and rural communities, and stressing the realization of human development and well-being through institutional and mechanism innovation. These important spirits and measures provide important directional guidance for community governance in the new era.

2.4 Review of Existing Research

As an important component of the national governance system, community governance is the manifestation of national governance in urban communities. From the current empirical reality, urban community governance urgently needs to cultivate and incubate social organizations to achieve "social collaboration," fully utilize information technology to expand participation channels and pathways to deepen "public participation," and also requires public spaces, fulcrums, and platforms to enable multiple entities to achieve "governance innovation" based on full consultation and communication. The goal of this book is to use "integrated governance" as the main line, through historical examination of Shanghai's community governance and empirical research on the current state of grassroots community governance, to reflect on the current practical dilemmas and deep-rooted causes of grassroots social governance, construct a community-based integrated service model, optimize the grassroots social governance system, and enhance governance capabilities.

2.4.1 Two Potential Directions in Community System Reform

Since the 1990s, under the influence of the "governance" concept, the community system, as the organizational form and management system of urban grassroots social management following the unit system and street-residence system, has begun to come to the forefront of history (He Haibing 2003; Liwen Hou et al. 2012). Many scholars, based on summarizing the practical experience of domestic system reform and innovation, have proposed the path of community system innovation around the core issue of "the relationship between state and social rights." Li Youmei (2007) summarized community construction as two paths: "grassroots regime construction" and "grassroots social development." Among them, Yang Min (2007) believes that the current community construction movement has constructed a state governance unit rather than a regional social life community that can promote the development of civil society; Xia Jianzhong (2003), through case studies of the emergence and role of urban owners' committees, proposed the possibility of their role as "the precursor of civil society." Shi Fayong (2010) also pointed out that the rise of owners' committees provides formal participation channels and community cooperation platforms for owners, thereby effectively promoting grassroots governance.

With the Third Plenary Session of the 18th Central Committee of the Communist Party of China as a watershed, there are several significantly different orientations in the connotation of social governance. One is the management-oriented social governance, which equates social governance with social management or public management at this stage. For example, Wang Puqu (2014) proposed that social governance is "governing society," referring to the management implemented by specific governance entities on society. The second is cooperation-oriented social governance. For example, Li Peilin (2014) pointed out that innovating the social governance system is to form a situation of co-governance by the government, enterprises, and society, better playing the role of social forces. The third is rights/service-oriented social governance, which emphasizes the service implications of social governance. For example, Wang Sibin (2014, 2015) explained the role mechanism of social work in social governance from the perspective of service-oriented governance.

2.4.2 *Multiple Entities and "Three-Society Linkage"*

In recent years, research on grassroots social governance innovation has paid more attention to the exploration and practice of separating government and society and cooperation mechanisms. "Community multi-entity cooperative co-governance" and "three-society linkage" are its core viewpoints. "The Three-Society Linkage" is an innovative community governance model summarized by community workers in China in recent years from their practical experiences. The aim is to connect the dispersed communities, social organizations, and social workers, coordinating interactions to form a synergistic force. "The Three-Society Linkage" emerged against the backdrop of China's social system reform—specifically the "separation of government and society"—and is closely linked to social governance innovation. It is also practice-oriented, carried out under the strong promotion of China's grassroots government, especially the Ministry of Civil Affairs of the People's Republic of China (hereinafter referred to as the "Ministry of Civil Affairs"). It is a government-led process involving social organizations and social workers in community construction. The large-scale implementation of "The Three-Society Linkage" began in 2013 when the Ministry of Civil Affairs identified it as a key task for grassroots social governance innovation, requiring its promotion in urban communities. Since 2015, 15 provinces and cities nationwide have held 23 special seminars. In October 2015, the Ministry of Civil Affairs held a national community social work and "Three-Society Linkage" promotion meeting in Chongqing, and in September 2017, the Social Organization Administration Bureau of the Ministry of Civil Affairs held a community social work and "Three-Society Linkage" symposium in Hangzhou.

On this basis, academia has also conducted related academic research. Xu Yongxiang et al. (2016) clarified "The Three-Society Linkage" as an academic concept from a theoretical and reflective perspective, based on summarizing practical experiences in academia. They believe that "The Three-Society Linkage" is a community governance activity carried out by neighborhood committees, social organizations, and social workers in the community field around community residents, aiming to improve residents' well-being, achieve grassroots democracy, and promote endogenous community development. There is a bidirectional interaction between the neighborhood committee as an autonomous consultation platform, social organizations as project operation carriers, and social workers as professional service providers. Community, social organizations, and social workers are the core components of the diverse subjects in the community field, and their "linkage" has significant constructive value and meaning for social governance innovation (Ye Nanke et al. 2010; Gu Donghui 2016; Xu Xuanguo and Xu Yongxiang 2016). Some scholars, based on practical experience, have proposed the concept of "multi-subject composite governance" on the basis of the "Three-Society Linkage" concept. For example, Chen Juan (2011) studied the innovative practice of "social composite subjects" in Hangzhou and believed that "composite governance" emphasizes the formation of multi-composite subjects by the government, market entities, and civil society organizations, jointly governing public affairs through cooperation, consultation, and other means.

2.4.3 The Highlighting of the Subject Status of Social Organizations

In the new round of community governance reform, both political and academic circles focus on the prominent role of social organizations as innovative subjects pointed out that the key to China's social governance innovation lies in further promoting the transformation of government functions, accelerating and decisively implementing the separation of government and society, striving to delegate power to society, and releasing more public space, thereby stimulating the vitality of social organizations and encouraging their extensive participation in social governance innovation practices at all levels. Social organizations are important subjects of social governance, and "social governance" emphasizes more on stimulating the vitality of social organizations (Li Youmei 2016).

In the discussions of the aforementioned scholars, we can clearly see that grassroots social governance reform constantly responds to the topic of government-society relations. Although it undergoes a series of shifts from management to governance, the "state in society" and "community as the basic unit of grassroots governance" remain real existences in the reform. The innovative practices, practical experiences, and institutional mechanisms in the new round of urban and rural community governance still lack systematic integration and theoretical enhancement. Based on existing research, the writing intention of this book is, firstly, to correct the "omnipotent" top-down approach of the government in grassroots society, focusing on the innovative models and practices presented in grassroots social governance practice, such as the "two bottom-up" mechanism innovations, "doorstep" services, and how "environmental remediation" as a top-down administrative task achieves the absorption and convergence of social forces, while paying attention to urban-rural differences for refinement and summary. Secondly, it aims to correct the theoretical community's divergent views, manifested in a comprehensive grasp of community governance principles and goals, explaining and analyzing the problems and dilemmas in grassroots social governance under the new normal, reflecting on the roles and functions of diverse subjects in governance, and constructing an integrated service model based on the community, achieving the connection and construction of theory and practice. This also constitutes the core content and significance of this book.

References

Chenxin Z (2001) Urban community construction, civil society, and political development (Part Two). J Lanzhou Jiaotong Univ (05):11–15

Deng Z (2008) State and society: research on Chinese civil society. Peking University Press, Beijing

Ding H (2015) The application and limitations of the "state and society" analytical framework—focusing on research in the field of sociology. Sociol Rev 3(5):15–23

Donghui G (2016) The connotation interpretation and logical deduction of 'three-sector linkage'. Academia Bimestris (03):104–110

He H (2003) The transformation of China's urban grassroots social management system: from the Danwei system, street-residence system to the community system. Manag World 6:52–62

He H (2006) Research on urban communities in China under the "state-society" paradigm framework. J Shanghai Adm Inst (4): 96–106

Jing Z (1998) Political sociology and its main research directions. Sociol Stud (03):17–25

Jing Z (2001) State power construction and rural autonomous units: issues and review. open times (09):5–13

Jing Y, Liu C (2007) Direct election of residents' committees and urban grassroots governance—an analysis of the 2006 Direct Election of Residents' Committees in Shanghai. Fudan J (Soc Sci Ed) 1:132–140

Jun L (2003) Community construction: broussonetia papyrifera building China's civil society. J. Hum(03):137–141

Kongfang Z (2003) On the institutional arrangement of community participation. J East China Univ Sci Technol (Soc Sci Ed) (01):13–17

Li Y (2007) Community governance: the micro-foundation of civil society. Society (2): 159–169, 207

Liping S (2002) Practical sociology and the analysis of market transition process. Soc Sci China (05):83–96

Ling M (2003) On institutional support for sustainable development. Theory J (04):117–118

Liu A (2015) Research on the state and society relationship at the urban grassroots in contemporary China and its theoretical reflection—an analysis based on the perspective of political sociology. Sociol Rev 3(5):24–37

Ma W, Gui Y, Luo T (2008) The state-society perspective in urban community research: limitations, experiences, and development possibilities. Acad Res (11): 62–67, 159

Meiping F (2001) Homeowners' committee and civil society in China. J East China Univ Sci Technol (Soc Sci Ed) (02):57–64

Mengying Z (2002) On organizational rationality. Sociol Stud (04):77–87
Na W (2003) Urban community construction and the development of community self-governance organizations. J Beijing Admin Inst (01):69–74
Ping L, Yingyuan Y (2004) Analysis of the development trends of administrative organizational models in the information age. Seeking Truth (S1):24–25
Shi F (2010) Homeowners' committees, quasi-factional politics, and grassroots governance—a case study of a Shanghai neighborhood. Sociol Res 25(3): 136–158, 245
Shijun T (1997) The temporal characteristics of civilized communities. Society (09):26
Sibin W (2014) The position and role of social work in the innovation of social governance system—a foundation-service oriented social governance. Soc Work (01):3–10+150
Tingyu L (2001) Community development and resident participation. Hubei Soc Sci (12):69–70
Wang P (2014) The meaning and interrelationship of national governance, government governance, and social governance. J Natl Acad Gov 3:11–17
Weidong C, Xueping L (2003) Community governance and the development of civil society. J Central China Normal Univ (Hum Soc Sci Ed) (01):27–33
Xiao Y (2014) From "state and society" to "institution and life": perspective shift in the study of social change in China. Chin Soc Sci 9(88–104):204–205
Xingzu P (1998) Reform trends in the management system of megacity urban districts—also on the concept of "Two-level government, three-level management". Polit Sci Res (03):53–58
Xuanguo X, Yongxiang X (2016) The 'tripartite collaboration' in grassroots social governance: connotation, mechanism, and practical logic—based on the exploration of h community in shenzhen. Soc Sci (07):87–96
Xu Y (2001) Community development theory. East China University of Science and Technology Press, Shanghai
Yalin T, Xianshu C (2003) Community autonomy: the return and promotion of grassroots democracy in urban society. Acad Circles (06):7–22
Yang M (2007) Community as a unit of state governance—a case study on resident community participation and community cognition in the urban community construction movement. Sociol Res (4): 137–164, 245
Ye L (2003) Public participation, community autonomy, and deliberative democracy: an analysis of public interaction behaviors in an urban community. Fudan J Soc Sci Ed (05):39–48
Nanke Y, Jincheng C (2010) Research on the mode selection and strategy of "Three-Society Linkage" in China. Nanjing J Soc Sci (12):75–80+87
Yihua B, Xiaogan Z, Yongying Z (1995) Investigation on strengthening the construction of neighborhood committees in gudong street. China Civil Affairs (07):16–17
Ying W (2006) Reconstructing the role of civil servants from the perspective of new public service theory. Soc Sci J (04):45–48
Youhong C (2005) The boundary Between administrative power and autonomous organization behavior urgently needs clarification. China reform (05):35–36+71
Youmei L (2016) Analysis of grassroots social governance innovation in China's megacities. J Party Sch Cent Comm C.P.C. (Chin Acad Gov) 20(02):5–12
Yong X (2001) On resident autonomy in urban community construction. J Central China Normal Univ (Hum Soc Sci Ed) (03):5–13
Zhuo Z (1997) The transformation of grassroots community organizations in China. Sociol Stud (04):15–25
Zhongliang M (2001) Urban community autonomy is a growth point of socialist new democracy. J Beijing Admin Inst (01):8–10

Chapter 3
Theoretical Foundation and Analytical Perspective

3.1 The Initial Origin and Conceptual Definition of Governance Governance

Originates from the Latin word "Gouvernail," which originally meant "steering, guiding, and manipulating." From an etymological perspective, the Latin words "Gouverne" (guidance, directing), "Gouvernement" (rule, government), and "Gouvernance" (governance) are the same. With the establishment of nation-states, the concept of "Gouvernement" (rule, government) gradually took shape, and after several evolutions, it was gradually replaced by "government" or "rule." After the revival of its original meaning, contemporary political scientists and sociologists have redefined "governance" from the perspective of their disciplines, leading to significant changes in its connotation and extension, far beyond its traditional classic definition.

Gerry Stoker is the first to sort out and summarize the currently popular governance theories. He points out that the existing definitions of "governance" mainly include five aspects. ① Governance implies a series of social public institutions and actors that originate from but are not limited to the government. It challenges the traditional authority of the state and government, suggesting that the government is not the only power center of the state. Various public and private institutions can become power centers at different levels as long as their exercised power is recognized by the public. ② Governance implies ambiguity in boundaries and responsibilities in the process of finding solutions to social and economic problems. This indicates that the boundaries and responsibilities between the state and society, and between the public and private sectors, are becoming increasingly blurred. ③ Governance explicitly acknowledges the power dependence among various social public institutions involved in collective action. Power dependence refers to the fact that organizations dedicated to collective action must rely on other organizations. To achieve their goals, organizations must exchange resources and negotiate common objectives; the outcome of these exchanges depends not only on the resources of each participant but also on the rules

L. Hou, *The Integrated Service in Urban Community Governance*, Public Economy and Urban Governance in China, https://doi.org/10.1007/978-981-96-6775-8_3

of the game and the environment in which the exchange takes place. ④ Governance refers to the autonomy and self-governance of actor networks. This autonomous network possesses authoritative command within a specific network, cooperating with the government in specific areas and sharing administrative responsibilities. ⑤ Governance theory posits that the ability to get things done does not lie in the power of the government, nor in the government issuing orders or exercising its authority. The government can use new tools and techniques to control and guide, and its ability and responsibility lie therein (Gerry Stoker 1999).

Rhodes believes that governance signifies a change in the meaning of government management, referring to a new management process or an altered orderly state of governance, a new way of managing society. Additionally, he lists six authoritative definitions of governance: ① The state reduces public expenditure to achieve maximum benefits at minimal cost, as governance of a minimal government; ② The organizational system that guides, controls, and supervises the operation of enterprises, as corporate governance; ③ Introducing market incentive mechanisms and private sector management methods into the public services of the government, as governance of new public management; ④ Emphasizing efficiency, rule of law, and responsibility in the public service system, as governance of good governance; ⑤ Cooperation and interaction between the government and civil society, and between the public and private sectors, as governance of the general social control system; ⑥ A social coordination network based on trust and mutual benefit, as governance of a self-organizing network.

The World Bank defines governance as the manner in which power is exercised in the management of a country's economic and social resources for development. The meaning of effective governance includes: ① Ensuring citizen safety and respect for the law, particularly through the rule of law; ② Proper and fair management of public expenditure, i.e., effective administrative management; ③ Political leaders being accountable to the people for their actions, i.e., implementing job responsibilities and accountability systems; ④ Information accessibility, allowing all citizens to be informed, i.e., political transparency.

The United Nations Global Governance Commission's definition of governance is highly representative and authoritative. It believes that governance is the sum of the many ways in which public and private institutions and individuals manage their common affairs. Governance is a continuous process of reconciling conflicting or different interests and taking joint action. Governance includes formal institutions and rules that have the authority to enforce compliance, as well as informal arrangements that people agree to or consider in their interest. Governance has four characteristics: ① Governance is not a set of rules or an activity, but a process; ② The basis of the governance process is not control but coordination; ③ Governance involves the public sector and also includes the private sector; ④ Governance is not a formal institution but a continuous interaction. Research on the Construction of Integrated Service Models in Urban Community Governance.

From a general perspective, governance is a management approach that involves cooperation between the public and private sectors to jointly address public issues. Ostrom (1990) believes that governance is a way of jointly determining rules to constrain individual and collective behavior; Bingham et al. (2006) consider governance as "the process of guiding decisions and actions that affect the private sector, public sector, and individual citizens." From a more precise meaning, governance is the decision-making process of collective action, involving a series of stakeholders, such as governments, business organizations, civil society, labor organizations, and others as pluralistic actors (Rasche 2010). From a deeper background, the rise of governance theory is related to the decline of traditional bureaucratic hierarchical organizations in the context of informatization and globalization. The strict hierarchy, rigid system, and weak flexibility of bureaucratic institutions contrast sharply with the autonomy of civil society and the efficiency of the private sector. Eliminating the monopoly power of bureaucratic organizations by introducing more actors into the decision-making and execution process of public affairs has become the core proposition of governance theory.

The concept of governance was introduced to China in the 1990s. Important early research includes Xu Yong's (1997) paper "GOVERNANCE: An Interpretation of Governance," Mao Shoulong et al.'s (1998) monograph "The Reform of Western Government Governance," and Yu Keping's (1999) paper "The Rise of Chinese Civil Society and the Transformation of Governance." The book "Governance and Good Governance" (2000), edited by Yu Keping, provides a relatively systematic introduction to the research achievements of foreign governance theories.

So, what exactly does "governance" entail? In what sense does it meet theintrinsic requirements and direction of the reform and innovation of China's community governance system? Yu Keping (2001), combining the definitions of many foreign scholars, points out that governance includes five aspects ofconnotation elements: First, it implies a series of social public institutions and action subjects that come from the government but are not limited to the government; Second, it implies ambiguity in rights and obligations in theprocess of seeking solutions to social and economic problems; Third, it affirms the power dependence among various social public subjects involved in collective action; Fourth, it implies that the participating subjects willeventually form an autonomous network; Fifth, it implies that the ability to do things well is not limited to the power of the government, nor is it limited to the government's issuing orders or exercising authority.

In the author's view, several core attributes of governance give it strong explanatory and application capabilities: First, it emphasizes multiple subjects rather than a single dominant one; Second, it emphasizes cooperation and consultation rather than issuing orders; Third, it emphasizes common goals rather than self-interest; Fourth, it highlights the multi-party win–win situation in participatory governance rather than the zero-sum game of power. It is in this sense that many typical practices of transitioning and upgrading from community management to community governance have emerged in the practical field, such as the so-called Shanghai model, Shenyang model, and Jianghan model.Specifically, Chen Weidong (2000) pointed out in his research on community construction in Jianghan District, Wuhan, that the fundamental issue of community construction is institutional innovation, which is to explore a brand-new urban grassroots social management system to replace the already ineffective unit management model. The community governance model explored and formed in Jianghan District under the background of community construction promoted by the Ministry of Civil Affairs has the following characteristics: the combination of administrative regulation mechanisms and community autonomy mechanisms, the complementarity of administrative functions and autonomy functions, the integration of administrative resources and social resources, and the interaction between government forces and social forces.

Under the guidance of the governance concept, the innovation of China's urban grassroots social governance system should follow the principle of "Party committee leadership, government support, community autonomy, and gradual progress." At the same time, the reform and innovation of the urban grassroots social governance system can be promoted from the following aspects. First, the leadership of the Party should shift from a "system guarantee type" to a "functional role type." Specifically, the functional positioning of the Party organization should shift from a system guarantee type institutional arrangement that fully intervenes in community governance to a functional role type institutional arrangement that promotes participation through Party building, creates conditions for grassroots mass autonomy, and guides and regulates community governance by leveraging the organizational resources of the ruling Party. Second, the government's role should shift from "direct intervention" to "macro-control and support." This is a key adjustment in the transformation of government functions and the way they operate, providing a more adequate environment and space for social governance innovation. Third, the development of society. Construct a specialized, autonomous social network system and social organizational forces, grant communities a high degree of complete autonomy, and promote the orderly undertaking of government-transferred functions by social forces, thereby meeting the growing needs of residents for a better life.

3.2 Social Work and Innovation in Grassroots Social Governance

Social work is an important institutional component and professional force in advancing social construction, innovating social governance, and promoting shared development (Xu Yongxiang 2005; Li Yingsheng 2008; Xiang Deping 2008; Wang Sibin et al. 2009; Guan Xinping 2017), and it holds significant constructive value and meaning for grassroots social governance. By the end of 2017, the total number of social work professionals exceeded 1 million, with 320,000 certified social workers, more than two-thirds of whom are active in communities. Social work plays an important role in supporting the improvement of people's livelihoods, innovating social governance, promoting social harmony, and consolidating the foundation of the Party's governance (Ministry of Civil Affairs 2017). It is evident that focusing on grassroots social governance is both an important aspect of examining Chinese social work and a key issue in the development of Chinese social work.

Firstly, the normative research on the governance function of social work. The social changes brought about by China's social transformation provide opportunities for the development of professional social work, while social governance expands the space for further development of social work. Some scholars believe that social work is a beneficial supplement to social governance (He Yun et al. 2016), and it has isomorphism with social governance (Han Qingxiang 2013; Ji Deshang 2015), and can play a unique role in social governance innovation (Xie Jianshe et al. 2012; Liu Zheng 2013; Li Yingsheng 2014). Other scholars believe that the governance function of social work should transition from disciplinary techniques to social construction (Guo Weihua 2014), ultimately moving towards "service-oriented governance" (Wang Sibin 2015).

Secondly, research related to the participation of social organizations in grassroots governance. One perspective is the "dependent" existence of social organizations from a structuralist viewpoint. Research often emphasizes the dominant influence of the state and government on social organizations, which is a mode of social governance that integrates social elements into the administrative system. Examples include "categorical control" (Kang Xiaoguang et al. 2005), "interest alignment" (Jiang Hua et al. 2011), and "administrative absorption" (Kang Xiaoguang et al. 2008). Another perspective is the development of social organizations as a "rational myth" from an action-oriented viewpoint. Social organizations can compensate for the deficiencies of the government and market, providing various social services (Wang Ming et al. 2010; Ge Daoshun 2011; Jing Tiankui 2012), and are important subjects in a multi-governance structure (Liu Zhenguo 2010; Guan Xinping 2011), serving as a horizontal order coordination mechanism (Li Youmei 2015).

In fact, the ideal function of social organizations is based on a series of complex conditions (Zhu Jiangang et al. 2013; Li Youmei 2017), and it is difficult to accurately depict the participation of social organizations in social governance without considering the multiple logics and institutional environment complexities of the emergence and development of local Chinese social organizations (Huang Xiaochun 2014, 2017).

Thirdly, research on the "embedding" of social work in grassroots social governance. The mainstream view in academia regarding the intervention of professional social work in communities is embedded development (Xiong Yuegen 2003; Sun Ying 2004; Wang Sibin 2011; Wang Ruihua 2011; Lu Shizhen et al. 2011); the path of social work participation in community governance is mainly reflected in the institutional design of "three-society linkage" (Yang Guihua 2015; Xu Yongxiang 2016). However, complex neighborhood power relations limit the deep embedding of professional social work (Zhu Jiangang et al. 2013), and in practice, embedding does not necessarily lead to development. "Embedded development" can only be reflected in structural functions, relatively neglecting the process of development and the dynamics of action strategies (Huang Xiaoxing et al. 2015), and research on "embeddedness" has not been fully developed at the "mechanism" level, thus losing analytical value due to being too general and broad, affecting the depth of theory and explanation.(Liu Shiding 2014). Research on "three-society linkage" also lacks emphasis and attention on "subjectivity" and "professional integration" based on it.

How to maintain professional autonomy and achieve "effective linkage" based on subject development becomes a key issue in reality.

Fourthly, community-based integrated social work. In recent years, some scholars have proposed from the perspective of action research to construct a "community-based social work" (Chen Tao 2011; Zhang Heqing 2011), with the core issue being to promote community-based integrated social work practice (Zhang Heqing 2016) and achieve resource integration. Some scholars have also attempted to construct a model starting from the community, focusing on relationship reconstruction, and using various service methods and knowledge traditions from the perspective of disaster social work.An effective integration into the main content of the integrated service model of social work aims to effectively expand the theoretical perspective and practical methods of integrated social work services (Wen Jun 2015, 2016).

Overall, the integration of social work into community governance has received certain attention at both practical and theoretical levels and has achieved fruitful research results. However, there are also some dilemmas that urgently need to be addressed and areas worth advancing. Firstly, at the theoretical level, existing research more or less shares the theoretical elements of the "state and society" relationship, lacking mid-level theories and analytical frameworks that can more accurately grasp the relationships between different subjects in the integration of social work and social organizations into grassroots social governance. Secondly, in terms of practical focus, existing research tends to emphasize fragmented action strategies and individualized, singular studies of contextual governance practices, with less attention to the mechanisms behind strategies and practices and the integration service model formed by the linkage and coordination between mechanisms. Finally, from the perspective of research preferences, existing research has also formed a consensus on "integration," but lacks due attention and research on the paths, mechanisms, and strategies to reach consensus, neglecting the value, strategy, and systematic unity of social work integrating into grassroots communities, and there is little discussion on the "integration mechanism" in the most practically meaningful "integration" process.

Therefore, this book uses the panoramic map and process of social organization participation in community governance as the narrative carrier, focusing on multi-subject comparative research and model integration refinement based on empirical research. It explores the specific and meso-level mechanism elements used by social organizations in the process of integrating into grassroots community governance and places them within an overall theoretical framework for construction, interpretation, and analysis, to extend the explanatory chain of existing analyses and construct a new community-based integrated social work service model at an intermediate level that can connect vertically and horizontally, optimizing the service efficiency and action strategies of social organizations participating in grassroots social governance.

3.3 Moving Towards a New Stage of Co-Governance: Cooperation Governance and Its Applicability in China

Tocqueville, in proving the necessity of social self-governance, believed that society was still at a low level of complexity, and the low complexity of society determined that the government could effectively govern a society. Even if the participation of social self-governance organizations in the process of social governance was needed, it was still centered on the government, with social self-governance organizations playing a role in assisting government governance. However, now, governance is no longer government-centered with social self-governance forces as auxiliary, but rather a cooperative governance between the government and social self-governance forces (Zhang Kangzhi 2006).

In fact, the concept of governance includes the attribute of cooperation. Due to the pluralistic and relatively independent characteristics of governance subjects, the conduct of governance activities inevitably requires participants to unite and collaborate with each other. American scholar Emerson et al. (2012) emphasized the interest association of cooperative subjects, pointing out that as a specific form of governance, collaborative governance refers to the institutional arrangement completed by many stakeholders participating together, which is used to determine common behavioral norms and coordinate interest relationships. Ansell et al. (2008) provided a classic definition of collaborative governance, considering it as the process where public and private actors jointly formulate the supply rules of public goods through various means, more specifically, bringing together a group of public and individual stakeholders through a public forum to make a consensus decision-making process. They also explained the six characteristics of collaborative governance: ① Cooperation is initiated by public departments or institutions; ② Participants in cooperation include non-government members; ③ Participants directly participate in the decision-making process, not just staying at the consultation stage with government departments; ④ The form of cooperation is formal, and decisions are made collectively; ⑤ The goal of cooperation is to make consensus decisions; ⑥ The focus of cooperation is on public policy or public management. From the above research, it can be generally seen that compared with the general meaning of governance, collaborative governance emphasizes more on the equal relationship and consensus decision-making among governance subjects, emphasizing the process where stakeholders make a joint discussion around public affairs to form the final plan (Chen Jiaxi 2015).

Jing Yijia (2014) believes that collaborative governance is a composite governance model between government governance and self-governance, characterized by the exchange and sharing of governance resources by different governance subjects to solve common affairs. The government can adopt tacit approval, invitation, authorization, or other methods to support. Encourage social organizations to participate in the consultation, decision-making, implementation, evaluation, and supervision of public affairs, jointly achieving the discovery, shaping, and response to public needs and social contradictions. In the process of collaborative governance, the government needs to address the mismatch between administrative governance and external demands, incorporating social governance resources to enrich interaction methods and identity aspects in public affairs, forming a complex governance structure and response capability. In Western countries, introducing social organizations often becomes a way to enhance government legitimacy. Although this is also a quietly growing trend in China, overall, social organizations still actively approach the government to gain legitimacy. Under the form of collaborative governance, the government and social organizations form a relationship of mutual agency or even mutual representation, jointly entering the process of consultation, evaluation, and decision-making.

China's urban communities are not merely autonomous units but also bear the connotation of national governance. Urban community governance is a collective decision-making process involving negotiation and cooperation between government extensions (community party organizations, community residents' committees) and other various community entities (community elderly associations, community volunteer organizations, etc.). The residents' committee has never been entirely a government agency and has always been in the dual tension between "administration" and "autonomy," sometimes "state," sometimes "society." Thus, the composite nature of community attributes, the diversity of governance subjects, and the consultative nature of the governance process undoubtedly strengthen the applicability of collaborative governance theory as an explanatory framework for China's community governance structure (Chen Jiaxi 2015). Collaborative governance theory has significant enlightening implications for promoting the optimization of China's urban community governance structure and achieving good community governance. Community governance is essentially the joint participation of various stakeholders, reaching consensus in the process of participation, and forming solutions to community public affairs. This participation itself also helps to enhance the community identity, subject consciousness, sense of responsibility, and sense of gain of each subject.

3.4 Analytical Framework and Approach

The author believes that social governance should be included in the structural system of social system reform for analysis, while it is linked with political system reform and economic system reform. Essentially, social governance is an important practical aspect of social system reform, meaning that the party, government, and society reach a new governance structure based on some consensual rules, thereby jointly striving to achieve the goals of social livelihood, social vitality, and social order. These consensual rules may be "party committee leadership, government responsibility, social collaboration, public participation, legal protection," and this new governance structure is a social governance pattern of co-construction, co-governance, and sharing by all people. Thus, social governance begins to move towards a new stage of "collaborative governance." The 19th National Congress of the Communist Party of China proposed to "create a social governance pattern of co-construction, co-governance, and sharing," to "strengthen the construction of social governance systems, improve the social governance system of party committee leadership, government responsibility, social collaboration, public participation, and legal protection, and enhance the socialization, legalization, intelligence, and specialization level of social governance," to further "strengthen the construction of community governance systems, promote the shift of social governance focus to the grassroots, play the role of social organizations, and achieve positive interaction between government governance and social regulation, and residents' autonomy," also further providing a realistic basis for "collaborative governance" under the leadership of the party. Therefore, based on the concept of "co-governance" and collaborative governance, this book proposes the following analytical approach from a theoretical perspective.

1. "Joint Governance" Based on the Separation of Government and Society

With "separation of government and society" as the principle, effectively transforming the government's social functions can achieve joint governance of society by the government and social organizations on the basis of division of labor and cooperation. China's current community construction system was formed under a special economic and social background, and the deepening of economic system reform is the initial driving force of community construction. The current "non-separation of government and society" community construction system is only a transitional system. With the development of the market economy, this system can neither play the role of a guarantor of state-owned enterprise reform nor adapt to the new trend of shifting the focus of urban social management downward. By adhering to the principle of "separation of government and society," effectively transforming the government's social functions, and achieving joint governance of society by the government and social organizations on the basis of division of labor and cooperation, it becomes the core of social system reform. The "two-level government, three-level management, four-level network" community system is a product of specific historical conditions and played an important role in the early exploration of community management and construction. However, as it is only an internal reform and innovation of the administrative system, it does not touch the social system itself of "non-separation of government and society" and "confusion of government and society," thus having structural defects that are difficult to overcome, making it increasingly difficult to play the institutional role of promoting social development, social management, and social services in grassroots communities. According to the principle of "separation of government and society," effectively transforming the government's social functions, achieving... The introduction of a modern social work system, establishing a division of labor and cooperation framework between the government and society, is a necessary condition for the innovation of community construction systems and mechanisms in our country (Xu Yongxiang 2006). The modern social work system, composed of the division of labor and cooperation between government and society, the support of the public financial system, and a professional and vocational work system, is an effective tool for social system innovation. It plays an important role in solving the difficulties of social members, resolving social conflicts, and maintaining social order. From the practice of community construction in our country, the introduction of a modern social work system is not only a necessary requirement for building a modern social management system and social development model but also the only way to enhance the overall social civilization and community service level. One of the directions of the reform of our country's social management system is to adhere to the principle of "separation of government and society," and to effectively transform the social functions of the government, striving to strip away the social service functions and some social management affairs that the government undertakes or directly engages in, and actively cultivate and develop various social organizations.

2. Governance System of Division and Cooperation Among Multiple Entities

The key to the reform and innovation of the social management system lies in effectively transforming the social functions of the government, actively cultivating civil social organizations, establishing a modern public financial system, and striving to construct a modern governance system of division and cooperation between the government and society. In the era of a planned economy, there was no community or social work in the modern sense in our country. With the establishment of the socialist market economy system and the disintegration of the "unit system society," community construction and social work have gradually gained the soil for survival and development. The current community construction system is the result of the government's reform of the urban administrative management system, but it is merely a redistribution of administrative power and functions within the government, lacking social attributes, and has not changed the structural defect of the traditional social system of "non-separation of government and society." In the new stage of building a harmonious society, this system is no longer able to undertake the institutional roles of community social development, social democracy, social governance, and social services. Therefore, the progress and development of society and the deepening of community construction all rely on the reform and innovation of the social management system.

It should be noted that community construction is the foundation or an important component of the entire harmonious society construction, and discussing the system of community construction cannot be separated from the study of the reform of the entire social management system. In other words, the reform and innovation of the community construction system should be incorporated into the macro perspective of the reform of the entire social management system, with a high emphasis on the significance of reform and innovation in the social management system, actively drawing on successful international experiences in social construction, and constructing a new community construction system needed for a harmonious society. Firstly, the principle of "separation of government and society" and the division and cooperation between government and social organizations based on it are fundamental elements of community construction system innovation. Secondly, effectively transforming the social functions of the government and addressing the issues of government function overreach and absence are important steps in achieving "separation of government and society." Thirdly, actively cultivating and developing non-governmental, non-profit social service organizations, especially professional social service institutions, is an important aspect of achieving "separation of government and society," transforming government social functions, and community development. Finally, reforming the traditional financial system and establishing a modern public financial system conducive to the innovative development of community construction is an important component of the social management system of "separation of government and society" and a material prerequisite for improving community social welfare and social service levels.

However, it is important to note that the leadership of the Party and the governance by multiple entities are organically unified. Social governance must achieve the unity of the Party's leadership, governance according to law, and the participation and co-construction of multiple social entities (Zhou Daming 1993; Ma Yili 2008; Tang Huangfeng 2008; Zhu Qianwei 2008; Wang Ming 2009; Kang Xiaoguang 2011; Yu Jianxing et al. 2012; Yan Jirong 2013; Zhou Zhiren et al. 2013). The role of Party organizations in community or social governance is receiving increasing attention, and scholars are striving to academicize this phenomenon. The result is the emergence of an analytical framework of "Party, State, and Society" or "Political Party, Government, Society" (Lin Shangli 2001; Xie Chuntao 2011; Jing Yuejin 2005, 2019) as an academic consensus. For example, Shi Guoliang's (2011) research found that the relationship among political parties, government, and society will affect the development prospects of social organizations. Lin Shangli (2001) studied the general relationship among the Party, State, and Society. Jing Yuejin (2005) studied the manifestation of the relationship among the Party, State, and Society in rural governance practice, arguing that compared to the framework of the Party, State, and Society, the framework of Political Party, Government, and Society is more suitable for analyzing social governance issues, and calls for "bringing political parties into the analysis of the relationship between the state and society" (Jing Yuejin 2019). The party is actually an important "integrative" force, a key force for the effective operation of grassroots social cooperative governance, and also the core with the most Chinese characteristics in China's grassroots social governance.

3. Innovative Mechanism Combining Grassroots Autonomy and Full Participation of Social Organizations

From the perspective of organizational co-construction in social governance, the population size of grassroots society is rapidly expanding, and the population structure is diverse. Facing governance dilemmas such as departmental function misalignment and overreach, heavy government regulatory administrative model, multi-dimensional differentiated governance status, and fragmented "innovation" that is difficult to replicate, it is necessary to achieve departmental coordination and administrative system adjustment. This should focus on departmental participation in social governance, exploring reforms in grassroots management systems, governance structures, governance processes, power allocation, resource allocation, power exercise, and personnel allocation. It should deeply explore the support system for grassroots autonomy and the collaborative role of social organizations in social governance, achieving the organic integration and linkage of "top-down" public service sinking, "bottom-up" grassroots autonomy, and "external embedded" social organization services, forming a three-dimensional, integrated service ecosystem.

4. New Pattern of Holistic Governance of Grassroots Society with Co-construction, Co-governance, and Sharing

Between the core of party organizations and the decentralization of other social organizations between the segmented administrative management system and complex social problems and needs, and between insufficient public participation of residents and fragmented grassroots governance, the serious fragmentation and closure of grassroots social governance make the linkage and systemic effects of grassroots social governance innovation increasingly important. Grassroots governance is not a single issue of social management and governance, nor is it an important mission that can be undertaken by a single department or social organization. It is under the social governance system background of "party committee leadership, government responsibility, social collaboration, public participation, and legal protection" that the innovation of the social governance system is realized, constructing a new pattern of grassroots governance with co-construction, co-governance, and sharing. It is a systemic reform and reorganization that "pulls one hair and moves the whole body." In this process, it is necessary to achieve a high degree of unity and integration of the political logic led by party building, the management (service) logic of shifting the focus of social governance downward, and the life logic of selective community participation (Wu Xiaolin 2019). Therefore, it is necessary to clarify the differences and unity between co-construction, co-governance, and sharing based on comprehensive investigation and in-depth research, extract the implementation path combined with grassroots governance of co-construction, co-governance, and sharing, and provide empirical evidence for better achieving grassroots social governance innovation.

References

Chen J (2015) Rethinking the structure of urban community governance in China—from the perspective of collaborative governance theory. J Wuhan Univ (Philos Soc Sci Ed) 68(1):71–76

Chen W (2000) The transition of urban grassroots social management system: from unit management model to community governance model—research on the goal model, system innovation, and feasibility of community construction in Jianghan District, Wuhan. Theory Mon 12:3–9

Gerry S, Huaxia F (1999) Governance as theory: five propositions. Int Soc Sci J (Chin Ed) 1:19–30

Guan X (2017) Analysis of the objectives and overall welfare level of China's current social policies. Soc Sci China (06):91–101

He Y, Wei X (2016) Social governance collaborates with social work: the formation of governance techniques and art combining rigidity and flexibility. J. Zhejiang Gongshang Univ (04):113–116

Jing Y (2014) From service purchase to cooperative governance—forms and development of government-society cooperation. China Adm Manag 7:54–59

Jing Y (2003) Administrative democracy: significance and limitations—The enlightenment from wenling's "Democratic Deliberation Meetings". Zhejiang Soc Sci (01):27–30

Jing Y (2005) The party, the state, and society: the relationship among the three dimensions—characteristics of chinese politics from the perspective of grassroots practices. J Central China Normal Univ (Human Soc Sci Ed) (02):9–13+29

Jing Y (2019) Bringing the party back in—reflection and reconstruction of the state-society relationship framework. Explor Free Views (08):85–100+198

Kang X (2005) Analysis of economic development issues in a harmonious society. Acad Exch (07):64–68

Kang X (2011) An analysis of brand building as the core competitiveness for the development of private enterprises—a case study of suning appliance. Econ Res Guide (20):49–51

Kang X, Han H (2008) Categorical control: a study on the relationship between state and society in mainland china. Open Times (02):30–41

Li Y (2008) Promotion strategies for the professionalization of social work in China. Soc Sci Res (05):109–114

Li Y (2014) Exploring effective pathways for social work to intervene in social governance innovation. Soc Work Manag 14(03):23–28+98

Ma Y (2008) Ritual interaction and the cohesive power of core values. Explor Free Views (04):6–7

Tang Huangfeng (2008) Returning to political buffer: a rational examination of the functional evolution of china's petition system in contemporary times. Wuhan Univ J (Philos Soc Sci) (04):573–579

Wang M, Le Y (2008) Analysis of the participation models of chinese civil organizations in public service procurement. J Party Sch CPC Zhejiang Prov Committee (04):5–13

Wu X (2019) Integration of governance power, service devolution, and selective participation: the "composite structure" of urban community governance in forty years of reform and opening-up. Chin Public Adm 7:54–61

Xu Y (1997) Governance: an interpretation of governance. Polit Sci Res (01):63–67

Xu Y (2006) Division and cooperation between government and society: research on the reform and innovation of community construction system. Southeast Acad Res 6:51–57

Xiang D (2008) The development orientation and reflection of social work education in China. Soc Sci (05):85–87

Xie C, Fan X (2011) Historical enlightenment of the popularization of marxism. Seeking Truth (08):19–21

Yan J (2013) Collaborative governance: the path to social management innovation—a theoretical reflection based on the state-society relationship. Chin Public Adm (02):58–61

Yu J, Gao X (2012) The behavioral logic and institutional foundation of local development-oriented governments. Soc Sci China (05):95–112+206–207

Yu K (1999) Introduction to governance and good governance. Marx Real 5:37–41

Yu K (2001) Governance and good governance: a new political analysis framework. Nanjing Soc Sci 9:40–44

Zhang K (2006) The historical process towards cooperative governance. Hunan Soc Sci 4:31–36

Zhou D (1993) On the urbanization of rural communities at the urban fringe—a study on urbanization in Guangdong (Part 1). Sociol Stud (06):13–20

Zhu Q (2008) From new public management to holistic governance. Chin Public Adm (10):52–58

Zhou Z, Jiang M (2013) Exploring interdepartmental coordination mechanisms of the Chinese government: a narrative and diagnostic framework. Econ Res.Guide 6(01):91–117+170

Chapter 4
Shanghai Model: Community-Based Service Integration

4.1 Logical Starting Point and Phased Development: Shanghai The historical evolution of innovative social governance

The innovative practice of grassroots social governance in Shanghai has been advancing in sync with the development and opening up of Shanghai's Pudong New Area (hereinafter referred to as "Pudong"). The development and opening up of Pudong, which began in the 1990s, is undoubtedly a milestone decision in Shanghai's modernization development and reform and opening-up endeavors. Over the past two decades of development and opening up, Pudong's economic and social construction has achieved tremendous success, rapidly transforming from a rural-dominated marginal suburb into a modern new urban area. These changes have further posed new requirements and challenges for social governance and construction, especially grassroots social governance.

Overall, the exploration of community governance in Shanghai has roughly gone through three stages. The 1990s was the initial stage of social governance in Shanghai. Entering the early twenty-first century, the continuously changing economic and social situation forced continuous innovation in grassroots social governance. After 2010, especially since the implementation of the Shanghai Municipal Party Committee's "No. 1 Project" in 2014, grassroots social governance has become a proactive behavior for simultaneous promotion and exploration in Pudong and all streets and towns. The in-depth promotion and practice of the "No. 1 Project" have constituted an important shaping force and variable, gradually incubating and constructing the "Shanghai Model" of community governance in the new era. The practical results of the "No. 1 Project" have also transformed into the intrinsic components of the Shanghai Model.

L. Hou, *The Integrated Service in Urban Community Governance*, Public Economy and Urban Governance in China, https://doi.org/10.1007/978-981-96-6775-8_4

4.1.1 "Two-Level Government, Three-Level Management": The Initial Formation of the National Basic Management Unit and the "Shanghai Model"

In the context of promoting urban community construction nationwide, how has the community construction in Shanghai evolved? In the community service and community construction practices since the 1990s, Shanghai's exploration… It played a demonstrative leading role nationwide. In order to adapt to the new situation of continuous deepening of reforms in Shanghai, ongoing opening-up, and the ever-changing socio-economic development of the city, effectively strengthening community management and grassroots government construction became a core issue of common concern for both the central government and the Shanghai Municipal Party Committee at that time. The community construction and management initiatives since the 1990s were the government's proactive attempt to reform the urban administrative management system in response to the disintegration of the "work unit system society" and the shift of the focus of urban management downward. Essentially, these initiatives aimed to build systems and mechanisms at the street and community levels to strengthen the consolidation of grassroots government, which is the process of building state power. In this political and historical context, "street communities" continuously formed, becoming a unique phenomenon in the construction of urban communities with Chinese characteristics, reflecting the integration and unity of government administrative functions and community social functions. This phenomenon is especially pronounced in Shanghai, which started the process of urban community construction and management earlier, where the entire city is accustomed to referring to streets as communities in terms of administrative system nomenclature, further highlighting the blurred boundaries and close relationship between streets and communities. In March 1996, Shanghai held its first-ever urban work conference, where then-Party Secretary Huang Ju delivered a report titled "Strengthening Community Construction and Management, Continuously Improving the Level of Urban Modernization Management," which comprehensively outlined Shanghai's community construction and management work in the new era, marking the transition from the previously single-attribute "work unit system" to a comprehensive and holistic community construction and management approach. This conference marked the beginning of urban community management and community construction in Shanghai and even nationwide.

In this context, starting in May 1995, Shanghai conducted a pilot of "two-level government, three-level management" in ten streets across ten districts, which later developed into the organizational system of "two-level government, three-level management, four-level network" for urban community construction and management in Shanghai (Xu Yongxiang 2001). Among them, the two-level government refers to the municipal and district governments, the three-level management refers to the management by the municipal, district, and street levels, and the four-level network incorporates communities in the sense of residents' committees into the community management framework. The development of the construction system is divided into two stages.[1] First, from 1996 to 2003, during the "two-level government, three-level management" model stage, the main focus was on decentralization, with the basic characteristic of strengthening the responsibilities and powers of the streets. In 1996, Shanghai proposed new measures for urban management reform with "two-level government, three-level management," further decentralizing some of the district government's powers to street offices. Although streets are not a level of government, they enjoy some management powers equivalent to those of urban governments. The core is the further downward shift of the focus of urban management (mainly public social management), forming a relatively complete hierarchical management system for streets, clarifying the streets' main responsibility status in social construction and management, i.e., streets taking the lead in unified organization, comprehensive coordination, and supervision and inspection of urban management, community services, comprehensive social security management, spiritual civilization construction, and street economic development, thereby forming a new management structure system. Second, from 2003 to 2006, during the "two-level government, three-level management, four-level network" model stage, the main focus was on decentralization, with the basic characteristic of de-emphasizing the economic function of streets and strengthening the social management function of streets and residents' committees. This was also the stage when grid management was proposed. In August 2004, the Shanghai Civil Affairs Bureau proposed the "General Report on Promoting Grid Management in Shanghai Communities," pointing out that since 1996, the Shanghai municipal government had established a "two-level government, three-level management, four-level network" management system. However, in practice, the real emphasis on the "four-level network," i.e., clearly incorporating residents' committees into the urban social management system practice sequence, was marked by the localized management centered on residents' committees during the SARS epidemic, which demonstrated the enormous social mobilization and organizational functions of this basic autonomous organization network. Thus, the idea of grid management began to fully permeate the practice of grassroots social governance in Shanghai.

Over more than a decade of practice, this system has become increasingly mature, becoming a major feature of Shanghai's community construction, forming a distinct "Shanghai model.“ Its basic characteristic is that Shanghai positions the community at the street level, maintaining the nature of the street as an agency of the district government, while appropriately delegating power to the street, achieving the downward shift of the focus of government administrative management, and strengthening the administrative power and administrative efficiency of the government at the street community level, i.e., the third level. Additionally, below the street level, in the residential communities affiliated with residents' committees, Shanghai has built a fourth-level management and service network (He Haibing 2012). On this basis, a street community management system combining leadership, execution, and support

[1] "Shanghai Model": The introduction of the two stages refers to the research materials from Feng Meng's "The Evolution of Community Governance (Innovation) in Pudong New Area". Special thanks are hereby extended.

systems has been constructed. Management system. Firstly, the community management leadership system is composed of the street office and the urban district management committee. This effectively clarifies the primary management status of the street office, achieving decentralization of power. Meanwhile, to effectively overcome the many issues brought about by segmentation, below the street office, an urban district management committee is established, led by the street office and jointly participated by the police station, environmental sanitation management office, industrial and commercial administration office, street hospital, housing management office, and city appearance inspection team, to discuss, coordinate, and supervise various matters of urban district management and community construction, and to formulate community development plans. This creates an organic synergy between specialized management in a linear form and comprehensive management in a block form. Secondly, within the street, a community management execution system is formed by four committees (Municipal Management Committee, Community Development Committee, Comprehensive Social Security Management Committee, and Financial and Economic Committee). The division of labor between different committees is clear, with distinct responsibilities and powers, providing a concrete organizational reliance for the street in handling and coordinating daily affairs. Furthermore, enterprises, social organizations, residents, and their autonomous organizations within the jurisdiction form the community management support system of the Shanghai model. They work through organizational forms such as community committees, community affairs consultation meetings, coordination committees, and residents' committees, mainly responsible for deliberation, coordination, supervision, and consultation, thereby providing effective support for community management. Finally, this model also uses the residents' committee, a mass autonomous organization, as a "four-level network" for social management, emphasizing the full role of the residents' committee as a network organization in practical work, promoting residents' participation in community management, and achieving effective community governance.

This system setup was highly innovative at the time and also had obvious institutional advantages and functional roles. Specifically, firstly, it initially streamlined the vertical and horizontal relationships of the government in grassroots community management, which is conducive to mobilizing and leveraging the enthusiasm of street offices and various government functional departments in community construction; secondly, it greatly strengthened the government's human, material, and financial resources on the front line of community construction, making the community a place of focus or inclination for various administrative resources for the first time; thirdly, it is conducive to community committee members being at ease and focused on community work, which is beneficial for the Party and government to manage and control grassroots communities; fourthly, the social service and social management functions that were separated from enterprises were relatively smoothly transferred to the street office and its affiliated community through this system (Xu Yongxiang 2006). The aim is to promote the decentralization and power devolution of municipal and district governments and relevant functional departments, with the street office as the main body, to strengthen the administrative effectiveness and efficiency of the government at the street community level.

It is not difficult to see that the unique community management system explored and formed by Shanghai has strong political, social, and economic development motivations, and this unique community management system has certain positive historical significance. Some scholars have pointed out that the community system reform since the 1990s means empowering street and residents' committee organizations, which is an important practice of bringing the street-resident system back from the marginal position to the mainstream framework of administrative power. This practice is a manifestation of the vertical extension of state administrative power downward, thus, to a large extent, reflecting the strengthening of the vertical order integration mechanism of community management (Li Youmei 2012). However, for a specific historical period, the strengthening of this vertical power order was an important means to cope with the risks brought by social transformation at that time, a temporary measure to promote stable social transformation and orderly operation of social power differentiation. From the specific practice process, due to historical and institutional inertia, the vertical order strengthening mechanism formed in a specific historical period still exerts strong inertial force in the new historical period, which in turn constrains the improvement of the horizontal coordination mechanism. For example, in the previous residents' committee re-election, the election, which should have reflected the autonomous nature of residents, showed a strong administrative color, leading to the continuous production and reproduction of administrative power (Geng Jing et al. 2011). This imbalance of the horizontal mechanism and the difficulties in vertical linkage are key issues facing contemporary community governance and are important tasks that should be focused on in the new round of innovative social governance and strengthening grassroots construction.

With the continuous advancement of social transformation, the original grassroots social governance reform has not evolved towards its social attributes that should be highlighted, but rather, in the specific Chinese context, a stronger community political connotation has emerged, leading to the so-called involution dilemma in grassroots governance (He Yanling et al. 2005). It is against this background that the "Shanghai model" has embarked on a new round of reform journey.

4.1.2 Grid Management: The "Shanghai Model" Solidifies and Takes Shape in Convergence[2]

In the exploration of reforms, the concept of grid management began to fully permeate the practice of grassroots social governance in Shanghai. The "two-level government, three-level management, four-level network" effectively managed grassroots society after the disintegration of the unit system, demonstrating significant institutional advantages and gradually evolving into the core essence of the "Shanghai

[2] Some content has been published in the "Academic Forum" 2014, Issue 12.

Model." However, as reforms deepened, the management form of urban communities underwent a transformation. Formally, the unit system gradually gave way to the community system, but the community system also exposed inherent issues of "excessive administrative integration and insufficient community autonomy," which affect the construction of urban grassroots social order. To eliminate these issues, various regions actively explored solutions, and the Shanghai Model also began new reform explorations. The basic premise is that district and street government powers are excessive, while grassroots social governance organizations (community committees) lack the capacity to undertake the social tasks transferred from unit organizations. Under this conceptual premise, the path advocates for the devolution of state power to community organizations like community committees, essentially attempting to advance social management through the optimized reorganization of power within the system. This is the practice of "grid management." Due to its inherent alignment with "grid management," the reform of the "Shanghai Model" continuously incorporates the thinking and practices of "grid management" into its own reform practices, demonstrating logical isomorphism.

Grid management refers to "using streets and communities as the foundation, dividing the management area into unit grids based on certain regions, establishing an urban grid management information platform, and managing urban components and events to achieve a four-level linkage management model and information resource sharing system among city, district, specialized handling departments, and grid supervisors." Essentially, it applies modern science and technology to effectively integrate community resources through community resource and information sharing, eliminating information asymmetry, and achieving community self-governance through community interaction, joint participation, and collective action, thereby improving social management efficiency. Grid management is a horizontal community self-governance form corresponding to the top-down vertical administrative management form, completing a three-dimensional, all-encompassing social management form that combines "vertical and horizontal." From an operational perspective, "grid management" involves dividing a jurisdictional area into several grid-like units according to certain standards, with dedicated personnel providing differentiated, specific, personalized, and continuous service and management for the needs and issues of residents within the grid. The main idea is to fully utilize modern information technology to break the boundaries between traditional urban management departments and administrative divisions, mimicking bureaucratic organizational design, and dividing the entire grid management process into six stages: information collection, screening and filing, task dispatch, task handling, result feedback, and evaluation and closure. This enables timely problem detection, sensitive crisis response, effective handling, scientific and efficient management, and specific service delivery within the precisely constructed "grid." The specific practice of grid management in urban community management systems is reflected in the following four points: First, using grassroots management units such as streets and communities as the foundation, dividing urban social management into several grids in a standardized manner; second, relying on information technology to strengthen communication and information exchange between different grids, establishing an integrated and linked platform for information resource sharing; third, establishing a unified resource scheduling and coordination mechanism to overcome "vertical and horizontal segmentation," integrating previously dispersed management and resources of various departments in an institutionalized manner to achieve efficient, scientific, and coordinated management; fourth, maintaining the compatibility and openness of the grid system, achieving "multi-network integration" and dynamic management through mutual compatibility between different grids (Zheng Shiyuan et al. 2005).

The grid management in Shanghai's Pudong New Area was developed based on the existing "two-level government, three-level management" framework. According to the requirements of the municipal party committee and municipal government, careful preparations were made, and Pudong New Area selected the Zhuyuan Community in Weifang New Village Street and the Lianyang Community in Huamu Street, which have strong representativeness, as the first batch of pilot communities.[3]

In grid management, the Zhuyuan Community established a "Community Party Committee/Community Governance Committee" structure. The party organizations in residential areas, community new economic organization party branches, and community mobile party member branches are managed territorially. The community party committee is elected by party representatives chosen from the community residential areas and community unit party organizations, implementing a permanent system for party representatives without setting levels, departments, or staffing. The community governance committee primarily integrates and coordinates various non-party organizations within the community, including six neighborhood committees, community workstations, and police stations, with a secretariat and community management committee, and social work committee office. The aim of this plan is to further improve the community management system, with the community party organization as the core, to enhance community cohesion and service capabilities, becoming a demonstration point for promoting grid management in traditional community types.

The Lianyang community plan is divided into two steps. The first step is to establish the "Community Party Branch/Community Management Committee" structure. The Community Management Committee (hereinafter referred to as the "Management Committee") directly corresponds to a large neighborhood committee, and the community party general branch only manages branches such as mobile party members and retired party members set up vertically according to attributes, without establishing horizontal community party joint meetings and other organizations. The second step, after the population reaches a certain scale and the community form is further improved, the community party general branch will manage several residential area party branches and party branches of new economic organizations established based on attributes vertically, and rely on the community party joint meeting and in-service party member council horizontally to integrate various party organizations within the community that have no subordinate relationship. The

[3] The "Shanghai Model" grid management pilot referenced the research data from Feng Meng's "Clues to the Evolution of Community Governance (Innovation) in Pudong New Area.".

community management committee implements a "three-in-one" system arrangement of administrative management, industry management, and resident autonomy, composed of representatives from the sub-district office, relevant functional departments' dispatched agencies, developers, property management units, and community unit representatives, to research and decide on community affairs, and lead the coordination of the property management association, governing several community workstations and neighborhood committees. This plan focuses on forming a model of multi-party participation and joint governance.

The core and most crucial aspect of grid management is achieving non-centralized control and the sharing and integration of resources and information. One of the difficult issues in community construction at the time was the "segmentation of lines and blocks, departmentalization of information and resources, and the widespread existence of isolated islands," which had become the main bottleneck of inefficiency and control failure. The proposal of the grid management concept was largely hoped to improve this situation. This is a brand-new resource integration mechanism, relying on which not only can the resources between various lines and blocks of the government be integrated, but also party and government resources, market resources, social resources, and personal resources can be integrated to form a synergy and vitality for community construction.

Specifically, the significant advantages of "grid management" are threefold. First, the decentralization of administrative power allows the connection of governmental power and social individuals at a more micro level, helping to improve the performance of administrative management, making administrative power reach vertically to the bottom, turning the past "thousand lines above, one needle below" into "thousand lines above, one net below," through which the voice of the party and the services of the government can extend to the grassroots of society, replacing the original "control" with "service," effectively eliminating the "blind spots" of social management. Second, the regular patrols and inspections by grid management personnel can timely grasp the demands and dynamics of the masses, turning the control of social sentiment and public opinion information from "passive acceptance" to "active collection," thereby greatly shortening the interval time of "collection and feedback" of information, allowing for timely intervention and problem-solving, winning people's hearts with high-quality and efficient services, and plugging potential loopholes that may lead to future crises, solidifying the mass foundation of the party's governance and enhancing the legitimacy of the party's governance. Third, grid management breaks through the scope of general management and services, adding a new level of "grid" under the "two-level government, three-level management" structure (regardless of the nature of the "grid" for now), forming a four-level responsibility system, namely "two-level government, three-level management, four-level network," causing a transformation in the grassroots social management system, which to some extent is conducive to forming a new social management pattern (thus, it can be seen that the Shanghai model and grid management have logical isomorphism).

From this perspective, grid management as an institutional innovation aims to solve the practical problems of "segmentation of lines and blocks, isolated island phenomenon" in community management, reflecting innovation in the original system, and has efficient and rapid advantages in responding to the contradictions and problems, needs, and services of the diversified and complex grassroots society. It is a downward supplement and improvement to the existing system. However, as the technical tendency of grid management becomes prominent, its ideological concept is still fundamentally about fully controlling grassroots order, "social stability above all else," "one rod to the end," and the institutional design basically follows the hierarchical administrative power's. The detailed logical construction is achieved under the premise of not altering the existing "street and neighborhood committee" system, by refining into smaller units under the community, namely "grids," to achieve a re-integration of administrative and service resources. Due to its value orientation and mindset focused on maintaining stability, the overall dominance strategy and hierarchical control thinking are still prominently present. This results in a dilemma where the grassroots social power structure lacks substantial community participation and subjects, showing an excess of "vertical structure" but insufficient "horizontal structure." The strong and rigid administrative power squeezes and engulfs the weak and resilient autonomous power, damaging social connections, and the operational structure within the field lacks flexibility, forming a rigid social coercion model that suppresses social vitality and reduces the society's ability to adeptly handle complex and uncertain social risks. Meanwhile, in social management, there is a significant downward shift of administrative responsibilities and tasks, but a lack of service resources and authority, leading to an imbalance of power and responsibility. This determines that grid management is difficult to change the hierarchical structure and monopoly of authoritative resources of government line departments, and it is challenging to bring about the horizontal integration and linkage of power and responsibility of government line departments in a macro sense, which is expected in public service governance.

Under the perspective of grid management, residents become objects managed and monitored by power, and the community transforms into a space where administrative power exercises its will within the grid, rather than a living community integrating stakeholders within the community. Therefore, how to dilute the administrative color of "grid management," achieve effective collaboration between community autonomy and government administrative power, eliminate the technical limits of "grid management," optimize the relationship between technological progress and social governance, and thus find the intersection between grid management and community autonomy, to achieve mutual construction and mutual strengthening for a win-win outcome, constitutes the direction and focus of a new round of innovation in community construction, community system reform, and social governance.

4.1.3 Innovating Social Governance and Strengthening Grassroots Construction: A New Round of Reform and Transformation in the Shanghai Model

With the continuous transformation and upgrading of the economy and society, Shanghai is also facing some new issues in the socio-economic field, such as accelerated economic transformation and development (industrial technology upgrading); a significant increase in the total population (approximately 24.28 million permanent residents in Shanghai, reaching saturation); a trend towards a diverse social structure (coexistence of multiple forces); complex demands for public interests (awareness of rights, interest protection, etc.); and profound changes in information dissemination (informationization, the internet era, big data, etc.). Especially since 2010, the degree of social individualization and atomization has been deepening, residents' needs have become more diverse, and the traditional management thinking and system of "two-level government, three-level management, four-level network" are difficult to effectively match and respond to. In the case of Pudong, this is even more so. Pudong's area is about one-fifth of Shanghai's, its population accounts for about one-quarter of Shanghai's, and its economic output accounts for nearly one-third of Shanghai's. This shows that Pudong's grassroots social governance is as a large urban district, large town area, and large community grassroots social governance. Relatedly, the basic background of social governance and grassroots construction in Pudong New Area presents three distinct characteristics.[4]

First, the region is vast, with many units, and the scope of grassroots governance is relatively large. Pudong's actual jurisdiction covers about 1,210 square kilometers, with 12 streets, 24 towns, 910 residential areas, and 365 villages; the permanent population is about 5.5 million; the average jurisdiction of a street is 7 square kilometers, and a town is 53.7 square kilometers. The largest street, Huamu Street (20.9 square kilometers, is about 19 times the size of the smallest street in the city, Shimen Second Road Street in Jing'an District, 1.1 square kilometers), and the largest town, Zhuqiao Town (160.2 square kilometers, is about 27 times the size of the smallest town in the city, Miaohang Town in Baoshan District, 5.9 square kilometers). The characteristics of large districts, large towns, and large streets are prominent.

Second, there are many types and differences, and the span of grassroots governance is relatively large. In Pudong New Area, relatively mature but constantly emerging new situations and challenges in urbanized communities (including international communities like Lianyang and Biyun, deeply urbanized communities like Lujiazui, and rapidly urbanizing communities like Huamu), and urban–rural junctions in a transitional period with various focused problems and contradictions (such as Beicai Town, Chuansha New Town, etc.), are high.Rapid advancement and numerous governance challenges urgently need to be addressed in large residential areas (such as Sanlin Town, Caolu Town, etc.) and in remote rural areas

[4] For details, please refer to the internal document "Report on the Work Achievements of the Pudong New Area Experimental Zone in Shanghai City".

with heavy development tasks and a pressing need to improve various supporting facilities and service resources (such as Datuan Town, Wanxiang Town, etc.). These diverse regional types coexist; additionally, there are 7 development zones within the district, each with different functional orientations and development stages. The relationships between the development zones and their respective towns, surrounding towns, and related towns are intertwined in terms of industrial development and urban management, with overlapping interests. Differences in urban and rural structures, north–south regional differences, and internal differences within towns are prominently highlighted. The diversity and differences lead to fragmented and atomized governance experiences, compounded by unbalanced and inadequate development, making it difficult to achieve integrated governance and service linkage.

Third, rapid changes and diverse demands make grassroots governance challenging. With the rapid development of the market economy, major projects like Disney and large aircraft are being intensively advanced, urbanization processes and large residential area constructions are deepening, various industrial forms and social management forms are emerging, various economic and social organizations are thriving, and large numbers of external populations are rapidly concentrated and introduced. The regional industrial structure, social structure, and population structure are changing rapidly, and the diverse needs of various entities are collectively emerging. Social governance, especially grassroots governance, must adapt to this rapidly changing and diverse demand pattern, which is understandably difficult.

To respond to the aforementioned background and challenges and to adapt to the rapidly transforming economic and social landscape, Pudong New Area is taking the lead in exploration, earnestly implementing General Secretary Xi Jinping's requirements for Shanghai to "adhere to the people-centered development philosophy, focus on promoting social governance innovation, and enhance the level of refined management in megacities." Former Party Secretary Han Zheng pointed out, "With the rapid development of Shanghai's economy and society, the grassroots situation changes rapidly every day, and new changes, new situations, and new problems arise, some of which we grasp, some only partially, and some not at all. The means to solve problems at the grassroots level are limited, resources are lacking, responsibilities are unlimited, and strength is severely insufficient. Many urgent problems cannot be solved by addressing them individually; there must be new breakthroughs in institutional innovation and new measures in policy arrangements. Through research, we can promptly identify problems, delve into them, concentrate wisdom from all sides, learn from successful grassroots experiences, and propose policy measures." At the same time, the exploration made by Shanghai in the field of social governance is also the central government's expectation for Shanghai, as a megacity, to promptly respond to various problems encountered in its development process. As Han Zheng pointed out, the Party Committee's "Number One Project" concerns the implementation of the spirit of the Third Plenary Session of the 18th CPC Central Committee, the consolidation of the grassroots foundation for Shanghai's current and long-term development, and the genuine promotion of social governance innovation and the strengthening of grassroots construction. The issuance of the "Number One Project" series of documents is the result of problem-driven, situation-forced, reform-driven, and institutional innovation as well as proactive actions.

Against the backdrop of the above multiple factors, at the end of 2014, the Shanghai Municipal Party Committee and Municipal Government issued the "Opinions on Further Innovating Social Governance and Strengthening Grassroots Construction" (hereinafter referred to as the "Opinions") and six special documents.[5] The "Opinions" point out that the core of social governance is people, the focus is on urban and rural communities, and the key is institutional innovation, actively exploring a new path of social governance that conforms to the characteristics and laws of megacities. These important decisions have made new responses to contemporary social governance, among which, adhering to the core of people is the fundamental starting point and foothold of social governance; adhering to governance according to law emphasizes the rule of law rather than rule by man; adhering to reform and innovation stimulates social vitality and shifts government functions; adhering to the focus on urban and rural communities. The "Number One Project" has innovated the community management and governance system in Shanghai over the past two decades, especially in grassroots community governance, with a series of new concepts and practices. At the 2016 Shanghai Municipal Party Committee's conference on promoting social governance innovation and strengthening grassroots construction, Comrade Han Zheng pointed out that all departments at the municipal and district levels must implement the "1 + 6" documents of the Party Committee, focus on solving specific problems, thoroughly change their mindset, and truly revolve everything around the grassroots, forming a "service-oriented" work mechanism. This indicates an emphasis on the grassroots, facing urban and rural communities, providing and delivering services, and thereby opening up service channels. The issue of the "last mile" for residents has become an important focus of "innovating social governance and strengthening grassroots construction."

From the perspective of its goal positioning, it mainly refers to two "further" aspects. First, "further improve the grassroots social governance system. In grassroots social governance, the Party's leadership is strong and effective, the government's leading role is fully played, all sectors of society participate in an orderly manner, the effectiveness of grassroots mass autonomy is evident, a positive interaction between government governance and social self-regulation, and resident autonomy

[5] At the end of 2014, the Shanghai Municipal Party Committee issued the "Number One Project" results, forming the "1 + 6" series of documents (hereinafter referred to as the "Documents"), including"Opinions on Further Innovating Social Governance and Strengthening Grassroots Construction," "Implementation Opinions on Deepening Street System Reform," "Implementation Opinions on Improving the Governance System of Residential Areas and Strengthening Grassroots Construction," "Implementation Opinions on Improving the Village-Level Governance System and Strengthening Grassroots Construction," "Implementation Opinions on Organizing and Guiding Social Forces to Participate in Community Governance," "Implementation Opinions on Deepening and Expanding Grid Management to Enhance Urban Comprehensive Management Efficiency," "Shanghai Community Worker Management Measures (Trial)".

is basically formed, and the multi-faceted synergy of social governance is significantly enhanced." Second, "further improve grassroots social governance capabilities. Improve grassroots coordination capabilities, reform and innovation capabilities, service to the masses capabilities, legal governance capabilities, organizational co-governance capabilities, guidance for autonomy capabilities, and informatization application capabilities, striving to make the grassroots social governance system more accessible to the channels of public demands, more responsive to public voices, more comprehensive in providing service management, more solid in carrying out mass work, more powerful in maintaining community safety, and more effective in creating a good environment." The first "further" lays the basic framework for the functional positioning and governance system of different subjects in grassroots society, while the second "further" clarifies the basic connotation and indicator composition of the modernization of grassroots social governance capabilities, thus pointing the way for a new round of grassroots social governance and community service innovation in Shanghai.

From the internal logic and reasoning of the reform, street system reform is the key and core of the "number one topic," and it is also a major initiative to innovate social governance and strengthen grassroots construction.[6]

First, cancel the street's investment promotion function and return to the "three public" positioning. The "document" points out, "The original community (street) Party Working Committee is renamed the Street Party Working Committee, serving as a dispatched agency of the district committee, playing a leading core role in regional social governance. Cancel the street's investment promotion function and corresponding assessment indicators and rewards, with street expenses fully guaranteed by the district government, promoting the street's work focus to truly shift to public service, public management, and public safety in social governance," thereby initiating a systematic reform of relevant elements in the street and street-residence system. In March 2015, according to the deployment arrangements of the municipal party committee and municipal government, the Pudong New Area District Committee and District Government issued the "Implementation Opinions and Responsibility Division on Further Innovating Social Governance and Strengthening Grassroots Construction," under the guidance and promotion of the District Committee Organization Department and the District Regional Work Committee, each street in Pudong New Area adhered to "grasping with both hands, promoting both," completing a series of prescribed actions such as agency listing, cadre adjustment, personnel placement, residential area secretary enjoying the establishment, salary treatment increase, and document policy issuance, while paying more attention to mechanism improvement and implementation effectiveness, and focusing more on the people's experience in the reform. Focus on solving the needs, expectations, and concerns of the people through system and mechanism reform, truly achieving

[6] The content of the "1 + 6" system reform, especially the case introduction in this part, specifically references and uses the research data of Feng Meng's "Pudong New Area Community Governance (Innovation) Change Clues," hereby acknowledged.

vitality at the grassroots level, effective management, and tangible benefits for the people.

Second, nested with the grid management system, the core leadership role of the Party organization at the grassroots level is more prominent. The "document" points out, "Further establish and improve the urban grid comprehensive management center, community Party building service center, and community comprehensive governance center," "establish and improve the resident area Party organization as the core leadership, improve the resident area joint meeting platform, implement the resident area Party organization part-time committee member system, enhance the resident area Party organization's ability to coordinate community resources, and effectively ensure that the residents' committee and owners' committee perform their duties according to law." Specifically, in terms of promotion, the street "abolishes two and establishes one," abolishing the original comprehensive Party committee and residential area Party committee, establishing a new community Party committee and using the Party building office as the daily office agency, using the community Party building service center as the work platform, with the community Party committee uniformly responsible for regional Party building, "two new" organization[7] Party building, and residential area Party building, greatly enhancing the ability to integrate and utilize Party building resources. For example, the Lujiazui Street Office uses The "Golden Link" new party-building model breaks the barriers between the "high-end" central business district and the "down-to-earth" residential areas. It uses residential areas and commercial buildings as units, relying on the existing grid-based comprehensive management responsibility areas and building comprehensive service stations to establish several regional party-building communities based on "building-residence" and "building-building" units. Through "two-building linkage and two-end extension," it complements each other's needs and resources, solving the previous issue of "one end cold, one end hot," and actively explores new ways of party-building in the financial city community. Weifang New Village Street has established a regional youth work co-construction committee, integrating resources from institutions like New York University Shanghai and China National Petroleum West–East Gas Pipeline Company. They adopt a rotating chairmanship system where the Youth League Committee Secretary of member units serves as the rotating chairman every six months to carry out related special activities, finding a new path to promote party-building and facilitate community cultural integration through the power of the community party committee.

Thirdly, the functional positioning and work approach of the street have become clearer. The document points out that the street mainly performs eight functions: strengthening party-building, coordinating community development, organizing public services, implementing comprehensive management, supervising professional management, mobilizing social participation, guiding grassroots self-governance, and maintaining community safety. The street system is reformed as follows: "The street party and government internal institutions are set up according to the '6 + 2'

[7] The "two new" organizations refer to new economic organizations and new social organizations.

model, namely, a unified setup of the party and government office, community party-building office, community management office, community service office, community safety office, and community self-governance office. At the same time, two additional work institutions can be set up according to the actual needs of the street." Thus, the organizational structure reform matches the functional positioning after the reform. This change has altered the previous situation where department settings simply corresponded to higher-level departments, and the division of sections was too detailed, to some extent solving the problems of overlapping functions and uneven workload. For example, through the street party-building office, party-building work is unified and centralized, integrating the previously scattered responsibilities of regional party-building, "two new" organization party-building, and residential area party-building, which were originally dispersed in community party-building joint meetings, comprehensive party committees, and residential area party committees. This is more conducive to playing the leading core role of party organizations in grassroots social governance and helps grassroots party committees integrate various resources.

Fourthly, establishing a professional system provides more security for grassroots teams. The document proposes establishing a professional system for community workers, stating that "based on job characteristics, years of service, education level, and relevant professional level, a job grade sequence for community workers should be established," and "a salary system linked to job grades and performance assessments should be established." In terms of the specific promotion practices of each district street, this reform not only introduced measures to improve the treatment of residential area party organization secretaries and social workers, such as allowing residential area party organization secretaries to enjoy staffing and increasing social workers' salaries, but also focused on comprehensively optimizing the career development system, enhancing the attractiveness of community service positions, and increasing community workers' sense of professional identity, honor, and pride, playing a motivating role. For example, each street has built a "reservoir" of reserve cadres for residential area party organization secretaries, where some outstanding comrades with both integrity and ability, outstanding performance, and public recognition are included in the training system, gaining opportunities for education and training, a stage to showcase themselves, and space for future development. Furthermore, by establishing a professional system, in addition to significantly increasing the income level of social workers, the street social work office directly signs contracts with social workers, giving them a "quasi-institutional" status, greatly enhancing the attractiveness of social worker positions in the job market, and helping to broaden the source of social worker teams.

Fifthly, consultative democracy highlights the synergy of grassroots self-governance and community co-governance. The document points out, "Fully leverage the self-governance function of the residents' committee under the leadership of the residential area party organization, innovate the content and form of self-governance based on residents' needs, and stimulate self-governance vitality." "Establish and improve a democratic decision-making mechanism focused on deliberation and consultation, effectively utilizing hearings, coordination meetings, and evaluation meetings, and improve the mechanism for forming self-governance topics and projects from the bottom up, guiding residents to participate in self-governance affairs throughout the process in an orderly manner." From this perspective, the reform emphasizes changing the previous "upward correspondence" and "responsibility to the top" to "downward correspondence" and "responsibility to the bottom," with relevant departments making every effort and taking the initiative to strengthen grassroots services. Each street changes its mindset, consciously shifting from the past "order-taking + order-issuing" work model to focusing more energy on front-line services and serving the people, forming a proactive adaptation at the district and street levels.Research on the Construction of Integrated Service Models in Urban Community GovernanceThe atmosphere of the new street system and grass-roots changes is more conducive to streets strengthening problem-oriented and demand-oriented approaches to solve actual grassroots issues.

In particular, the "two bottom-up" mechanisms established in this reform (the bottom-up self-governance project formation mechanism and the co-governance agenda formation mechanism) have pointed the way for streets to carry out community co-governance and resident self-governance work. Especially in terms of streets playing a core role in forming and implementing co-governance agendas and self-governance projects through the "two bottom-up" mechanisms, it has effectively guided and encouraged broad social participation. For example, Jinyang New Village Street has established a "dual governance" council in residential areas, which is elected by a residents' representative meeting, has legal status, and a standardized charter. It provides a "four-coordination" functional platform for consultation, coordination, collaborative management, and joint advancement among various governance entities in the residential area, forming a "dual governance" operational mechanism where residents identify problems, experts discuss countermeasures, the council makes decisions, and teams execute them. Dongming Road Street, by guiding residential areas to formulate self-governance rules or conventions, adopts "public discussion" community self-governance, menu-style legal education, selective legal advisors, incubative legal training, and grid-style legal publicity, integrating and permeating legal elements into community self-governance and co-governance, enhancing the scientific level of community construction.

Sixth, deepening grid management significantly enhances the efficiency of urban comprehensive service management. The "document" proposes to "fully integrate the security patrol and prevention network, armed emergency response network, mass prevention and control network with the urban comprehensive management grid to ensure that various grids such as urban management and social security can overlap and reduce crossovers," "promote the integration of grid management with joint operations, and establish a relatively standardized and unified citywide grid comprehensive management system," "urban grid management mainly undertakes the inspection, dispatch, handling, supervision, and assessment of components and event issues in areas such as urban management, market supervision, and street security that can be discovered through patrols, strengthening the leading coordination and handling responsibility for urban management stubborn problems that require multi-department collaboration," and subsequently, "promote the shift of focus downward, the sinking of forces, and the delegation of power, facilitating linkage and collaboration across sectors."

From the practical results, on one hand, it has basically achieved full coverage of grassroots comprehensive management, making streets more capable of mobilizing resources and smoother in operation mechanisms; on the other hand, it has achieved the simultaneous advancement and innovation of problem discovery and problem-solving mechanisms, focusing on the handling and resolution of issues. For example, through the deep integration of urban grid comprehensive management with large-scale joint operations and linkages, Pudong has expanded the scope of grid comprehensive management from the narrow field of urban management to areas such as social security (participating in crime fighting), food safety, and fire safety, initially achieving "one-stop acceptance and joint handling," changing the previous situation of "each department working independently and separately."The previous situation of "each department working independently and separately" has been changed; the responsibilities, resources, and forces of relevant street departments have been delegated to workstations, achieving full-process, all-round, and full-coverage information communication and work linkage from the street to the community, from management to law enforcement, from discovery to handling, initially realizing the linkage of urban routine management and emergency response.

On this basis, in March 2017, the "13th Five-Year Plan for Social Governance in Shanghai" (hereinafter referred to as the "Plan") was introduced, marking Shanghai's first five-year special plan for social governance. The goal system of the "Plan" is for grassroots social governance to be more vibrant, social organization development to be healthier, the social security comprehensive governance system to be more complete, the urban operation system to be safer, and the social work talent growth environment to be more optimized. Among them, making grassroots social governance more vibrant means more actively stimulating and mobilizing the potential vitality and advantageous resources of grassroots communities, which is an important innovation in transforming communities from passive governance objects to active governance subjects. Meanwhile, in April 2017, the "Shanghai Residents' Committee Work Regulations" (hereinafter referred to as the "Regulations") were issued, becoming the first local regulation in the country concerning residents' committee work. The "Regulations" further emphasize the role of residents' committees in self-governance, emphasizing their guidance and supervision of owners' committees, property management, and other entities. The above provisions further strengthen the exploration of new requirements and initiatives for grassroots community self-governance and co-governance under the "No. 1 Project" background, further institutionalizing and normalizing the "Shanghai Model 3.0" of innovative grassroots social governance in the new era.

In summary, the new round of grassroots social governance reform in Shanghai has undergone deep innovation in systems and mechanisms, forming a rich variety of specific practices, practical features, and project brands, achieving positive results.The effectiveness of governance.

4.2 In-Depth Exploration and Practical Logic: The New Era the Shanghai Experience in Grassroots Social Governance

The "Shanghai Model 3.0" is essentially a progression based on previous governance experiences. It continuously responds to new situations and problems encountered in grassroots social contexts and practices. It is also a continuous exploration and advancement of "innovative social governance and strengthening grassroots construction." This model is the result of ongoing exploration and expansion based on the relentless pursuit and effort towards the people's aspirations for a better life and sense of gain. Gradually, it has formed a "new model" of grassroots social governance innovation and service under the new normal of social governance. The author believes that "Shanghai Model 3.0" refers to "cooperative co-governance" based on "government-society division of labor."At its core, it focuses on the organic integration of party building and social governance as the main line, institutional innovation and team building as important supports, people-centered development and a sense of gain as value guidance, and the continuous downward shift of governance focus and the effective cultivation of social organizations as characteristics. It has initially realized the socialization, legalization, intelligence, and specialization of social governance, and on this basis, the positive interaction of government governance, social regulation, and residents' autonomy, as well as community-based integrated grassroots social governance innovation practices.

4.2.1 The Core of the Shanghai Model: "Cooperative Co-Governance" Based on "Government-Society Division of Labor"

The issue of government-society relations is a core and key issue in grassroots social governance innovation. The relationship between the government and society, as well as the internal mechanisms and dynamic evolution processes behind this relationship, are important clues for understanding social governance. They are also important theoretical premises for promoting and optimizing the positive interaction of government governance, social regulation, and residents' autonomy. Therefore, understanding the new era Shanghai model requires analyzing whether there are significant differences and innovations from the perspective of the nature of government-society relations.

The government and society (organizations) belong to two different operational fields, with different operational mechanisms and internal logics. Therefore, how to avoid conflicts between the two and achieve positive interaction has become an important topic of concern for scholars. In fact, since the 1980s, the issue of government-society relations has become an analytical paradigm and knowledge base for many social science studies. The academic community has accumulated rich academic knowledge on this topic and achieved a series of important research results. From Evans et al. (1985) and Putnam (2001) discussing specific paths to achieving positive interaction between government and society, to Skocpol (2008) understanding state capacity in government-society interactions and attempting to "bring the state back in," to Migdal (2013) proposing a new research path of "state in society" in macro examinations of state-society interactions, the issue of government-society relations has also shifted from macro institutional structures to micro interaction mechanisms.

From the perspective of institutional structure research, pluralism, corporatism, and authoritarianism are three traditional influences. Pluralism is a complex theoretical system. Theoretically, pluralism emphasizes that society and the state should be separate, and civil society is an autonomous activity field. In policy design, pluralism advocates that citizens' rights and freedoms are of primary importance. To avoid state interference, it emphasizes that there should be a distance between the state and society (Whyte 1992). In the relationship between the state and society, pluralism views society as preceding the state, external to the state, and having a unique operational logic that is not influenced by external factors. Society has value priority. The state should be an institution representing the will of society, gaining legitimacy through empowerment by society (Liu An 2009). This can be reflected in theories on the origin of the state and the relationship between civil (citizen) society and the state. In terms of power allocation, pluralism has two assumptions: first, there are various organizations (interest groups) in society; second, due to the highly dispersed power resources, a multi-centered pattern emerges (Jing Yuejin 2003). In practical reality, the "society-centered" (civil society) concept of pluralism has a dominant influence on the actual political operations in Western societies, especially in the United States, and is the mainstream of Western political thought.

Corporatism advocates that society and the state should be integrated, and the corporatized group formed by their integration… The fabric should serve as the intermediary for the smooth operation of the entire society; the boundaries between interest groups and the state are relatively blurred, and their connections are institutionalized, routinized, and compulsory. The state should be an active and proactive actor, transcending these diverse groups and integrating them into the national decision-making structure to achieve an organic integration between the state and society (Chen Jiajian 2010; Wu Jianping 2012). Schmitter (1974) believes that "corporatism can be defined as a system of interest representation, in which the constituent units of society are organized into a limited number of singular, compulsory, noncompetitive, hierarchically ordered, and functionally differentiated categories. These categories, created by the state, are recognized or certified by the state and granted a monopoly of representational status within their respective domains. However, as an exchange, the state enjoys a certain degree of control over their leadership selection and demand expression."

Authoritarianism, as a theoretical trend, emerged in the 1930s, existing in opposition to totalitarianism. Generally speaking, we can understand authoritarianism as a type of modern political system, a relatively mild form of autocratic regime situated between totalitarian and democratic regimes. Authoritarianism once had considerable explanatory power for Chinese politics, even if not completely. From its proposal in the 1930s, to the systematic definition and refinement of its connotations in the 1960s, and then to the first wave represented by bureaucratic authoritarianism and the second wave represented by the expansion of authoritarianism (including the sub-concept of soft authoritarianism), authoritarianism has demonstrated significant theoretical penetration in the study of real politics. However, as authoritarianism develops in a new phase, integrating and absorbing various institutional factors and theoretical elements, the internal tension of its theory is increasing, and its future development is highly unstable. For example, Yu Jianxing (2012) pointed out that the theory of decentralized authoritarianism cannot effectively explain the behavioral patterns of local governments in China.

In fact, the above three ideological trends all interpret and practice the reform of the Chinese system to some extent, and they all have limitations in their interpretations. Due to the unique characteristics of China's development model, its unique growth and transformation model is destined to face the dilemma of effectiveness when relying on Western contexts and values and constructing analytical theories based on existing Eastern and Western experiences. From the perspective of interaction mechanism research, before the 1990s, the understanding of the relationship between government and society was always influenced by a one-way thinking, tending to believe that government and society were in a zero-sum game relationship, that is, a strong government necessarily meant a weak society, and a strong society necessarily meant a weak government. After the 1990s, academia discovered that the zero-sum game relationship between government and society is not inevitable, especially for developing countries. Often, the government can form an interactive cooperative relationship with society, and further research found that the interaction between government and society can lead to mutual empowerment in specific environments (Wang Jinjun 2015), meaning that on one hand, the government's capacity can be effectively enhanced, and on the other hand, the autonomy of society can be effectively developed. The division of labor and cooperation between government and society can bring about many spaces for reform and innovation. Cooperative governance has rapidly grown in the practice of public domain governance in recent decades, becoming an important theoretical framework for understanding the interactive practice between government and society (seeChapter 2 literature review, not elaborated here). On one hand, effective governance by the government requires the full development and participation of society to provide legitimacy support and foundation; on the other hand,society also needs the government to gradually grow into an important force in the field of social governance on the basis of actively relinquishing power, to achieve effective protection of "society." From this perspective, the positiveinteraction between government and society will not only not weaken the power of the government but will also achieve cooperative co-governance and good governance between government and society through interaction.

Brinkerhoff (1999) proposed five specific steps for the government in promoting cooperation with society. First, construct administrative structures, processes, and mechanisms conducive to the establishment and operational arrangements of partnerships, with decentralization being the primary focus. Second, carry out institutional capacity building for effective cooperation between the public sector and civil society forces, including providing relevant resources and incentives to the public sector to fully interact with civil organizations and non-governmental organizations. Third, as a necessary requirement for capacity building, provide relevant training for public institution personnel to make them adept and committed to cooperation with social forces, including strategic management, policy implementation, community relations and outreach, stakeholder consultation, and confirmation.

Ensuring service quality and supervision, etc. Fourth, establish the necessary legal framework to promote the participation of social organizations and public–private partnerships, including legal recognition of non-state institutions (such as NGOs, interest group associations, etc.), and the establishment of financial and government service procurement mechanisms related to partnership activities. These mechanisms need to go beyond standard contracts, focusing on issues such as power sharing and joint decision-making among potential collaborators. Fifth, develop community and public relations strategies to make society aware of the government's intentions and cooperation plans, and ensure stakeholder participation in cooperative arrangements and policy processes. This means that the cooperation between the government and society is more of a constructive process that needs to be built in specific practices, rather than a spontaneous order.

Therefore, to understand the relationship between the state and society in China, it is necessary to turn to China's practices, especially the grassroots society as the intersection of government and society, and the coexistence field of state and social forces, which becomes an important observation point for observing the practice of government-society relations. From the governance practices in Shanghai, especially since the introduction of the "No. 1 Project," a series of measures such as further streamlining of government functions, further decentralization of services, and further cultivation of society are all responses to and solutions for this proposition, namely how to better achieve "division of labor between government and society" and the effective cultivation of "society" by the government, and on this basis, achieve "cooperative governance." This is typically reflected in the re-positioning of street functions in Shanghai's new round of governance reform, the upward shift of investment promotion functions, and the continuous advancement of community committee and grassroots community construction, as well as the continuous cultivation and incubation of social organizations, all of which are optimizing government-society relations and constructing a cooperative governance mechanism and pattern. Below, I will use the experience of community governance in Pudong New Area as an example to explain the governance logic and practical innovation embedded in the new round of reform of the Shanghai model.

From the governance experience of Pudong, on the one hand, it has begun the attempt of "division of labor between government and society" from the system, which provides the basic premise for cooperative governance. First, streamline functions and completely cancel the street investment promotion function. The "document" points out, "Cancel the street investment promotion function and corresponding assessment indicators and rewards, and the street's financial expenditure is fully guaranteed by the district government, promoting the street's work focus to truly shift to social governance work such as public services, public management, and public safety.“ This “removing the firewood from under the pot” strategy effectively solves the “operator, broker” role of grassroots government, achieving the positive construction of a “service-oriented government,” making social construction and grassroots governance and service provision the daily work of the government, thereby achieving orderly transfer of government functions and service advancement. Second, solidly promote street system reform under a service-oriented approach. “According to the requirements of street function positioning and innovative system, the street party and government internal institutions are set up in a ‘6 + 2’ model, that is, a unified setup of the party and government office, community party building office, community management office, community service office, community safety office, community autonomy office, and at the same time, according to the actual needs of the street, two additional work institutions can be added.“ Expanding the street’s “three centers” to “six centers”,[8] each center is a carrier for the street to perform basic duties of “public service, public management, public safety,” a window for serving the masses, and a platform for promoting community co-governance and autonomy. Such a layout makes the positioning of each street center more accurate and the functions more complete. On this basis, further clarifying the internal setup of the street “6 + 2” “six centers” and other institutions, clarifying the number of street leadership positions, division of labor, and staffing quotas, providing policy support and institutional guarantees for street system reform.

On the other hand, Pudong New Area is also continuously strengthening the process of institutional innovation, forming a system and mechanism for joint consultation and governance of grassroots public affairs, which provides a method guarantee for the effective implementation of cooperative governance. Its main practices include three points. First, the introduction of a grassroots joint consultation and governance system. The “Several Opinions on Promoting Joint Consultation and Governance of Grassroots Public Affairs in Pudong New Area” was introduced, clarifying the scope of joint consultation and governance, participating subjects, platform carriers, procedures, work mechanisms, etc., encouraging the public to participate in joint consultation and governance topics. Second, improve the town-managed community model. In terms of improving the township governance system, the “Guiding Opinions on Promoting Town-Managed Community Work in Pudong New Area” was introduced, strengthening town-managed communities, “establishing community centers as work platforms for town governments to serve residents, providing administrative affairs and basic public health, culture, and other services nearby for residents,” clarifying the four main functions of town-managed communities: coordinating regional party building, carrying out community services, guiding residential (village) work, and organizing joint consultation and autonomy, with town functional

[8] Expanded from the original “community affairs acceptance center, community cultural activity center, community health service center” to “community affairs acceptance center, community cultural activity center, community health service center, urban grid comprehensive management center, community party building service center, and community comprehensive governance center.“.

departments and town-managed... The operational mechanisms between communities, town-managed communities and residential (village) areas, and within town-managed communities among the "two committees and one center" (community party committee, community committee, and community center). Thirdly, advancing the construction of basic management units. By issuing the "Opinions on Improving the Allocation of Basic Public Service Resources in Town-Managed Communities in Pudong New Area (Trial)", the basic management units are solidified, "allocating corresponding public service resources and administrative law enforcement, professional management forces, establishing community affairs acceptance service centers, community health service centers, community cultural activity centers, and urban grid comprehensive management centers or service points," proposing specific goals for the construction of basic public service facilities from five aspects: basic education, health, culture and sports, elderly care, and community affairs acceptance centers, and formulating relevant safeguard measures.

From this perspective, the key to innovation in grassroots social governance in Pudong is the orderly repositioning and transfer of government functions, and on this basis, the establishment of a system and mechanism for co-discussion and co-governance of grassroots public affairs. In continuous exploration, a governance mindset, institutional constraints, and organizational structure of "cooperative co-governance" have been formed, becoming the "core" and "soul" of the in-depth advancement of the Pudong model.

4.2.2 Party Building Leading Governance Innovation: Organic Integration and Mutual Construction of Party Building and Social Governance

The 19th National Congress of the Communist Party of China pointed out that the Party's leadership over all work must be upheld. "The Party, government, military, civilian, and academic; east, west, south, north, and center, the Party leads everything" "improving the Party's ability and determination to set direction, plan the overall situation, formulate policies, and promote reform, ensuring that the Party always oversees the overall situation and coordinates all parties," which includes the Party's strategic positioning of "leadership," the "all-domain" coverage, the "integration" in functional nature, and the "four-dimensional" layout content, specifying the direction and core for innovative social governance in the new era. Shanghai, guided by Party building, integrates Party building into all aspects and the entire process of social governance, actively constructing comprehensive leadership and guidance of the Party over various undertakings, focusing on the exploration and innovation of grassroots systems and mechanisms, fully reflecting the important strategic significance of Party building leading governance innovation for the modernization of urban governance systems and capabilities. Pudong's distinct feature is also reflected in the mutual construction and coupling of Party building and social construction, that is, governance expansion under the leadership of the Party committee, continuously constructing the coupling and embedding of Party building work and grassroots social governance, achieving mutual construction. Below, the author analyzes the relevant practical exploration themed "Internet + Party Building" in H Street.[9]

Firstly, supported by the Party building network, the collaborative effect in social governance innovation is strengthened, enhancing the overall governance capacity of mega-cities. Firstly, strengthening Party building leadership, constructing an optimized and powerful grassroots Party organization system. On one hand, Pudong New Area, following the requirements of the municipal Party committee, conducts comprehensive pilot projects of community Party building and community construction, exploring the formation of a grassroots Party building work network of "three verticals, three horizontals" (vertically forming three levels of community Party working committee, residential area Party general branch, and directly managed Party members, horizontally forming three interfaces of community Party building work joint meeting, residential area Party building joint meeting, and in-service Party members), and using the "three services"[10]activities as a starting point, focusing on promoting the construction of grassroots Party organizations, Party member teams, and system construction. Governance Establishing a strong political and organizational guarantee for harmonious community construction. On the other hand, continuously strengthening the core leadership role of grassroots Party organizations. In 2007, Pudong New Area formulated the "Opinions on Strengthening the Leadership of Community Party Organizations and Actively Building Harmonious Residential Areas (Trial)," further clarifying the responsibilities and relationships of organizations such as residential area Party organizations, residents' committees, property companies, and owners' committees. In 2012, Pudong New Area formulated the "Implementation Opinions on Fully Playing the Role of Party Organizations in Grassroots Mass Autonomy."Establish and improve a grassroots party organization leadership system that is close to reality, conforms to rules, and reflects characteristics, creating a vibrant system of mass autonomy. Strive to achieve effective connection and positive interaction between the party's leadership, government management, and grassroots autonomy. As of now, Pudong New Area has explored and formed a four-level linkage system and network for party building work at the city, district, street, and residential area levels, achieving a synergy of institutional innovation in social governance at different levels. Secondly, relying on regional party building to strengthen "vertical" and "horizontal" coordination and promote the participation of various units in community governance. To solidly advance regional party building, Pudong New Area has issued opinions on implementing the responsibility system for grassroots party building work, exploring multi-dimensional and

[9] The experience of Party building governance in H Street, Pudong New Area, referenced Dr. Xu Xuanguo's research report "Party-Society Mutual Construction: Innovation of Internet + Community Governance Model under the Leadership of Party Building — An Empirical Study Based on Shanghai H Street," with thanks.

[10] "Three services" refers to the Party's higher-level organizations serving grassroots organizations, grassroots organizations serving Party members, and all levels of Party organizations and Party members serving the masses.

three-dimensional party building responsibility assessment content, and completed the renaming of street party committees and the establishment of community party committees, with all district, street, and town party building service centers renamed and listed. Through regional party building platforms and mechanisms, units in each jurisdiction are effectively integrated into the field of grassroots social governance under the guidance of party building, forming an important component of social governance. From the perspective of governance effectiveness, this linkage mechanism of party building work constructs a comprehensive governance network that combines vertical and horizontal elements, ensuring close coordination of different levels, types, and units on the party building platform, jointly enhancing urban governance capabilities. This reform exploration fully taps into the political and organizational resources for governance innovation in the unique context of China, effectively enhancing the systematic and holistic level of current urban governance transformation.

Secondly, adhere to the party's leadership over all work, and practice the political guiding function of grassroots party organizations at multiple levels, promoting the standardized and orderly development of community publicness and public space. Essentially, it is necessary to ensure the party's political guiding power in various fields of grassroots social governance, as well as its practical governance ability and determination to set direction, plan the overall situation, formulate policies, and promote reform. This is also the key design for achieving the coupling and mutual construction of party building and community governance, requiring overall planning and systematic implementation. This mainly manifests as a core and multiple subjects, constructing a governance pattern under the guidance of party building. In practice, H Street, combining the spirit of superior documents and the actual situation of H Community, has formed a party building pattern of "three innovations" and "three transformations." Among them, the "three innovations" mainly refer to innovation in the concept of Internet + community autonomy under the guidance of party building; innovation in the form of Internet + serving the masses under the guidance of party building; and innovation in the channels of Internet + resource integration under the guidance of party building. The "three transformations" include the following content. The transformation of party building guidance from "performing" to "setting the stage." This transformation reverses the previous "dislocation phenomenon" where the party organization played the leading role and the masses participated as supporting roles, and also avoids the phenomenon of "absence" of party organizations in many grassroots governance. The transformation of serving the masses from direct care to resource integration. For the diversified needs of residents, it requires the party organization to step out of the walls to seek resources, making the cohesion and integration of various resources an advantage of the party organization at the grassroots level, promoting the integration of service resources and innovation of service carriers for units stationed in the district and street-side merchants, changing the traditional work path of relying solely on party organizations and party members to directly serve the masses. In serving the masses, residents transform from the original single role of being served to the role of self-service and serving others, highlighting their subjectivity and ownership characteristics. The transformation of uniting people's hearts from brand promotion to mass teams. By cultivating the masses' own teams, promoting the integration of the masses into teams, changing the past single promotion model of party building brands, and exploring corridor and community resources, innovative and colorful mass cultural activities are further integrated into effective carriers for party building to unite people's hearts. Among them, brand services such as micro-wishes and team party building are practical innovations carried out in the process of the above-mentioned transformation of party building ideas, which is an important exploration of H Street in optimizing the ideas and models of party building work.

The above "three innovations" and "three transformations" are all firmly based on the "three major leadership cores" of street community party organizations as pointed out in the "Opinions." The "three major leadership cores" refer to ensuring that street community party organizations become the leadership core for implementing the party's line, principles, and policies at the urban grassroots level, the leadership core for urban grassroots social governance, and the leadership core for uniting and leading the masses to jointly create a better urban life. In this way, the effective leadership of the party over community work is also guaranteed.

Thirdly, strengthen the close connection between party building work and community "burden reduction and capacity enhancement," the allocation of public resources, and the implementation of livelihood projects, enhancing the awareness and governance capabilities of community residents as autonomous subjects, further strengthening the organic connection between the party and the people. First, reduce burdens and lighten autonomy. According to the principle of "reduce what should be reduced, merge what can be merged, and reduce as much as possible," solidly promote the "burden reduction and capacity enhancement" of residential (village) committees.The establishment of the resident (village) committee account directory and the assistance list for government affairs has been streamlined, with the basic directory of accounts dispatched to the resident (village) committees reduced from over 80 items to 11 items for resident committees and 12 items for village committees. This has been achieved by instituting a "conditional access" collaborative approval mechanism, regular inspection mechanism, and special inspection mechanism for the accounts. Secondly, a comprehensive social governance information service platform has been developed, known as the "Thousand Points, Three Cores, One Platform" model.The term "thousand points" refers to the system's extensive coverage, which encompasses 36 street towns, over 1200 resident (village) committees, as well as various district-level departments and units. The "three cores" denote the foundational information core, the data application core, and the decision analysis core. The "one platform" refers to the integrated social governance information platform that is utilized by users at all levels. The "thousand points, three cores, one platform" framework has achieved the integration of large-scale datasets, including basic population data, housing data, agricultural information, and elderly information, directly serving the daily operations of street towns and resident (village) committees. It has effectively addressed issues such as the multiple reporting and repetitive filling out of resident (village) committee ledgers, thereby alleviating the workload at the grassroots level. The innovative development of information technology has enriched the means of innovation in grassroots work.Thirdly, financial security and the promotion of self-governance are emphasized. In accordance with the overarching approach of "project-based management and participatory governance," which is characterized by "residents autonomously determining the purpose, participating in expenditures, and assessing and sharing the outcomes," the "Interim Measures for the Use and Management of Working Funds of Residents' Committees in Pudong New Area" have been promulgated. This has increased the financial support for the construction and self-governance of residents' committees, with the self-governance work funds reaching 80,000 yuan per committee per year.Fourthly, the supervision is strengthened to improve self-governance. Efforts are being made to advance the public disclosure of community affairs and democratic management, thereby continuously enhancing the ability of residents' (villagers') committees to conduct mass self-governance and perform mass work.

The implementation of the aforementioned work has also been accomplished with the active participation of resident district party building, resident party members, and volunteers. In fact, grassroots party building cannot be discussed in isolation from party building itself, nor can governance be discussed without the context of party building. Only through the organic integration and synergy of party building and governance can both be advanced in tandem. Therefore, H Street and the entire urban grassroots party building in Pudong emphasize that party organizations at all levels should focus on enhancing the sense of gain among the people when promoting party building work. The party building mechanisms are closely integrated into community service projects such as neighborly community construction, white-collar stations, 15-min living service circles, resident self-governance fund projects, and community self-governance services. These practices have significantly enhanced the organic connection between the party and the people, as well as the public's sense of identification with and participation in urban governance.

Fourthly, under the guidance of party building, the "Pareto optimal" improvement of community order and vitality is achieved. This mainly involves exploration in two aspects: first, how community order is maintained and how multiple stakeholders achieve positive interaction with each other; second, where the community's momentum comes from and how to stimulate the innovation of different stakeholders to promote the realization of good community governance. This requires the formation of a sustained attention to public issues by various stakeholders, leading to the establishment of a long-term and stable participation mechanism, as well as a rational and responsible spirit of participation. The effective resolution of this issue also involves, at a deeper level, the core issue of constructing community publicness. Huang Xiaochun (2017) believes that publicness refers to the process of people stepping out of the private domain to discuss and act on issues of common concern, thereby transforming from private to public, and forming a consciousness of concern for community public affairs. However, it should be noted that the construction of publicness requires certain entry points and is carried out under the active leadership of residents' committees and party members, especially in the discovery of public needs, the formation of public issues, the formulation of disposal plans, and the resolution of public problem troubles, all of which require communication and interaction among multiple stakeholders such as party building, residents, and residents' committees.

Pudong's approach of leading grassroots self-governance and co-governance through urban grassroots party building has precisely formed a new pattern where the party's embedded working mechanisms promote a positive interdependence between vitality and order. In turn, the continuous advancement of grassroots self-governance also consolidates and constructs the legitimacy and authority of the party organizations. By rebuilding the party's legitimacy through service, this has become an important path for grassroots party building in the new era, and it is also an important manifestation of the party's social and service nature.[11] On one hand, the existing party building work needs to achieve a transformation in methods and pathways, shifting from traditional political party building to a social and service-oriented party building leadership. This shift places greater emphasis on the multi-level leadership functions of the party, focusing more on "soft" value leadership, service leadership, professional leadership, project leadership, and talent leadership. This approach helps to maintain effective order in grassroots self-governance and co-governance while embedding flexible leadership, which is conducive to the orderly maintenance of grassroots autonomy and co-governance.

It is particularly important to focus on achieving "silent and subtle" permeative leadership by strengthening the social and service foundations of the Party. This should become a normalized method in the Party's work in the new era. On the other hand, new media technology is a new force for innovating traditional Party building, which means embedding and absorbing new era factors to enhance the effectiveness of Party building work. For example, by building a more open Party building work network, an information-based Party building platform, and a diversified Party building linkage mechanism, it provides important coupling carriers and mechanism channels for forming the public nature that autonomy and co-governance rely on. This also facilitates the diversified diffusion of community governance platform channels and the continuous stimulation of governance vitality.

In essence, in grassroots social governance, Pudong has constructed a governance network that extends Party building in multidimensional spaces through continuous innovation in Party building work, achieving precise governance of urban society and continuously practicing the "Pareto optimal" improvement of community order and vitality under Party leadership. In response to the changes in the Party building situation and environment in the new era, Shanghai's grassroots Party building work not only focuses on forming a comprehensive Party building work network but also emphasizes forming precise work paths and platforms targeting different nature spaces in urban economic and social life. For example, in building spaces, a relaxed

[11] The issue of the party's social and service nature is a significant assertion and an important dimension of party building in the new era, which highlights the need to reconstruct the social nature of the party in the construction process.

Party building network is formed around core areas of concern for modern organizations such as public welfare, charity, and culture; in internet spaces, cutting-edge methods such as agenda setting and guiding public attention distribution structures are constructed. The issue of the Party's social and service nature is an important assertion and an important dimension of Party building in the new era, which is to highlight the reconstruction of the Party's social nature in construction. In urban community governance, the construction of an open yet cohesive Party building network is emphasized; in mobile spaces, a mobilization network is formed around focal issues such as public service delivery. Through these flexible yet precise mechanisms, urban grassroots Party building can further effectively absorb the social spaces that "overflow" traditional administrative governance networks (Huang Xiaochun 2017). The layout of these new Party building work fields effectively realizes the Party's governance leadership in various tasks and fields in the new era, continuously consolidating and expanding the horizontal and vertical penetration of the Party organization network, and reconstructing the Party's core leadership by continuously absorbing new factors and expanding new spaces.

In summary, the innovative practice of Shanghai's Party building leading social governance, and the paths, work logic, and service fields formed or being formed in exploration undoubtedly have great research and exploration value. They are not only of great significance for finding new ways for social governance innovation in megacities but also provide important support and construction significance for shaping the micro-foundation of national governance capacity during the transition period.

4.2.3 Practical Exploration of Shifting the Focus of Governance Downward: "Two Bottom-Up" in Pudong's Innovative Social Governance in Pudong's Community

Governance and service innovation, emphasis is also placed on system and mechanism innovation to promote the continuous downward shift of the focus of social governance. From a practical perspective, since the implementation of the "1 + 6" document, various grassroots streets and towns in Pudong have fully focused on the important ideas emphasized by the municipal committee, such as "looking downward," "focus on the community," "the key is system innovation," and "the core is people," in the implementation of the strategic deployment of "innovating social governance and strengthening grassroots construction." This has formed a pattern of comprehensively deepening the transformation of government functions, comprehensively promoting governance mechanism innovation, comprehensively stimulating grassroots autonomy vitality, and comprehensively strengthening government self-construction (the four "new" comprehensives). At the same time, more emphasis is placed on problem orientation, scientific and refined management, strengthening linkage and coordination, and enhancing the construction and professional function of grassroots social worker talent teams. In the process of demand-based services and experiential governance, the focus of governance is continuously shifted downward, thereby achieving and implementing the "people-centered development philosophy" and the sense of gain and happiness of residents (villagers).

The municipal committee's "No. 1 topic" pointed out when proposing "promoting resident autonomy and stimulating community grassroots vitality" that it is necessary to deepen the resident autonomy mechanism, fully play the autonomous function of the neighborhood committee under the leadership of the residential area Party organization, and innovate the content and form of autonomy based on resident needs to stimulate autonomy vitality. It further emphasizes "improving the bottom-up autonomy agenda and project formation mechanism," orderly guiding residents to participate in autonomy affairs throughout the process; "establishing and improving the bottom-up neighborhood committee work evaluation system." The focus is on residents' awareness, participation, and satisfaction, strengthening residents' evaluation and supervision of the neighborhood committee and its members. This has led to the formation of a "two bottom-up" mechanism. Specifically, the so-called "two bottom-up" mechanism refers to the bottom-up mechanism for forming residents' self-governance issues and the bottom-up "self-service" project evaluation mechanism. The bottom-up mechanism for forming residents' self-governance issues aims to clarify the boundaries between government and residents' self-governance, further expanding the channels for grassroots participation in community self-governance and co-governance, striving to achieve the goals of "cultivating a group of subjects, exploring a set of mechanisms, providing a series of services, and creating a batch of brands." The bottom-up "self-service" project evaluation mechanism involves entrusting professional third-party social organizations to conduct comprehensive monitoring and evaluation of the "self-service" projects, including daily evaluation, mid-term evaluation, and final evaluation of project implementation, project effectiveness, and financial management, and incorporating the evaluation results into the application work for the next year.

At the community governance level, H Street combines its actual characteristics and real needs in its governance process, exploring and forming a multi-faceted H Street community governance model through a series of community co-governance and residents' self-governance practices that integrate guidance, distinctiveness, and growth. The most notable measure is actively implementing the spirit of the "two bottom-up" mechanism of the municipal committee, formulating and issuing the "Implementation Opinions on the 'Two Bottom-Up' Mechanism (Trial)" and the "Overall Process of Practicing the 'Two Bottom-Up' Mechanism in H Street (Trial)" based on the actual situation of H Street. Since 2015, H Street has launched a pilot project for "self-service," with the first batch of three projects achieving good results, discussed and approved at the 2015 community representative meeting, and fully promoted in 33 residential areas of the street in September 2015 with the "Adding Blessings and Longevity" elderly care self-service project. Further, in 2016, 36 self-service projects were identified. Residents' self-governance work has become an important characteristic brand of H Street community governance. In this, community social work plays an important role in professional guidance, resource linking, and project cooperation, effectively exploring a path for community social work to participate in grassroots community self-governance and co-governance.

At the beginning of 2016, when the Organization Department of the Pudong New Area District Committee conducted research on the implementation of the "two bottom-up" mechanism in H Community, it required the street to improve the structural system, strengthen institutional design, and refine operational processes, and to quickly produce a complete set of replicable and promotable rules and regulations.[12] Specifically, it required H Street to adhere to the following four directions when improving the "two bottom-up" mechanism. First, it should reflect the leadership of the Party, playing the core role of Party members and organizations in practice, further embodying the characteristics of self-governance, co-governance, and regionalization. Second, it should improve the structural system, exploring the needs of different subjects such as individual residents, residential areas, and teams, as well as streets, in a layered and classified manner, and responding through different carriers and methods. Third, projects should be used to timely connect the "two bottom-up" mechanisms, effectively reflecting the formation process of residents' self-governance issues and projects, as well as the project evaluation process, through clear flowcharts, defined time nodes, and standardized review elements, promoting effective linkage of relevant subjects. Fourth, it should refine the implementation steps and processes, forming an effectively operating system that becomes an operable and replicable community governance model. Under the guidance of the above municipal committee's document spirit and the specific requirements of the district committee, H Street, based on its actual situation, formed relevant opinions on the "two bottom-up" mechanism, namely, formulating and issuing the "Implementation Measures for Further Promoting the 'Two Bottom-Up' Mechanism in H Street" (hereinafter referred to as the "Implementation Measures"),[13] institutionalizing the "two bottom-up" mechanism to strengthen and implement it. The "Implementation Measures" emphasize adopting the development concepts of "innovation, coordination, green, openness, and sharing," actively exploring the practical application of the "two bottom-up" mechanism in the community, guiding multiple subjects to participate in grassroots co-governance and self-governance, further expanding orderly participation, promoting information disclosure, strengthening deliberation and consultation, and enhancing power supervision, effectively playing the grassroots foundational role of streets and neighborhood committees in social governance. It has set the goals of reducing grassroots pressure, stimulating grassroots vitality, gathering grassroots synergy, increasing grassroots motivation, and enhancing grassroots capability, by establishing and improving the "two bottom-up" mechanism, widely

[12] Cited from FW: "Implementing 'Two Bottom-Up Approaches' Must Reflect Party Building Leadership," District Organization Department Website, January 8, 2016. With modifications when cited.

[13] Cited from the internal document "H Street's Implementation Measures for Further Advancing the 'Two Bottom-Up' Mechanism.".

mobilizing, widely soliciting opinions, widely participating, and widely benefiting, further deepening grassroots. The vibrant grassroots community co-governance and mass autonomy led by the Party organization comprehensively promote the modernization of the community governance system and community governance capabilities, striving to forge a new path of community governance with H Street characteristics, and accelerating the realization of the "community dream" of demand-oriented services and experiential governance.

In fact, the "two bottom-up" mechanism aims to shift the focus of social governance downward, deeply engaging in service and governance work within residential areas, and achieving "refinement" in governance and service performance. This is also one of the core features of the "Shanghai Model 3.0" in community governance.

4.2.4 The Value Orientation of Pudong's Exploration: People-Centered Development Thought and Sense of Gain

The people-centered development thought does not come out of nowhere; it has deep roots in Marxist theoretical sources and the practical foundation of socialism with Chinese characteristics. It is a systematic refinement and summary of our Party's theories on economic, political, cultural, social, and ecological civilization development (Cai Fang 2016), particularly embodied in the Xi Jinping Thought on Socialism with Chinese Characteristics for a New Era formed at the 19th National Congress of the Communist Party of China. In the "Constitution of the Communist Party of China," the Party's fundamental purpose is "to serve the people wholeheartedly," while also requiring "development for the people, development relying on the people, and development results shared by the people."

Accordingly, the people-centered development thought, when implemented at the grassroots level, is "centered on the people's good life." In practice, it can be transformed into "the people's yearning for a better life is our goal of struggle," with plain language and resounding promises reflecting the Party's governance philosophy of "adhering to the people-centered development thought." From the perspective of grassroots society, the sense of gain and happiness of residents is the test of the effectiveness of the "people-centered development thought." From the grassroots exploration experience in Shanghai, the people-centered development thought and the sense of gain of residents (villagers) based on it have become the value concept and pursuit behind the Pudong model. On one hand, the promotion of grassroots social governance is service and demand-oriented, with residents (villagers) as the center of development and governance; on the other hand, the exploration results of grassroots social governance innovation are judged by the satisfaction and sense of gain of residents (villagers). This activates and forms the endogenous motivation for innovative social governance, achieving the unity of value pursuit, conceptual action, and governance practice.

Firstly, from the perspective of value pursuit, demand-oriented grassroots social governance has become the norm. The innovative exploration of property governance in Gaohang Town, the resource department integration practice of the "Zhangjiang 613" urban operation system, the "Harmonious Home in a Snail Shell" in Yongye First Residence of Jinqiao Town, and the "Menu-Style Service for the Masses" work method in Heqing Town are all grassroots governance practices originating from the diversified orientation of residents' (villagers') needs. The governance process distinctly reflects the "people-centered development thought."

For example, the exploration practice of the "Menu-Style Service for the Masses" work method in Heqing Town. The "Menu-Style Service for the Masses" work method was developed on the basis of Party building leadership and villagers' autonomy. It was created by the village Party general branch in response to the difficulties and demands encountered by villagers in their daily lives. To enrich service carriers and improve service quality, the Party branch uses a "points system" as a means of supervision and assessment, gradually forming a new service model of grassroots Party organization where "the masses place orders, the branch places orders, and Party members take orders." Over more than two years of practice, it has continuously adjusted and innovated, providing precise services to villagers and receiving unanimous praise from the masses. Its approach can be summarized in four points.

(1) Conducting visits and research, villagers "place orders." Since the implementation of the "Menu-Style Service for the Masses" work method in 2015, the village Party branch secretary has led members of the "two committees," village representatives, and Party group leaders in conducting "thorough" and "carpet-style" research work through various forms such as home visits, regular discussions, and care visits. They directly face the issues and opinions of the masses, with each household listing their problems and needs, which village cadres summarize to create an annual list of "urgent, difficult, and worrying" issues for the masses, and make it public. On one hand, Party members and cadres fully understand the needs of villagers, which helps them always remember their mission and responsibility, achieving comprehensive coverage and zero omission in demand research; on the other hand, comprehensive the research has realized the participation of all people in grassroots self-governance, ensuring villagers' rights to participate in managing collective affairs and co-building a beautiful homeland, which is conducive to enhancing villagers' sense of belonging and pride.
(2) Demand classification, branch "ordering." After the visits and research, party members and cadres classify and organize villagers' needs, establish a list of issues, and form a service menu that includes major sections such as poverty alleviation and assistance, public welfare services, safety construction, environmental improvement, and acts of kindness. At the same time, the party branch holds meetings with the "two committees" leadership, party members and cadres, and village group leaders to jointly discuss service content. Through multi-party consultation and joint participation, they develop a list of needs that

combines commonality and individuality, determine issues that require coordination and support from higher-level departments, issues that need to be included in the annual work plan, and identify long-term service content and personalized issues. They adopt a method of reasonable planning and breakthrough one by one for demand classification, adding a self-recommendation section for villagers on the basis of several fixed sections, fully considering villagers' personalized services, thereby continuously enhancing villagers' sense of gain and satisfaction, increasing their trust in cadres, and strengthening the image building of the party organization.

(3) Publicity and mobilization, party members "taking orders." The "menu-style service for the masses" work method emphasizes the advanced and exemplary role of party members. Through various channels such as party member meetings, community bulletin boards, blackboard newspapers, WeChat public accounts, and party member WeChat groups, it promotes and mobilizes party members to actively participate in "taking orders," achieving a shift from task assignment to voluntary acceptance by party members, and strengthening the close connection between party members and the masses. Adhering to the principles of "personal voluntary application, acting within one's means, prioritizing specialties, and using spare time," it fully leverages the initiative of party members, with cadres leading party members and party members leading the masses to participate. At the same time, a signing ceremony for the "menu-style service for the masses" is held, where the information of those who claim the "service menu" and their completion status are all "posted on the wall," standardizing the service quality of party members in an institutionalized manner and promoting the effective development of service work.

(4) Points management to ensure quality. To ensure the quality of party members serving the masses under the guidance of the "menu-style service for the masses" work method, the village party branch specifically sets up party member points indicators and adopts a classified points method. It refines service content, reasonably quantifies scores, and uniformly creates a party member service points management book for each party member and cadre, distributing the "menu-style service for the masses handbook." Using "party group grid management" as a starting point, the party group leader evaluates and scores party member services against assessment standards, implementing the management principle of "one person, one file; one matter, one record." At the same time, party member points and ranking situations are publicly displayed, forming a positive competition among party members, enhancing their sense of responsibility and honor. The party group is also responsible for the informatization collection and points grading work of party member service, strengthening the supervision and management of the quality of party members serving the masses. Party member service points will also serve as an important basis for the annual quantitative assessment of party members, thereby stimulating their work motivation.

Second, from the perspective of concept and action, the co-governance system is continuously improving, and the concept of integrated governance is deepening. Through exploration in recent years, the co-discussion and co-governance of grassroots public affairs in Pudong New Area has been systematically promoted. The scope of participating subjects is becoming increasingly clear, and the procedures are becoming more standardized. The results of co-discussion and co-governance have been truly transformed and implemented, forming typical cases such as the "tidal parking" in Tangqiao Street, "building group party building" in Weifang New Village Street, "nursing home without walls" in Zhoujiadu Street, and the "three actuals" information platform for managing the floating population at Nanmatou, "centralized unified management" in Gaodong Town, and "external management by external means" in Gaoqiao Town. For example, the co-governance result "tidal parking" is a practical exploration by Tangqiao Street to solve the community's "parking difficulties and disorderly parking" issues. It incorporates community subjects such as grassroots mass self-governance organizations, local units, social organizations, corporate legal entities, and people from all walks of life into the community governance and service system. Through cross-departmental cooperation with traffic police and municipal functional departments, various social and market resources are brought into the public service field, improving service quality. From the initial staggered parking pilot to the later "tidal parking," and then to the comprehensive expansion of work content, the "parking difficulties" project ultimately explored a path of integrated governance for community co-governance. Similarly, Shanggang New Village Street solved the problem of disorderly parking blocking fire lanes in old communities with the slogan "unblocking the lifeline." To establish a communication and contact mechanism with the places where people come to Shanghai, Gaoqiao Town established a management service workstation for people from Pingyi, Shandong, in Luling Village, implementing community-based management and participatory co-governance, achieving good results.

Thirdly, from the perspective of governance practice, the experience of autonomy is continuously being promoted. Pudong New Area is not only content with cultivating autonomous models but also focuses on expanding the results of reforms and promoting exemplary experiences, turning "bonsai into nurseries, and nurseries into forests." For example, the promotion of the "1 + 1 + X" autonomy working method in Heqing Town ("1 + 1 + X" autonomy working method was initially explored and formed as a village autonomy model by Heqing Town, where the first "1" refers to the leadership of the party organization; the second "1" refers to the village autonomy charter; "X" refers to the implementation rules formulated according to the autonomy charter). Since the promotion of the "1 + 1 + X" autonomy working method, the leadership of the party organization has been further strengthened, the relationship between cadres and the masses has significantly improved, and many difficulties in rural social governance have been effectively addressed, solidifying the grassroots foundation. Additionally, in Zhongjie Village of Beicai Town, villagers were guided to participate in the supervision of village affairs, successfully resolving the issue of reserved land compensation, a problem that had persisted for over 30 years since the late 1970s. In Jingshi Village of Datuan Town, village cadres used the "grassroots constitution" as a golden key to successfully persuade villagers on land transfer, establish family farms, and prevent the resurgence of "three violations."

At the same time, the promotion of the autonomy fund management method is also an important achievement, using the "autonomy fund" as a leverage point to drive innovation in community governance. Since 2011, Lujiazui Street has been exploring innovative residential community autonomy management models through project-based operations. After five years of practice and exploration, a total of 649 autonomy projects have been implemented, involving funds of 6.023 million yuan, covering various fields of residential area construction such as building group construction, cultural education, people-benefiting projects, and mass organization cultivation, forming a batch of highly recognized, influential, replicable, and promotable brand projects. At the same time, the level of community services has been further enhanced. According to the requirements of the effectiveness of social management and the equalization, accessibility, and convenience of public services, Pudong New Area has now fully formed a community comprehensive service framework with "3 + 1" centers ("3" refers to the community affairs acceptance service center, cultural activity center, and health service center that have been built and are operational, and "1" refers to the community life service center that is being vigorously promoted) as the main content, forming a one-stop service network covering the entire district with "1 + 36 + X" ("1" is the district-level platform, "36" are the 36 street and town acceptance platforms, and "X" are the sub-centers). Meanwhile, Pudong New Area is accelerating the construction of public social undertakings and large residential community projects, significantly improving the balanced allocation level of public service resources in fields such as education, health, culture, sports, civil affairs, and housing security. For example, in terms of public cultural resource allocation, a four-level public cultural facility network system covering urban and rural areas has been formed at the district, regional, street (town), and village (residential) levels, with the current per capita public cultural facility building area exceeding the average level of Shanghai.

Fourthly, from the perspective of governance effectiveness, the sense of gain among residents (villagers) has been significantly enhanced. For example, the governance practice of Heqing Town's "menu-style service for the masses" working method has solved a series of "urgent, difficult, and worrying" problems for villagers, significantly enhancing the image of the party and solidifying the party's credibility at the grassroots level, further forming a combined force for grassroots social governance. The "menu-style service for the masses" working method implements a model where party members and cadres proactively claim problems, discover problems, and solve problems in a timely manner, providing services while also offering suggestions and advice. It incorporates party members and the masses into grassroots service and management, forming a model where cadres take the lead and party members actively participate in services. At the same time, it introduces multiple stakeholders into grassroots social governance, continuously expanding the volunteer team, consolidating community synergy, and establishing a long-term management mechanism for village areas, forming organizational strength for community construction and social governance under the leadership of the party organization. For example, in

Zhangjiang Town, urban governance adheres to the actual problems and difficulties faced by the masses as the orientation, prioritizes the needs of the masses, and takes the terminal experience of the masses as the focal point, using "experience-based service" as the basic method of mass work and as a standard for measuring the effectiveness of various work. The effectiveness of the service ultimately relies on the masses for testing and evaluation, continuously improving and perfecting the mechanisms for expressing demands, responding to demands, and participating in evaluation, thereby ensuring seamless connection between service providers and service recipients' needs, and organic unity between service motivation and service effectiveness, achieving a transition from "refined governance" to "experience-based service."

4.2.5 The Continuous Shift of Governance Focus Downward and the Strong Cultivation of Social Organizations

The 19th National Congress of the Communist Party of China advocated for "strengthening the construction of community governance systems, shifting the focus of social governance to the grassroots, leveraging the role of social organizations, and achieving a positive interaction between government governance, social regulation, and residents' self-governance." The shift of the focus of social governance is an important strategy and fundamental trend for achieving social reintegration and reorganization since the disintegration of the unit system. The shift in governance focus signifies the continuous strengthening of the importance of the grassroots, which requires the full development of multiple entities within grassroots communities and the effective undertaking of transferred government functions. As one of the incremental entities, the vigorous cultivation and role of social organizations (especially community social organizations) in grassroots communities have become key to the new era Shanghai model. In practice, grassroots social governance in Pudong essentially involves the interaction and cooperation of different governance entities within the grassroots community field, with the orderly participation of social organizations being a distinctive feature and highlight of the Pudong model.

Overall, to cultivate and develop social organizations and further enhance the vitality of social development, Pudong has introduced a series of policies and measures. (1) The issuance of the "Guiding Opinions on Further Promoting the Development of Community Social Organizations in Pudong New Area" (Pudong Government Office [2015] No. 14) clarifies four key development areas: providing community life services, promoting community mutual aid and assistance, meeting cultural and sports needs, and promoting grassroots governance and community participation. These provide paths and support for streets and towns in creating a development environment, solidifying service management, and strengthening work guarantees. Relevant measures have been incorporated into the "13th Five-Year Plan" social organization support policies in Pudong New Area. (2) Exploring and improving the government purchase service mechanism in Pudong New Area. A directory of qualifications for social organizations to undertake government-purchased services has been formulated, promoting the standardization and professionalization of public welfare service projects through platforms such as "demand docking · one-stop service." (3) Achieving full coverage of street and town social organization service centers. A network linkage platform for social organization service centers has been constructed, strengthening interaction, pairing, and guidance training among centers, fully utilizing the early warning network, auxiliary management, public welfare project service, and capacity-building support functions of street and town social organization service centers. It guides the healthy development of various mass activity teams in streets and towns and residential (village) areas. (4) Strengthening the construction of public welfare demonstration bases. Efforts are made to build the Pudong public welfare demonstration base, composed of the Pudong Public Welfare Service Park, Pudong Foundation Service Park, Pudong Public Welfare Street, and Community Public Welfare Service Park, into an incubation and growth park for public welfare social organizations in Pudong, a service platform for government-society cooperation and demand–supply docking, a distribution base for public welfare projects and product development, a gathering center for public welfare organizations and talents, and a highland for the output of public welfare concepts and culture. It strengthens the exchange and cultural dissemination of public welfare organizations, organizes activities such as the social organization public welfare activity month, and further enhances the function of social organizations in participating in community co-construction and co-governance.

Under the strong promotion of the above set of policies, social organizations in Pudong's grassroots social governance have fully developed, their professional roles have been continuously highlighted, the social governance pattern has been continuously optimized, and the division of labor among various entities has been orderly, with cooperative development. This has initially achieved a positive interaction between government governance, social regulation, and residents' self-governance. (1) Various community social organizations have been continuously growing, and community development foundations have been generally established. By the end of 2015, community development foundations were fully established in all streets and towns in Pudong New Area, with a total amount reaching 118 million yuan. The establishment, management, and use of the funds have been further standardized, effectively promoting the collection of charitable funds and social integration. (2) The social organization service centers in Pudong streets and towns have achieved full coverage, and on this basis, a group-style mutual aid mechanism construction attempt has been made. In 2016, Pudong New Area identified six street and town social organization service centers, including Tangqiao Street, Chuansha New Town, Lujiazui Street, Puxing Road Street, Jinyang New Village Street, and Yangjing Town, which had developed well, practiced fully, and had complete functions, as the core of network development, with other streets and towns belonging to six network groups. Each group regularly conducts training, holds meetings, exchanges learning, and interacts with visits, initially forming a companionship, mutual aid, and growth plan for social organization service centers in Pudong New Area, innovatively establishing a group-style mutual aid mechanism. The Pudong New Area Civil Affairs Bureau innovates interaction mechanisms and leverages typical experiences to form an interactive platform and network group for the "passing, helping, and leading" of social organization service centers in each street and town, gradually establishing an interactive empowerment development model with Pudong characteristics.[14] (3) The group-style mutual aid mechanism has achieved significant results, effectively promoting the expansion and play of the professional functions of social organizations. By the end of 2017, the entire district had been evaluated for the of social organizations. There are a total of 285 social organizations rated 3A and above, accounting for about 15% of the total number of social organizations. Among them, 139 are community social organizations rated 3A and above, making up about 49% of the total number of community social organizations. Four social organizations from Weifang Xincun Subdistrict, Chuansha New Town, Jinyang Xincun Subdistrict, and Puxing Road Subdistrict have been awarded the second and third "Shanghai Advanced Social Organization" titles. The social organization service centers in Chuansha New Town, Kangqiao Town, and Hangtou Town actively promote the establishment of special development funds and community special funds to carry out community public welfare venture projects and support the development of social organizations. The social organization service centers in Tangqiao Subdistrict and Chuansha New Town have drafted several opinions on government procurement of social organization services, project lists, and opinions on supporting the development of social organizations, assisting subdistricts and towns in supporting social organizations and public welfare development. The social organization service centers in Tang Town and Gaohang Town have also integrated the demand and resource lists of each residential (village) committee with the "Doorstep" service system, introducing social organizations in a targeted manner, thereby enhancing residents' awareness and acceptance of social organizations. Social organizations have gradually become an indispensable element in grassroots communities in Pudong, effectively promoting the modernization of grassroots social governance capabilities and systems.

References

Brinkerhoff DW (1999) Exploring state-civil society collaboration: policy partnerships in developing countries. Nonprofit Volunt Sect Q 28(4):59–86

Cai F (2016) Using "people-centered development thinking" to solve problems in the field of people's livelihood. Labor Econ Res 4(3):3–15

Evans PB, Rueschemeyer D, Skocpol T (1985) Bringing the state back in. Cambridge University Press, London

Chen J (2010) Corporatism and contemporary Chinese society. Sociol Stud 25(02):30–43+243

Jing Y (2003) Administrative democracy: significance and limitations—The enlightenment from Wenling's "Democratic Deliberation Meetings". Zhejiang Soc Sci (01): 27–30

[14] Cited from "Pudong Street Town Social Organization Service Centers Achieve Full Coverage," Eastday, November 14, 2017.

Li Y (2012) Problems encountered in the new pattern of social management in China—a perspective based on mesoscopic mechanism analysis. Acad Mon 44(7):13–20
Migdal JS (2013) State in society: how states and societies transform and constitute one another (trans: Li Y, Guo Y). Jiangsu People's Publishing House, Nanjing [American]
Putnam RD (2001) Making democracy work (trans: Wang L, Lai H). Jiangxi People's Publishing House, Nanchang [British]
Skocpol T (2008) Bringing the state back in: retrospect and prospect The 2007 Johan Skytte Prize Lecture. Scand Polit Stud 31 (2): 109–124
Wang J (2015) The construction of cooperative governance: the generation mechanism of positive interaction between government and society. Polit Sci Res 4:98–105
Wu J (2012) Understanding Corporatism—With a Discussion on its applicability in the study of state-society relations in China. Sociol Stud 27(01): 174–198+245–246
Xu Y (2001) Community development theory. East China University of Science and Technology Press, Shanghai
Xu Y (2006) Division and cooperation between government and society: research on the reform and innovation of community construction system. Southeast Acad Res 6:51–57
Yu J, Gao X (2012) The behavioral logic and institutional foundation of local development-oriented governments. Soc Sci China (05):95–112+206–207
Yu J, Ren Z (2012) Collaborative governance in contemporary Chinese social construction: an analytical framework. Acad Mon 44(08): 23–31
Zheng S, Xu H, Wang H (2005) Overview of grid and grid management. Syst Eng 3:1–7

Chapter 5
The Shift of Social Governance Focus and Service Integration Practice

5.1 "Doorstep" Service: The Pudong Practice of Shifting the Focus of Social Governance

5.1.1 "Doorstep" Service: Connotation, Value, and Significance

The "Doorstep" service is a highlight livelihood project in Pudong New Area in 2017, representing an innovative integrated service paradigm in grassroots social governance. It is a response to General Secretary Xi Jinping's call for "adhering to a people-centered development philosophy, focusing on promoting social governance innovation, and enhancing the refined management level of megacities." It is also a key measure to implement the "1 + 6" documents of the Municipal Party Committee and the spirit of the 11th Congress of the Communist Party of China in Shanghai.

In summary, the "Doorstep" service aims to build a social governance system compatible with an open, innovative, and high-quality Pudong New Area. It follows the path of comprehensive coordination, system integration, and self-governance and co-governance, using the construction of residential (village) "Doorstep" service stations as a starting point. It focuses on deepening the grassroots governance system and mechanism, promoting platform, carrier, function + project, mechanism, and team building. Relying on residential (village) party building service stations, it constructs a "Doorstep" service system at the residential (village) level through standardized construction, standardized operation, information support, and professional support, achieving "small life matters do not leave the residential (village), education services are nearby," and solving the "last mile" problem of serving the masses as a systematic project.

The "Doorstep" service is both an extension of social governance and service at the grassroots level and a key measure to solve the "last mile" problem of serving the masses. It holds significant value and meaning in Pudong's new round of service

L. Hou, *The Integrated Service in Urban Community Governance*, Public Economy and Urban Governance in China, https://doi.org/10.1007/978-981-96-6775-8_5

innovation. In terms of conceptual value, it fully realizes the "people-centered development philosophy." It is a direct service transformation of Xi Jinping's Thought on Socialism with Chinese Characteristics for a New Era. In action, it is also a deep extension and advancement of the previous round of Pudong's innovative community governance and service innovation experimental zone work.

In terms of its significance, the construction of the "Doorstep" service system mainly has two aspects of significance.[1] On one hand, it is an important measure to implement and promote the "shift of the focus of social governance to the grassroots" proposed by the 19th National Congress of the Communist Party of China, and it is a deep implementation of the "1 + 6" documents of the Shanghai Municipal Party Committee. The 19th National Congress proposed "strengthening the construction of the community governance system, promoting the shift of the focus of social governance to the grassroots, playing the role of social organizations, and achieving a positive interaction between government governance and social regulation, and residents' self-governance." At the same time, "shifting the focus, sinking resources, and delegating power" and "everything revolves around the masses" are the basic principles of the Municipal Party Committee's innovation in social governance and strengthening grassroots construction. To implement the requirements of the Municipal Party Committee, the Pudong New Area District Committee proposed the "three shifts" work concept, namely, departments revolve around subdistricts and towns, subdistricts and towns revolve around residential (village) committees, and residential (village) committees revolve around the masses. Promoting the "three shifts" cannot be done in a vacuum; it must have a grasp and be implementable, and the construction of the "Doorstep" service system is a key move. On the other hand, it is the service to the masses "last "A kilometer" livelihood project. During grassroots research, the district committee discovered that there are still many areas in need of improvement in serving the public, which can be summarized in three words. The first word is "far." Although each street and town has established "three centers," due to the large area of Pudong New District, especially in suburban rural areas, many residents (villages) cannot enjoy the convenience of a "15-min living service circle." The second word is "scattered." Although residential (village) committees have some service functions and resources, they are scattered across various lines, and residents often cannot find the corresponding point or person for their needs. The third word is "virtual." Some residential committees have dozens of signs, but many are "signs without services," with services not being implemented, leading to public complaints and dissatisfaction. The construction of the "doorstep" service system aims to address these three issues, providing more accessible, convenient, and practical services for the public.

---

[1] Quoted from the speech of Leader M at the "Meeting on Implementing the Spirit of the Urban Grassroots Party Building Conference to Promote the Construction of the 'Doorstep' Service System" on August 23, 2017.

5.1.2 "Doorstep" Service: Realistic Advancement and Practical Logic

The "doorstep" service is a systematic livelihood project for social governance and service innovation in Pudong New District. Its advancement process is divided into three progressive stages. The first stage is systematic planning and concentrated pilot phase, with the main task of forming a construction plan for the "doorstep" service system and selecting four streets and towns for concentrated trials. Research on the Construction of Integrated Service Models in Urban Community Governance The second stage is the coordinated deployment and comprehensive promotion phase, with the main task of mobilizing deployment and work training, promoting it comprehensively across 36 streets and towns in the district, and conducting evaluation and acceptance. The third stage is the summary reflection and improvement phase, with the main task of achieving district-wide coverage and comprehensively enhancing the refined level of social governance in Pudong New District's residential (village) areas.

First Stage: Systematic Planning and Concentrated Pilot (Early March 2017—End of May 2017).

First, the leading department for the service system proposal is the District Work Committee, with participation from other member units of the promotion group and various towns, to form a district-level work plan, district-level service resources, and service project list (Early March 2017—End of April 2017). Led by the District Work Committee, with cooperation from relevant functional departments, a work plan for the construction of the "doorstep" service system at the residential (village) level in Pudong New District, a district-level service resource list, and a service project list were formed based on scientific research and systematic demonstration, providing guidance for practical operations in streets, towns, and residential (village) areas.

Second, conduct concentrated pilots (End of April 2017—End of May 2017).

Conduct concentrated pilots simultaneously in Chuansha New Town, Lujiazui Street, Puxing Road Street, and Shuyuan Town, selecting 1–2 residential (village) committees to promote the construction of "doorstep" service stations, forming exemplary leadership. Second Stage: Coordinated Deployment and Comprehensive Promotion (Early June 2017—End of 2018) First, hold work deployment and training meetings (Early June 2017—Mid to Late June 2017). In early June, hold a work deployment meeting for promoting the construction of the "doorstep" service system in Pudong New District, issuing work plans, service resource lists, and service project lists, and conducting comprehensive mobilization and deployment. In mid to late June, hold training meetings, visit the four pilot street towns on-site, and invite line departments for relevant training. Second, comprehensively promote in each street and town (Early July 2017—End of 2018). Each street and town sorts out and forms a list of residential (village) needs, community resource lists, and service project lists, integrating existing service functions of residential (village) committees to promote the construction of "doorstep" service stations. By the end of 2017, more than 30% of residential (village) areas completed construction; by the end of 2018, more than 80% completed construction.

Third Stage: Summary Reflection and Improvement (Early January 2019—End of 2019).

In 2019, the "doorstep" service stations achieved district-wide coverage, further summarizing experiences, improving mechanisms, and comprehensively enhancing the refined level of social governance and service quality for residents (villages) in Pudong New District. At the same time, a new round of construction was launched on topics such as service content expansion, service upgrades, and institutionalized construction, striving to take the lead in achieving governance modernization.

The above practice advancement of the "doorstep" service also presents a clear internal logic, essentially integrating and enhancing the grassroots social governance and service practice experiences and innovative approaches since 2014. This is a multidimensional integrative attempt at service resources, service platforms, and service forces, as well as a service delivery system, which is a people-centered service integration practice.

(1) System integration, coordinating scattered service resources. This mainly refers to the integration function of "at your doorstep" services as a platform. First, comprehensive coordination to promote the decentralization of departmental resources. A prominent issue in current grassroots social governance is how to bridge the "last mile" of services to residents. In Pudong New Area, community public service resources are distributed across multiple departments such as education, health, and civil affairs, mostly concentrated at the district and sub-district levels. When people need services, they often "can't find the right way" and cannot obtain services nearby and quickly. To address this, Pudong New Area has "prescribed the right remedy," comprehensively sorting out district-level service resources that can be decentralized, covering seven major categories: party and mass, government affairs, life, law, health, culture, and community management, involving 19 district-level departments and 42 service items, forming a district-level service resource list and service item list. At the same time, following the principle of "departments provide the list, grassroots connect as needed," a public service resource block connection mechanism is established, allowing communities to select services based on actual needs, achieving "service forward movement." Second, party building leads to the integration and development of social resources. Through regional party building, the service resources of stationed units and market entities serving the community are integrated, for example, co-building with municipal enterprises to introduce greening maintenance resources; cooperating with community service companies like "Dianbangbang" to introduce market-oriented service resources. Through the party building of "two new" organizations, the service resources of new economic organizations and new social organizations are integrated, for example, introducing resources from local law firms and mediation social organizations. Through residential area party building, endogenous

service resources are stimulated. Pudong's exploratory practice has highly integrated and fully merged social resources such as social organizations, market enterprises, and community capabilities, maximizing the expansion of the total amount of public service resources, and establishing a "resource pool" for providing diversified community services. Third, project operation promotes the on-site transformation and use of service resources. Pudong New Area adheres to a project-based operation method, integrating departmental decentralized resources and social coordinated resources, launching "basic + characteristic" service modules based on community service demand points and key difficulties in community governance, transforming abstract service resources into specific service projects. For example, party and league relationship transfers, subsidy application, utility payment, legal consultation, health consultation, cultural activity guidance, etc. In addition, each community, based on actual conditions, explores and cultivates characteristic service projects and brands, achieving efficient use of service resources.

(2) Functional integration, combining scattered service platforms. This mainly refers to the integration function of "at your doorstep" services as a brand. First, breaking segmentation to achieve service platform reintegration. Previously, community committees had 20 to 30 plaques. However, these platforms "operated independently, with segmented sites and scattered resources," unable to provide high-quality, refined services to the public. To solve the above problems, Pudong New Area widely listened to opinions from sub-districts, communities, and the public, deciding to integrate various platforms at the community level, relying on community party building service stations, to build a highly open, fully functional, vertically and horizontally connected "at your doorstep" one-stop service platform, promoting service optimization through spatial optimization, achieving the reorganization and reconstruction of the grassroots service system. Second, precise services to achieve platform function classification and implementation. In the construction process of "at your doorstep" service stations, the general requirement is to achieve functional integration through platform integration. Pudong New Area, based on the diverse types of communities and the diverse service population, has created different categories of service function blocks. For example, in rural areas, there are services such as writing housing applications and handling employment guarantees; in highly urbanized areas, there are technical guidance services such as mural painting, micro-landscapes, and green plant maintenance; for office workers, staggered and extended work systems are established, with services such as WeChat processing platforms; for the elderly, agency service systems are established, with services such as water, electricity, and gas agency payment, and purchasing daily necessities and fresh vegetables. Third, utilizing "Internet + ," achieving informatization and intelligence of service platforms. Strengthening the effective application and comprehensive utilization of technology in community services, allowing the public to enjoy the multiple services brought by "Internet + " at their doorstep. For example, in conjunction with the construction of "Pudong Cloud," extending software service systems such

as sub-district community affairs acceptance centers and party building service centers to community points, accelerating the promotion of self-service government services, and providing precise and convenient life services for community residents through the "Pudong Easy Life" online and offline platform; actively playing the role of the "Pudong e-Home" platform, further improving the comprehensive information service platform for social governance, continuously promoting the informatization construction of community committees, and promoting the integration and sharing of information resources.

(3) Autonomous co-governance, bringing together dispersed service forces. This mainly refers to the integration and cohesion of diverse forces in "doorstep" services. First, resident autonomy, truly providing service projects "centered on the people." The construction of service stations adheres to a bottom-up approach, combining with the actual situation of the residential (village) area, led by the residential (village) area, using the "1 + 1 + X" grassroots autonomy mechanism. Through hearings, consultations, and evaluation meetings, the choice, decision, and evaluation rights of service projects are handed over to the masses, strengthening the awareness and responsibility of residents (villagers) to participate in community services, creating a good atmosphere for grassroots democratic consultation and participation in autonomy.In the extraction of needs, residents (villagers) and stakeholders are invited to accurately grasp community service needs through questionnaires, WeChat collections, and other forms. In project selection, residents (villagers) choose which projects enter the service station through forms such as co-creation meetings and open space discussions. After a project has been running for a period, services are timely adjusted and improved based on public evaluation. Second, multi-party co-governance, strengthening the backend support of community services. Deepen regional party building, promote the construction of community committees, achieve two-way exchange of regional resources, and demand docking; improve the "thousand-listening" mechanism for government officials to contact residents (villages), and the research mechanism for grassroots common problems; establish a grassroots invitation system, where residents (villages) can invite district or street-town functional departments, district-owned enterprises, and institutions to jointly promote the resolution of community "urgent, difficult, and worrying" issues, constructing a new pattern of party-led grassroots governance, forming a community of interests, life, and culture that integrates autonomy, co-governance, moral governance, and rule of law. Third, promote "all-post access," strengthening the team guarantee of "doorstep" services. To ensure the realization of "doorstep" one-stop services, Pudong New Area has developed a community worker training manual, appointing retired secretaries with rich experience in mass work as supervisors, providing guidance and support throughout the process of community worker team building. Gradually introduce and implement an assessment system that combines bottom-up public evaluation and third-party independent evaluation for community workers, fully playing the role of the "command baton" of assessment, guided by the "all-post access" service concept, promoting the standardization of residential (village)

systems, construction standardization, and management informatization, implementing the first inquiry responsibility system, designated responsibility system, and bottom-line responsibility system, comprehensively promoting community workers to be "specialized in many skills, accessible in all posts," continuously improving the ability and level of serving the masses. Fourth, autonomous homeland, enhancing the level and capability of grassroots social governance. A vibrant "doorstep" service station not only requires broad participation and interactivity but also should focus on stimulating the public spirit and rule awareness of community residents, reflecting the warmth of the community "home." The construction of "doorstep" service stations not only solves residents' needs by introducing external resources but also needs to continuously stimulate the release of endogenous resources within the community, promoting residents to orderly, effectively, consciously, and capably solve their community governance needs, from enhancing residents' sense of participation and gain to building a civic sense of responsibility, achievement, and belonging in an autonomous "ecosystem," gradually promoting community autonomous co-governance.

In addition, the construction of the "doorstep" service system further sorts out and improves the organizational network, carriers, teams, projects, and mechanisms of residential area autonomous co-governance work. For example, the introduction of a crowdfunding mechanism in the autonomous fund work shifts from "project" participation to "funding" participation, not only achieving diversity in funding sources and stimulating the responsibility awareness of autonomous teams but more importantly, greatly increasing the socialization degree of community public welfare promotion, further effectively allocating community funds and resources, providing public space for the use, management, and distribution of social public welfare funds, and promoting the optimization and enhancement of grassroots governance structure and autonomous capability.

5.1.3 "Doorstep" Service: Practical Achievements and Logical Tension

Firstly, from the perspective of the practical achievements of promoting "doorstep" services,[2] the coordinated promotion of "doorstep" services is powerful, and initial results are beginning to show. In 2018, more than 700 residential (village) areas in 36 streets and towns were piloting the promotion, and the results can be summarized in three aspects.

[2] Refer to the speech by Leader F on August 23, 2017, at the "Implementing the Spirit of the Urban Grassroots Party Building Conference to Promote the 'Doorstep' Service System Construction Meeting," and the speech by Leader W at the "Pudong New Area Building 'Doorstep' Service System Mobilization and Deployment Meeting.".

(1) The "three lists" continuously consolidate the professionalism and social nature of services

The "three lists" are the standard configuration of "doorstep" service stations. The "three lists" refer to the demand list, resource list, and project list. In constructing "doorstep" service stations, first, a demand list must be formed. Services should be demand-oriented, and the extraction of needs should adhere to a "bottom-up" approach, through holding hearings, coordination meetings, evaluation meetings, discussion forums, and opinion solicitation meetings are various forms used to widely collect and categorize feedback from different organizations and groups within residential (village) areas. In the initial phase of centralized pilot projects in residential (village) areas, the first step is to assess needs. For example, the Puxing Road Subdistrict conducted an online questionnaire survey to create a "Community Residents' Needs Survey Report," which identified and summarized the demand for seven categories of services, prioritizing which needs should be met first, making it clear and targeted. Secondly, a resource list must be formed. The regional work committee has repeatedly solicited opinions and suggestions from functional departments to sort out public service resources that can be delegated to residential (village) areas, forming the Pudong New Area "Doorstep" district-level service resource list, which is distributed during training sessions for reference. At the street and residential (village) levels, it is also necessary to sort and identify market, social, and self-governance resources within the residential (village) area, combining public and endogenous resources to form a resource list with the characteristics of the specific residential (village) area. Thirdly, a project list must be launched. Once the needs and resource lists are available, they can be matched to form a project list. The formed Pudong New Area "Doorstep" district-level service project list is available for selection by streets and residential (village) areas, and it is also distributed during training sessions. Each street and town, based on the combination of the "three lists," launches several service projects that meet the actual needs of residential (village) areas, satisfying different groups. To meet the diverse service needs and effectively improve the professionalism and socialization level of services.

(2) Three types of mechanisms to solidify the normalization and institutionalization of services

The construction of "Doorstep" service stations is combined with the standardization of neighborhood committees and the promotion of the "All-Post Access" model. During the construction process, attention must be paid to future normalized and long-term management, establishing and improving three major mechanisms. First, the mechanism of responsibility for the people. Combined with the promotion of "All-Post Access," service stations must set up "one-stop" and counter-style front desk receptions to facilitate public affairs. To promote accountability and implementation, the first inquiry responsibility system, designated responsibility system, and bottom-line responsibility system must be implemented to ensure that all work responsibilities are assigned to individuals and implemented effectively. Second, the classified project service mechanism. Each of the seven service sectors has a corresponding service management mechanism. It is particularly important to emphasize that government services must establish and improve staggered work systems, extended work systems, and "All-Post Access" service systems. Health services must establish a mechanism for general practitioners to conduct patrol visits to residential (village) areas and improve residents' health self-management mechanisms. Third, the work support mechanism. Among them, one is the self-governance and co-governance mechanism, especially adhering to the "1 + 1 + X" grassroots self-governance mechanism, establishing the "three meetings" system of hearings, consultation meetings, and evaluation meetings; the second is the information support mechanism, as online expression of community residents' needs has become the norm since the new era, it is necessary to integrate various information platforms and keep pace with the times, combining the construction of "Pudong Cloud," "Pudong Easy Life," "Pudong e-Home," and the comprehensive social governance information platform, increasing the application of "Internet + " management services at the residential (village) level; the third is the assessment and evaluation mechanism, increasing the weight of street and town evaluations and public evaluations in assessments, fully playing the role of the "command baton" in assessments, guiding departments at all levels to enhance service awareness.

(3) Restructured and recreated residential (village) functions, achieving service integration

Firstly, the service system was integrated. The "Doorstep" service station integrates existing stations such as party building service stations, community affairs residential (village) agency offices, and volunteer service stations, highly merging government, social, and market forces, gathering public resources, service resources, and self-governance resources into one terminal, achieving a combination of online and offline services, and combining resident services with residents' self-services. Secondly, it reflects comprehensive functionality. The "Doorstep" one-stop service platform built at the residential (village) level integrates seven major service functions, including party-mass, government affairs, life, law, health, culture, and community management, maximizing the use of the limited office space resources of residential (village) committees. For example, Tangbei Village in Shuyuan Town, based on rural realities, centralizes all manageable affairs into the service station, such as issuing, replacing, and supplementing medical record books, handling social security business, processing residence permits, and providing special administrative services like collecting images for elderly people with mobility difficulties, allowing the public to experience comprehensive services. Thirdly, the projects are well-aligned. Functional departments comprehensively sorted out seven categories of service resources that can be decentralized, forming a district-level resource list, identifying 42 service items, and providing them for community (village) selection. For example, the District Women's Federation conducted two rounds of detailed surveys, identifying the top five needs specific to women (in order: rights protection consultation, elderly assistance, life skills training, maternal and child healthcare, psychological counseling), and designed service projects for grassroots women's federations to choose from. Each street and town, through "three meetings," namely hearings, consultations, and evaluations, handed over the choice, decision, and evaluation rights of service projects to the public, reflecting the characteristic of "projects are not about quantity, but about relevance."

In terms of its internal logic, the "Doorstep" service is essentially an innovative integrated service paradigm for grassroots social governance in Pudong. It integrates and enhances the experiences and innovative practices of grassroots social governance and service since 2014, attempting a multidimensional integration of service resources, platforms, and forces. From its recent practical explorations, it has also achieved significant service effectiveness, namely the continuous strengthening of professionalism and sociality under the "three lists," the construction and consolidation of service normalization and institutionalization in the linkage of three mechanisms, the functional reorganization and service integration of communities (villages), and on this basis, the effective improvement of community (village) residents' satisfaction and sense of gain. Meanwhile, the "Doorstep" service also encountered tensions in practice and difficulties in further advancement.

(1) Mismatch between the form and content of decentralization

The "Doorstep" service aims to provide seven categories of services nearby for residents, which aligns with the 19th National Congress of the Communist Party of China's proposal to "shift the focus of social governance to the grassroots." However, further reflection and research are needed on what exactly the shift in governance focus means, what is being shifted, how to shift, and the potential issues that may arise after the shift. The "Doorstep" service in Pudong New Area has not yet effectively considered and answered these questions, nor has it reached a basic consensus on the specific matters, construction standards, and ideal state of service decentralization. During field research, relevant community (village) leaders expressed concerns and doubts about the upcoming evaluation. Therefore, there may be mismatches between concepts and services, inconsistencies between understanding and action, lack of coordination between the form and content of decentralization, and asynchrony between communities (villages), leading to the suspension of "Doorstep" services and the detachment of community services.

(2) Tension between standardized service projects and differentiated community (village) realities

The standardized group service system should better consider the specific differentiated needs of residents.

How the "Doorstep" service projects can further dynamically and flexibly consider the needs of other groups (higher-level needs), especially how to achieve dynamic matching and coupling adjustment with people's needs for a better life, is a logical tension in the construction of the "Doorstep" service system. For example, leaving enough room and flexibility for local adjustments of special projects, arranging a mechanism for absorbing and feedback of flexible and diverse resident needs during operation and execution, and introducing third-party social work service agencies into the standardized service platform to achieve linkage in service provision may be important measures to resolve this tension.

(3) Unidirectional transmission between service provision and reception

Community (village) "Doorstep" services mainly involve seven categories: party-mass, government affairs, life, legal, health, culture, and community management, aiming to provide precise and convenient services to the public, achieving "daily services at your side, emergency services with one click," improving grassroots governance levels and the ability to serve the public. However, this "top-down" unidirectional service delivery from the government may also cause community (village) residents to become "unrelated neighbors," becoming "passive recipients" of services. On one hand, it may lead to "service dependency" and "service inflation" among community (village) residents, resulting in unreasonable higher expectations of the government; on the other hand, it also causes the shrinkage and delay of community (village) residents' service participation and service capabilities, which is not conducive to the precise and effective provision of services. This means that how to mobilize residents' active participation and how to involve community (village) residents in the provision of "Doorstep" services are directions that need further consideration. It is particularly important to be vigilant and avoid the formation of passive behavior, dependency mentality, and unreasonable expectations among residents in the "Doorstep" service.

(4) Integration of service projects and the segmentation and personalization of line services

The "Doorstep" service system encompasses seven major categories of services, including party and mass services, government affairs, daily life, legal, health, culture, and community management. While providing one-stop services brings great convenience to residents, it undoubtedly increases the demands on staff capabilities and inevitably faces difficulties in coordination and integration from different lines. More seriously, some service stations have shown opportunities for the downward transmission of business from line functional departments, which requires sufficient attention. Therefore, in this sense, the "Doorstep" service urgently needs to clarify its functional positioning and nature, strictly following the "list system" approach to service provision, and institutionally cutting off the possibility of administrative business being passed down.

5.2 "Neighborhood Gathering": Xuhui's Exploration in Social Governance Innovation

In contrast to the "Doorstep" service in Pudong New Area, Xuhui District focuses on grassroots party building and the needs of grassroots people, gradually forming the "Neighborhood Hub" brand model through continuous exploration. "Hub" in the academic sense refers to gathering and integrating, which is a linkage based on the integration of various subjects, aiming to gather and unite multiple forces in community governance, thereby constructing a community governance community. The specific approach is to establish 1 to 2 "Neighborhood Hub" centers in each street or town, integrating residents' self-organizations, social organizations, community foundations, and volunteer groups to provide community life services, elderly services, health services, cultural services, childcare services, legal services, and more for Xuhui District residents, effectively facilitating their daily lives. In this process, grassroots party organizations continuously promote resident organization, fully playing the leading role of grassroots party organizations. From the brand connotation, practical logic, and governance effectiveness of "Neighborhood Hub," this is also an integrated service practice in real practice.

5.2.1 The Concept and Positioning of the "Neighborhood Hub"

Model The construction and operation of the "Neighborhood Hub" is a deep understanding of the requirements mentioned by General Secretary Xi Jinping in the report of the 19th National Congress of the Communist Party of China, which is to "address the most immediate and realistic interests of the people" and "make the people's sense of gain, happiness, and security more substantial, more secure, and more sustainable." By setting up corresponding public spaces in the community and integrating service resources within the community, it better serves the daily life needs of community residents. The main concept of "Neighborhood Hub" work is to serve residents and benefit the people's hearts. The following discussion is based on the research of Q Street.

Q Street took the lead in exploring and innovating the development practice of "Neighborhood Hub," focusing on the word "Hub" to form a unique "3HUI" working method, which is the value goal and practical strategy of "benefiting the people, gathering neighbors, and enriching life" upheld by Q Street in community governance and service innovation. Specifically, Q Street deeply grasps the people-centered development core of "Neighborhood Hub" (benefiting the people), regards meeting neighborhood needs, mobilizing resident participation (gathering neighbors), and realizing a better life for residents (enriching life) as the value guidance and development direction of Q Street's "Neighborhood Hub," and concretizes it into the "Four Hubs Linkage" practice of gathering needs, gathering services, gathering residents, and gathering people's hearts. This action helps explore the working mechanism of subject and service linkage, enrich and develop the connotation of contemporary grassroots social governance and service innovation, and helps improve the modernization and refinement level of social governance.

(1) Gathering Needs: Accurately collecting, benchmarking, and meeting needs. Whether it is material and cultural needs or the need for a better life, both are key points of the party and the country's governance and administration at different stages, that is, the party and the country meet the needs of the people through the social welfare system. The "Neighborhood Hub" model is essentially a space for grassroots public services and social governance, accommodating welfare funds, resources, and organizations through this space to provide good public services to residents and promote public participation in grassroots social governance. Gathering needs refers to collecting and summarizing residents' needs, mainly including five stages: collection, integration, classification, response, and evaluation. To effectively gather needs, Q Street designed mechanisms such as community life party-building joint meetings, using the community as a spatial base, and responding to community needs through "Neighborhood Mini Hubs." By using building party-building points, urban white-collar workers can conveniently meet their dining, entertainment, and leisure needs, making the party-building points very popular. In the "Neighborhood Hub," Q The street has introduced the Shenyang professional elderly care institution to provide a good living, entertainment, and socializing place for the elderly in the area, significantly improving their quality of life. At this time, the main focus is on the street and community neighborhood committees working together to utilize a series of need-collection mechanisms to gather and integrate the needs of the public. They respond to these needs using existing governance resources and systems, thereby satisfying the residents' needs. In this process, the neighborhood committee's work increasingly wins the hearts of the community, and the street's promotion of various tasks in the community becomes smoother.
(2) Service Integration: Innovating supply models and building a closed-loop service system. To meet the people's needs for a better life, it is important to focus on supply-side reform in the process of innovating social governance. This includes not only increasing the input of supply resources but also changing the way services are provided. By leveraging the expertise of professional organizations and workers in fields such as social work, psychology, gerontology, and nursing, the professionalism of public services is enhanced. At the same time, the social nature of social governance is expanded by using a variety of social activities to attract public participation and support.

Therefore, the essence of service integration is to design a comprehensive public service system that meets the needs of the people, promoting a sense of gain among the public during the implementation of the "Neighborhood Hub" development. In the process of promoting the development of the "Neighborhood Hub," Q Street emphasizes being district-based, flexibly using multiple resource chains to purchase different service project contents according to the characteristics of its district. Q Street gathers many urban elites and purchases the "Shanghai Dialect Class" service project from the "Nine O'clock Social Work Station" through bidding, teaching Shanghai dialect to new Shanghai residents and their families every weekend to help them better integrate into Shanghai culture. The Q Street Community Foundation annually funds 1 to 2 service projects for each community's autonomous team in its district, using community volunteer teams to provide corresponding public services, thereby enhancing community well-being and stimulating community vitality.

(3) Resident Integration: Enhancing residents' participation in the service process. General Secretary Xi Jinping proposed at the 19th National Congress of the Communist Party of China to build a social governance system of co-construction, co-governance, and sharing, ensuring both order and vitality in society. The "co" in co-construction, co-governance, and sharing not only refers to government, enterprises, social organizations, and foundations but also to the public. The public should fully integrate into the social governance process, continuously improving their participation ability and willingness, to grow and develop into active participants in grassroots social governance.

Resident integration means that residents can autonomously and spontaneously enter the "Neighborhood Hub," willing to participate in building the "Neighborhood Mini Hub" public space, making the "Neighborhood Hub" public space popular and allowing more residents to participate in the "Neighborhood Hub" projects. Resident integration involves three steps: First, the service activities provided by the "Neighborhood Hub" and "Neighborhood Mini Hub" are what residents need, so they can gather a wide range of community residents to participate when activities are held. Second, promote the further publicization of the "Neighborhood Hub" and "Neighborhood Mini Hub" spaces, making them the community's public living room, a good place for weekend leisure, and a fixed location for hallway neighbors to chat, continuously gathering community residents' popularity. In this process, strengthen residents' goodwill towards public spaces, enhance the social capital of the community or building, and increase the attractiveness of party organizations and social organizations to the public, preparing for the next step of integration. Finally, based on previous interactions, not only is the attractiveness and cohesion of the "Neighborhood Hub" to community residents strengthened, but the public's enthusiasm and initiative for participation are also enhanced, making the public active participants in daily processes and establishing increasingly close connections in the "Neighborhood Hub" public space.

(4) Heart Integration: Strengthening the leading capacity of grassroots party organizations in the service delivery process. General Secretary Xi Jinping said during his inspection in Shanghai, "The people have a scale in their hearts. If we put the people in our hearts, the people will put us in their hearts." Currently, in promoting the development of the "Neighborhood Hub" and its related social governance, grassroots party building is a core element and its ultimate destination. In the process of providing public services, allowing party organizations to play a more important role can ensure that the public feels a sense of gain while closing the psychological distance with the party and government.

Q Street emphasizes integrating party building elements into the social governance framework, focusing on integrating party building space and public… Space integration allows party organizations to be visible and accessible, becoming a part of the daily lives of the public and urban white-collar workers. By prominently displaying their identity and providing friendly services, they have won the hearts of the public and urban white-collar workers, encouraging them to voluntarily participate in the governance process. The Q Street Party Building Service Center regularly hosts a white-collar book club on Fridays, where urban white-collar workers gather to discuss national affairs and actively learn new ideas and theories from the party organization. Community reading groups have gradually developed into community self-governing councils, with veteran party members in the community, driven by their belief in their identity and love for the community, becoming proactive actors and helpful assistants to the neighborhood committee, helping to solve complex issues within the community. Such success is attributed to Q Street's commitment to making "Neighborhood Gathering" the ultimate goal of development, ensuring that the public sees it not only as a platform for providing social services but also as a public space for establishing good social relationships, and more importantly, as a significant platform for participating in social governance and realizing their social value. At this time, grassroots party building work, leveraging the strength of party organizations and outstanding party members, gradually enters the hearts of ordinary people, awakening and empowering them, making party building gradually gather people's hearts and become an important growth pole for maintaining vitality in grassroots social governance.

5.2.2 *The Operating Mechanism of "Neighborhood Gathering"*

In the process of promoting street social governance, Q Street focuses on territorial party building and networked participation as the main points of innovation and breakthrough. This is to promote the leading role of grassroots party organizations in different functional spaces while promoting networked participation of diverse subjects, ensuring that the goals of order and vitality in the social governance process advance together.

In specific practice, Q Street mainly explores through four practical methods and tools: party building leadership, demand-based approach, project-driven initiatives, and neighborhood gathering. These four are not only the goals in the governance process of "Neighborhood Gathering" but also constitute the components of a people-benefiting project with corresponding practical attributes.

(1) Party Building Leadership. Party building leadership should fully utilize the functions and roles of ideological party building, organizational party building, and institutional party building. Ideological party building, as the name suggests, shapes the recognition of cadres and the public towards the party's governance strategies through services and standardized party member activities, thereby ensuring the party's ruling position at the grassroots level. Organizational party building means fully utilizing grassroots party organizations as the central hub

for coordinating interests and planning actions. At the street and town level, this means viewing the party committee and party building office as the central structure for coordinating various departments and lines of social governance and integrating resources from enterprises and institutions within the jurisdiction, avoiding resource duplication and ensuring the systematic and holistic nature of social governance. At the community level, it means fully utilizing the functions and roles of the community party general branch to mobilize ordinary residents, community self-organizations, homeowners' committees, and property companies to jointly discuss and resolve community affairs, strengthening the authority of the party general organization in the hearts of residents and improving the efficiency of community governance. Institutional party building means making grassroots party building the central work and core element of constructing a co-building, co-governing, and sharing social governance system, fully institutionalizing the effective social governance experiences under party building leadership previously explored, thereby forming standardized guidelines to ensure the continuous generation and effectiveness of social governance outcomes.

(2) Demand-Based Approach. "Neighborhood Gathering" essentially belongs to the provision of grassroots public services to ensure the people's needs for a better life. Therefore, demand becomes the ultimate goal in the overall work advancement. Firstly, a demand-based approach means "Neighborhood Gathering" should continuously explore and categorize community residents' needs by establishing a community demand collection mechanism, ensuring that the needs commonly reflected by the public are known to grassroots political organizations, categorized, and addressed at the community level. Matters that can be resolved within the community should be promptly responded to and resolved through "Neighborhood Mini-Gathering." If the needs cannot be met within the community, they should be reported to the street office, utilizing "Neighborhood Gathering" and other street resource carriers to meet them. Secondly, a demand-based approach means "Neighborhood Gathering" should continuously institutionalize to steadily and sustainably meet the residents' growing needs for a better life. Currently, Q Street, similar to many central urban areas in Shanghai, faces common demands generated in the modernization process, such as the elderly care needs caused by an aging society, the need for parent–child relationship adjustment due to increased work pressure, and the need for population integration due to the influx of migrants. Q Street continuously leverages the overall "Neighborhood Gathering" framework to address these needs. Integrate resources and satisfy them through project-based approaches, such as "Shanghai Dialect School," "Four-thirty Classroom," and "Shenyang Institution for Elderly Care." These projects fully leverage the professional advantages of social work and continuously provide residents with high-quality social services.

(3) Project-driven. Essentially, project-driven is a service supply method, which involves integrating and packaging people, events, and resources, and entrusting them to relevant professional institutions to provide services to the public. The project-driven approach is designed to adapt to the unequal situation where street

governance resources are gradually decreasing while public demand is gradually increasing. By transferring non-core government functions to social organizations and enterprises, and using third-party evaluation agencies to supervise and assess the projects, it not only helps to enhance the flexibility of grassroots governance but also promotes more professional and efficient service supply. The generation of projects is strongly related to residents' needs, meaning that by scientifically collecting and integrating residents' urgent and pressing needs, these needs are disseminated into the social service market. Professional social organizations and enterprises are invited to bid, and the most professionally qualified institutions are selected to carry out the services.

(4) Neighborhood Convergence. Neighborhood convergence is the ultimate value aim of the "Neighborhood Convergence" governance brand, with a dual meaning. On one hand, neighborhood convergence aims to overcome the "atomization" status of modern social life, aiming to enhance the public nature of social life. By establishing public spaces such as "Neighborhood Convergence," "Small Neighborhood Convergence," and party-building service centers, community residents, urban white-collar workers, parents and children, and the elderly are gathered in public spaces. Through activities, interpersonal barriers are broken, allowing people to become more familiar with each other, enhancing social capital in individuals and society, making the community a community of acquaintances, and making Q Street a warm community. On the other hand, neighborhood convergence aims to leverage the role of enthusiastic community members, promoting the emergence of more active actors, and making grassroots social governance more vibrant. In the early stages of "Neighborhood Convergence" development, the main goal was to gather popularity through public spaces, allowing the public to fully enjoy public services as customers. However, in later stages, the public is viewed as citizens, empowering them to balance their awareness of rights and responsibilities. At this point, "convergence" is not just about gathering residents and popularity but about gathering the co-construction, co-governance, and shared framework of a wide range of social governance entities.

5.2.3 Integration and Dilemmas in "Neighborhood Convergence" Governance Innovation

The 19th National Congress of the Communist Party of China pointed out that social governance innovation should pursue the establishment and improvement of a co-construction, co-governance, and shared social governance system, fully realizing the professionalization, socialization, legalization, and intelligence of social governance. How to identify and understand these discussions on social governance and transform the central value expectations into specific practical measures is a major challenge in grassroots social governance.

Grassroots affairs are the aggregation of "a thousand lines from above," making it easy to fall into a very chaotic and difficult-to-clarify situation, especially in the current context of social governance innovation and grassroots party building. Various top-down value advocacies and other advanced practices can easily cause confusion in grassroots social governance innovation. Social governance innovation has two aspects: one is the increase of governance elements to better mobilize the resources and advantages of multiple domain entities; the other is to attempt to integrate governance entities, governance resources, and governance methods into a governance system on this basis, to better play the role of these elements.

"Co-construction, co-governance, and sharing" is the value goal of social governance, highlighting the word "co," meaning that social governance is by no means the internal management of administrative or enterprise management but rather emphasizes the division of labor and cooperation between organizations, pursuing the governance path between organizations. "Co-construction" refers to the multiple organizations such as the government, social organizations, communities, and enterprises, which should maintain an equal pattern in the governance process to fully exert their powers and advantages. "Co-governance" is to improve and design the social governance system, avoiding the awkward situation of a single administrative entity leading, and should provide each organization with a structural position to exert its advantages and resources in the governance system, making it a governance entity. "Sharing" is to ensure that all governance participants can meet their interests and needs in governance, especially for new organizations, providing good incentives for enterprises to participate in social governance and good economic conditions for professional social organizations, to ensure that professionals do professional things.

The specialization, socialization, legalization, and intelligence of social governance also have rich meanings. Specialization refers to the continuous introduction of professional forces such as social work and public management into the grassroots governance team, while incubating, cultivating, and introducing professional social organizations to effectively transform work concepts, methods, and models, thereby enhancing the professionalism of grassroots social governance. Socialization is distinguished from administration by adopting a "one core, multiple elements" work model, promoting the growth of diverse entities to become the main bodies of social governance, linking multiple forces to jointly solve social problems. Legalization aims to ensure and strengthen the institutional foundation of grassroots social governance, advancing government service procurement, volunteer management, grassroots cadre selection and appointment, community consultation, etc., all with regulations to follow, avoiding disorderly conduct. Intelligence refers to streamlining platform mechanisms and systems, fully realizing the functions of diverse entities, and improving the ability of grassroots social governance to quickly collect and process information and respond to emergencies through the introduction of artificial intelligence and big data technology.

In comparison, there is still room for further optimization in the process of innovative social governance in Q Street.

Firstly, the integration of "Neighborhood Hub" with grassroots party building development is minimal. In the process of innovating grassroots social governance,

Q Street emphasizes two elements: grassroots party building and "Neighborhood Hub," and gradually adopts a "dual-track" approach to steadily advance each element. Grassroots party building gradually expands from the original community party building to public rental housing community party building and enterprise party building, with the "Party Building Plus" project in Green Valley New Space being a distinctive governance brand. In the process of developing "Neighborhood Hub," Q Street adopts a "1 + 9 + 20" advancement method, establishing and using "Neighborhood Hub" and several "Neighborhood Mini Hubs." However, it is worth noting that the two directions have initially shown differentiation, which may lead to the problem of duplicate investment in governance resources, reducing the efficiency of grassroots social governance.

Q Street should highlight the value and function of "Neighborhood Hub," making it the main goal of street social governance innovation. "Neighborhood" in the aforementioned explanation is not only the neighborhood of the community but also the neighborhood of buildings and the jurisdiction. Therefore, "Neighborhood Hub" should be understood from a broad perspective. On this basis, "territorial party building" should be an important governance element of "Neighborhood Hub," helping it link different organizational entities, coordinate mutual interests, and mediate conflicts in specific contexts, avoiding potential conflicts among diverse entities. Although in reality, grassroots party building and "Neighborhood Hub" advancement are managed by different departments, it is necessary to flexibly coordinate the advancement of both in practice, coordinate the use of governance resources to avoid duplicate investment, and view governance spaces ("Neighborhood Hub," "Neighborhood Mini Hubs," and party building service centers, etc.) as public spaces open for sharing, allowing residents to easily access public services and participate in the social governance process. The practical purpose of doing so also has another significance, as most grassroots party building work would inevitably become formalistic without "Neighborhood Hub." Therefore, the goal of combining the two is to break down the boundaries between communities and enterprises and institutions within the jurisdiction, promoting further integration and discovering a smoother and more convenient governance resource circulation network.

Secondly, from the organizational structure perspective, "Neighborhood Hub" and "Neighborhood Mini Hubs" have not effectively connected. In exploring the development of "Neighborhood Hub," Q Street has gradually started to establish "Neighborhood Mini Hubs" in the community, but lacks corresponding understanding of the relationship between the two, resulting in little significant business interaction and connection despite their similar names. The lack of connection is mainly reflected in two aspects. First, the roles of "Neighborhood Hub" and "Neighborhood Mini Hubs" are not clear. "Neighborhood Hub" is a project space carrier purchased at the street level, while "Neighborhood Mini Hubs" are space carriers based on the community level to meet residents' needs. Although they belong to the street and community levels, how can the services they provide be divided and coordinated to effectively meet residents' needs? For example, "Neighborhood Hub" conducts similar community activities, and "Neighborhood Mini Hubs" also conduct corresponding community activities, causing functional overlap and difficulty in providing differentiated functions and resources. Secondly, "Neighborhood Hub" and "Neighborhood Mini Hubs" have not been institutionalized in terms of information and work methods. "Neighborhood Hub" is more set by the street as a professional elderly care service institution and holds community activities regularly. However, whether it is elderly care services or community activities, they can only attract residents from surrounding communities to participate.This issue is mainly manifested in the fact that "Neighborhood Hub" does not have the right to suggest or evaluate the development of "Neighborhood Mini Hub," which is more like a working resource under the community residents' committee.

Thirdly, there is a relative lack of professional social organizations and social enterprises as governance entities within the jurisdiction, which has not yet effectively formed service collaboration and governance integration. In the process of social governance innovation, Q Street's shortcomings are reflected in the lack of corresponding governance resources, insufficient professional social organizations, and the absence of its own public welfare park. With few social governance resources, the government's promotion of social governance innovation lacks effective allied partners. At the same time, the small number of social organizations and social enterprises makes it difficult for the government to adopt a competitive purchasing method for services, thus hindering the efficiency of service procurement.

Fourthly, Q Street lacks corresponding third-party evaluation agencies, and the government itself has insufficient governance experience, making it difficult to effectively judge the performance of social organizations and community social organizations. In this situation, it is necessary to rely on third-party evaluation agencies to help the government supervise and evaluate project service performance.

Looking to the future, the integrated governance of Q Street needs to further integrate diverse governance tasks and consolidate consensus on governance innovation. Currently, in promoting social governance innovation led by "Neighborhood Hub," there are actually multiple governance tasks, mainly including the construction of "Neighborhood Hub," "Neighborhood Mini Hub," Green Valley New Space, and Xinjiayuan. The objectives are also different: the construction of "Neighborhood Hub" aims at the street-level elderly service function and coordinating the functions of "Neighborhood Mini Hub," while "Neighborhood Mini Hub" construction targets the community-level public service supply. The construction of Green Valley New Space is for building party-building services in enterprise parks, and Xinjiayuan construction targets party-building services in public rental housing communities.

On the surface, the social governance innovation promoted by Q Street includes two levels: street and community, and two tasks: "Neighborhood Hub" and party-building work. At the same time, the functional division between "Neighborhood Hub" and "Neighborhood Mini Hub" in street and community is not clear, as both carry out community cultural activities and community elderly services, with the difference being that "Neighborhood Hub" can provide more professional care services. Party-building work is not simply about posting slogans or constructing red spaces but focuses on exploring the use of services to achieve the objectives and connotations of grassroots party-building. If these elements appear mixed on the surface, most of the governance process can only result in "treating the symptoms rather than the root cause," lacking systematic and robust advancement in social governance. Such a lack of clear top-level design can lead to an involution effect in social governance investment, resulting in low efficiency of grassroots government financial input.

Therefore, it is necessary to clarify the relationship between grassroots party-building and "Neighborhood Hub" tasks from a substantive level and consciously and effectively promote them in practice. The primary objective of grassroots party-building is political, hoping to maintain the public's trust in grassroots government and community party branches and to leverage our party's grassroots organizations' coordination capabilities in grassroots society. However, to achieve this objective, it is also necessary to consider the social characteristics of the new era, where the public gradually detaches from the unit system, making it difficult for political parties to effectively manage the large public through units. In other words, it is necessary to attract broad resident participation through forms that the public loves, effectively playing the political guiding and rallying role in this process. Therefore, contemporary grassroots party-building mainly relies on service elements to achieve its objectives.

Although "Neighborhood Hub" is committed to playing a social role in grassroots social governance, designing and providing different services for different groups to gain residents' enthusiastic support for "Neighborhood Hub" and "Neighborhood Mini Hub," it is necessary to strengthen the volunteer service mindset of the public in this process, transforming them from passive service recipients to providers of informal support. However, to avoid the disorderliness of community social organizations and enthusiastic residents conducting activities, it is necessary to strengthen the guiding ability of grassroots organizations, transforming the richness of governance resources into effective social services. Therefore, in the process of service, "Neighborhood Hub" also needs to leverage party-building elements to achieve the value goals of gathering needs, services, residents, and public sentiment.

In summary, grassroots party-building and "Neighborhood Hub" should be closely integrated into a unified task, and by leveraging the "Neighborhood Hub" brand, absorb and integrate Q Street's governance experience to achieve Q. The goal of holistic street governance. On a practical level, it is necessary to promote different governance locations to leverage their social spatial attributes, enabling spaces to achieve multiple functions with the support of interior design, allowing residents to access social services provided by the street nearby, and avoiding the duplication of governance resources.

At the same time, based on the division of labor among street offices, the coordinating role of the Party Working Committee should be strengthened, integrating the functions of different offices, consolidating the resources and advantages of various departments, and formulating medium- and long-term as well as annual social governance plans. This should be done step by step to support relevant governance entities in participating in the governance process, ensuring that the entire street level has a stable expectation of the future direction of social governance development. Subsequently, the regionalized party-building mechanism should be actively utilized. After the annual social governance plan is completed, a regional party-building joint meeting should be convened to announce the annual social governance plan and special social governance projects, allowing each entity in the jurisdiction to understand the subsequent planning direction and their participation direction. This enables them to connect, integrate, and use resources more strategically based on consensus. Particularly for Q Street, which has a series of large enterprises internally, releasing its annual social governance plan before the enterprises' annual planning helps leverage the investment of corporate social responsibility funds and attract more social funds into the social governance service resource pool.

Chapter 6
Integration Practices of Social Organizations Participating in Grassroots Governance

6.1 The Strategic Position and Governance Function of Social Organizations in the New Era

With the accelerated advancement of China's social and economic system transformation, the state's attention to the social field is increasing day by day, and the role of social organizations is increasingly highlighted. Since the 18th National Congress of the Communist Party of China, innovative social governance has become a powerful driving force for promoting sustainable social development and has clearly proposed to fully leverage the positive role of social organizations in social governance, enhance their ability to participate in public services and grassroots governance, and accelerate the construction of a modern social organization system characterized by the separation of government and society, clear rights and responsibilities, and legal autonomy. The 19th National Congress of the Communist Party of China clearly proposed to create a social governance pattern of co-construction, co-governance, and sharing, promoting the participation of multiple entities in social governance practices, strengthening the construction of social governance systems, and improving the socialization, legalization, intelligence, and specialization of social governance. It also proposed accelerating the separation of government and society, stimulating the vitality of social organizations, overcoming the tendency of administrativeization of social organizations, and further shifting the focus of social governance to the grassroots level, leveraging the role of social organizations to achieve a positive interaction between government governance and social regulation, and residents' self-governance. In 2017, the Ministry of Civil Affairs issued the "Opinions on Vigorously Cultivating and Developing Community Social Organizations" (hereinafter referred to as the "Opinions"), proposing overall requirements and deployment for cultivating and developing community social organizations. It is evident that reforming and optimizing the governance functions of social organizations is of significant value and importance for promoting the transformation of government functions and collaborative governance between government and society. It is an

L. Hou, *The Integrated Service in Urban Community Governance*, Public Economy and Urban Governance in China, https://doi.org/10.1007/978-981-96-6775-8_6

important part of deepening the reform of Party and state institutions and advancing the modernization of the national governance system and governance capacity. The "Decision of the Central Committee of the Communist Party of China on Deepening the Reform of Party and State Institutions" in 2018 emphasized the need to stimulate the vitality of mass organizations and social organizations and promote the reform of social organizations. This clearly Chapter 6: Integration Practices of Social Organizations Participating in Grassroots Governance 105 proposed the necessity, urgency, and reality of reforming the social organization system in the new era.

Over the more than 40 years since the reform and opening up, the development of social organizations in China has gone through five distinct stages, namely the "germination development period," "tortuous development period," "stable development period," "accelerated development period," and the "reform development period" initiated since the 19th National Congress of the Communist Party of China. The development, functions, problems encountered, and aspects needing adjustment of social organizations in different stages have significant differences. In the new period and new stage, the governance functions of social organizations have shown significant progression and focus, reaching a consensus on their governance functions, namely that social organizations are an important component of national governance modernization, an important responder to people's aspirations for a better life, a core area of social service supply-side reform, an extension area of in-depth market economy advancement, an important carrier of the co-construction, co-governance, and sharing social governance pattern, an important component of the social governance reform reverse mechanism, and a key link in achieving positive interaction between government governance and social regulation, and residents' self-governance.

6.2 Structural Optimization and Governance Innovation: The Development Trend and Characteristics of Social Organizations

In the New Era Having experienced the "accelerated development period" since the 18th National Congress of the Communist Party of China, social organizations have made progress in structural optimization, reform consensus, Service purchasing and governance innovation have undergone some new changes. In order to adapt to these new changes, it is also necessary for people's understanding to undergo synchronous adjustments and changes.

Firstly, while the number of social organizations is increasing, there is also optimization in structure and function. The number of community social organizations active in urban and rural grassroots communities has significantly increased, becoming an important and indispensable governance force in grassroots social governance. In the process of incremental reform and stock development of social organizations, different types of organizations have achieved a certain degree of development. Supportive and hub-type social organizations, as well as numerous social work service agencies, have realized governance that "crosses community boundaries," beginning to grow into important carriers after the transfer of government functions.

Taking Shanghai's Pudong New Area as an example, as of July 31, 2018, the total number of social organizations in Pudong New Area reached 2,228, including 389 social groups, 1,835 private non-enterprise units, and 4 foundations. Among them, more than 1,780 social organizations are active in fields such as education, culture, health, sports, social services, and ecological environment in Pudong New Area, accounting for nearly 80% of the total; nearly 200 industry associations and chambers of commerce, and technology-related social organizations serve the industrial and scientific research fields of Pudong New Area. Various types of registered community social organizations have also achieved varying degrees of increase in numbers. More encouragingly, the business interconnection and intercommunication of different types of social organizations are gradually forming a network, with horizontal connections continuously strengthening, becoming an important growth point for the horizontal linkage mechanism of social order. Thus, the logic of "atomization" and "fragmentation" in the development of social organizations is changing in the horizontal linkage and functional complementarity of diverse social organizations. In modern social governance, the government is no longer the sole subject of social governance; social organizations, urban and rural community social organizations, and the general public have all become important subjects of social governance, initially forming a pattern of co-construction, co-governance, and sharing in social governance.

Secondly, the reform of the social organization system has become an irreversible trend, with consensus on reform continuously consolidating and practice continuously expanding. On one hand, there is the consolidation of reform consensus in the national strategy. "Accelerating the formation of a modern social organization system" is an important theoretical proposition put forward by the 18th National Congress of the Communist Party of China. To strengthen social construction, it is necessary to accelerate the promotion of social system reform and to accelerate the formation of a modern social organization system with separation of government and society, clear rights and responsibilities, and legal autonomy. The Third Plenary Session of the 18th Central Committee further proposed to accelerate the modernization of the national governance system and governance capacity, innovate the social governance system, and stimulate the vitality of social organizations. The 19th National Congress emphasized the need to accelerate the implementation of the separation of government and society, stimulate the vitality of social organizations, and overcome the tendency of administrativeization of social organizations. From this perspective, the principles, direction, content, and goals of social organization reform have gradually become clear, and the consensus on reform has been effectively consolidated. On the other hand, there is the pioneering and trial implementation, achieving continuous accumulation and expansion of governance innovation practice, with the practice of reform continuously deepening. In 2009, Pudong New Area began implementing public welfare project bidding, exploring the establishment of a social organization integrity system, and establishing a list of social organizations undertaking service projects and a list of high-quality social organizations. In 2013, a "supply–demand docking · one-stop service" platform for public welfare service projects was launched, promoting the growth of social organizations through project docking, process monitoring, project evaluation, and project guidance. In 2015, the "Guiding Opinions on Further Promoting the Development of Community Social Organizations in Pudong New Area" was issued, adding more than 100 community social organizations, and achieving full coverage of social organization service centers in 36 streets and towns in the city. In 2016, the district government issued the "Financial Support Opinions on Promoting the Development of Social Organizations in Pudong New Area during the 13th Five-Year Plan Period," allocating nearly 20 million yuan in support funds over two years. At the same time, the construction of community foundations was vigorously promoted, with 13 street and town community foundations established by 2017. In 2017, community social organization federations were piloted in 6 streets, and in 2018, they were fully rolled out in 36 streets and towns in Pudong New Area, further building a district social organization party-building platform to fully leverage party-building in guiding community social organizations to participate in urban grassroots governance.

Thirdly, the government continues to increase efforts in cultivating and developing social organizations, with the purchase of social organization services becoming a normalized mechanism. Government procurement of services is an important mechanism for the transformation of government functions and market-oriented reform in the field of public services, and it is an important channel for social organizations to obtain resources, having become a government The construction of cooperative relationships between the government and social organizations is crucial for the stable development of social organizations. Particularly during the process of shifting the focus of social governance downward, the convergence of various resources at the grassroots level has significantly alleviated the financial bottleneck pressures that constrain the development of social organizations. According to statistics from Pudong New Area, for registered community social organizations, government procurement of services accounted for 57.8% of the income of such organizations in 2017. Meanwhile, data from the "Shanghai Pudong New Area Social Organization Development Report" indicates that in 2016, the proportion of income from private non-enterprise units directly or indirectly through government procurement of public services and subsidies was 32.4%. Excluding other types within the sample data of registered community social organizations, it is still evident that the intensity of government procurement is continuously increasing, and government procurement of services is becoming normalized. Through this mechanism, the resource situation of social organizations has undergone significant changes, achieving stable development expectations. From the perspective of the main resource conditions for the development of record-type community social organizations, community autonomy funds have played a certain role, with 38.7% of record-type community social organizations indicating that autonomy funds are their main source of funding, 33.0% relying on member self-funding, and the proportion of subsidies from communities and streets being relatively small, at only 1.95% and 1.3%, respectively, indicating that the funding sources for social organizations are relatively diverse.

Overall, through government procurement and diversified socialized fundraising channels, the total amount of resources for social organizations has increased, the sources have become more numerous, the resource structure has tended towards rationality, and the situation of resource shortages has significantly improved, greatly enhancing the ability to respond to diverse needs. Correspondingly, issues such as the capacity building of social organizations and the specialization of services have become a new mission for the reform and development of social organizations in the new era.

Fourth, under the technological means of self-media and big data, the development environment of social organizations is constantly being reshaped, with opportunities and challenges coexisting. On one hand, new technological means have expanded the space and fields for social organizations to provide and carry out services, forming an important dimension of social service governance innovation; on the other hand, new technological means have also continuously promoted the transparency and openness of the entire process of service provision by social organizations, subjecting them to multiple pressures of standardization, credibility, and specialization, further constituting a source of motivation for their reform and innovation. Research on the construction of integrated service models in urban community governance.

6.3 New Social Organizations: Connotation, Characteristics, and Development Principles[1]

6.3.1 Definition of the Connotation of New Social Organizations

New social organizations have emerged and grown as a result of the advancement of social transformation and the optimization of the governance environment. As a product of social organizations reaching a new stage of development, new social organizations are an important vehicle for deepening reform and innovating social governance.

Therefore, research on new social organizations should "re-root" (Re-Root) from the historical continuum of social organization emergence, and on this basis, propose the "genesis" of new social organizations to understand their proposal, connotation nature, and functional positioning.

1. Background Field: Social Transformation and System Transition

The transformation of society and the transition of systems, along with the deepening of reforms, have led to profound changes and adjustments in the relationships

[1] Some content has been published in "Learning and Practice," Issue 7, 2015.

between the state and the market, and between the state and society. This is the basic background field for understanding the development of social organizations during the transition period, meaning that the emergence of social organizations is an inevitable result of reform and opening up and social transformation. Before the reform and opening up, society was essentially a "total society" (Total Society) (Sun Liping 1994). Its main characteristic was that the state, through institutional arrangements of urban social unitization and rural social collectivization, monopolized the control and allocation of social resources, with individuals being restricted by a series of rigid status-segmenting systems such as the unit system, household registration system, and identity system, resulting in limited space for activities. Society had the distinct feature of a "strong state, weak society," with only the state and no society. Therefore, non-governmental organizations, especially so-called social organizations, had no space or environment for survival and development.

After 1978, China successively carried out economic system reform, political system reform, and social reform, initiating an "unprecedented great change." Firstly, the "market" gradually developed as a second domain independent of the "state," with the socialist market economy rapidly developing, the market economy system being basically established, and replacing the planned economy system as the main theme in the national economic field; secondly, "society" As an independent third domain outside of the "state," it has also gained autonomous space. The streamlining of government institutions and the transformation of their functions continue to progress through exploration, establishing the vision of "small government, big society" as the guiding principle for governance. Thirdly, with the miniaturization of the "state," the standardization of the "market," and the independence of "society," various entities and components within the social field gradually develop and grow, objectively providing opportunities and space for the development of social organizations.

After more than 30 years of reform, a relatively rich, free, and open association ecosystem has gradually formed. Social organizations, as their main institutional form, have also become more standardized. They have created a rich social platform in promoting individual participation, realizing social value, and expanding the public domain, becoming an indispensable constructive force in China's social transformation and governance innovation.

2. Conceptual Analysis: Understanding Convergence and Differentiated References

With the development of social organizations at the practical level, academia has also conducted multidisciplinary research on social organizations. Whether in academic articles or government documents, frequently used and cross-used concepts generally involve non-governmental organizations, non-profit organizations, civil organizations, intermediary organizations, etc. Generally speaking, these different terms do not have substantial differences, but from a strict semantic perspective, there are differences that cannot be ignored. Therefore, when recognizing and understanding the concept of new social organizations, it is necessary to strictly analyze related concepts to clarify their meanings.

(1) Non-Governmental Organizations. Non-governmental organizations are mainly relative to governmental organizations, aiming to emphasize the non-official

nature of social organizations, indicating that social organizations do not belong to the category of governmental organizations. However, as Yu Keping (2006) pointed out, there are two major misconceptions in the use of this concept in reality. One is the belief that only those important organizations formally approved and registered by relevant departments belong to social organizations. In contrast, a large number of informal organizations existing in society are excluded from the category of "non-governmental organizations," not treated as an important part of the social organization system. The second is the extreme interpretation of the "non-governmental" nature of "non-governmental organizations" as having no relationship with the government, or even being opposed to the government, which is not conducive to establishing a healthy government-society relationship.

(2) Non-Profit Organizations. The concept of non-profit organizations is mainly relative to enterprise (market) organizations, aiming to emphasize the difference between social organizations and market organizations such as enterprises and companies, as they do not operate based on "market rationality." However, in reality, it easily blurs the boundary between the necessary paid services and profit-making activities that social organizations engage in for their survival, leading to misunderstandings about the credibility of non-profit organizations and affecting people's enthusiasm for working in non-profit organizations. This further results in criticism and questioning of their non-profit nature and credibility, with non-profit organizations facing the fate of "trapped charity." The key issue lies in people's definition and standard of "non-profit."

(3) Civil Organizations. Civil organizations are also relative to "top-down" government organizations, emphasizing their grassroots nature. The bottom-up formation path indicates that the driving force for the formation of social organizations comes from civil society. Due to China's long-standing "official-oriented" culture, social organizations spontaneously formed by civil forces face many difficulties in development. For example, civil organizations face issues of legitimacy. Since they originate from the grassroots and lack "top-down" government authorization, they do not possess "legitimacy," and their status as independent legal entities is problematic, leading to serious deficiencies in their "acceptance" and "recognition" in society, thereby hindering their development.

(4) Intermediary Organizations. Intermediary organizations are mainly discussed from the perspective of their position and role, aiming to emphasize their bridging role in connecting resources and information, without clearly defining the nature by which they achieve this function. Therefore, most intermediary organizations in reality operate based on a "profit-oriented" logic, such as law firms, accounting firms, and real estate agencies. Rather than being considered social organizations, they are more accurately described as market organizations. In the process of accelerating the establishment of a socialist market economy system in China, such organizations will continue to increase with the development of the service industry, playing important roles in economic life but differing completely from social organizations.

(5) Mass Organizations or People's Organizations. These concepts mainly pertain to the Chinese political system. It is a specific political category under the existing system, primarily encompassing trade unions and women's federations under the leadership of the Communist Party of China, as well as a few other special groups such as the China Association for Science and Technology and the China Disabled Persons' Federation. Their typical characteristics include a strong political and administrative nature, corresponding administrative levels, personnel formally allocated by the state, and certain administrative management and service functions. In terms of their status in society and the functions they perform, they resemble government organizations more than non-governmental organizations, differing fundamentally from the concept of social organizations. However, based on China's national conditions, they are mostly classified as social organizations.
(6) Third sector organizations. The third sector mainly refers to the category outside the "government" and "market," corresponding to which third sector organizations primarily refer to organizational forms active in this field, emphasizing their differences from government and corporate organizations. However, the third sector is a political science category imported from the West, and in reality, there is a lack of basic understanding and cognition of what constitutes the third sector, leading to considerable confusion and ignorance regarding third sector organizations.
(7) Volunteer organizations. Volunteer organizations are mainly in contrast to the "bureaucratic nature" of modern organizations, formed based on people's voluntary union, with the logic of their actions primarily being spontaneous and voluntary by members. Generally speaking, they have a low degree of organization, lacking clear rules, schedules, and institutional arrangements. However, voluntariness is a relatively broad concept without specific behavioral subjects and is not unique to social organizations; some party agencies and organizations also emphasize the voluntariness of their members' participation. Therefore, using this concept to refer to social organizations is also inappropriate in many ways.
(8) Concepts such as social groups or associations. These concepts more or less indicate the "social" or "civil" nature of social organizations, which are distinctly different from government and corporate organizations. Specifically, concepts like social groups and associations emphasize the social nature of social organizations; concepts like civic groups and civic organizations highlight the political nature of social organizations, defining them from the perspective of political rights. These concepts have their unique applicability in Chinese society and are largely used interchangeably. The aforementioned different concepts do not have substantial differences; they emphasize certain aspects of modern society from different angles. However, as the author mentioned earlier, in the profound historical process of comprehensively advancing the modernization of national governance, the ambiguity and arbitrariness in the basic understanding of the concept of social organizations may become a "knot" in advancing social governance reform, leading to divergences or obstacles in the path selection and implementation plans for comprehensively advancing social system reform.

Therefore, it is particularly necessary to scientifically define social organizations from the perspective of connotation and extension. Alternatively, a new concept could be created to distinguish from the existing confusion in the field of social organization concepts, thereby aligning with the current social system reform.

3. Conceptual Deduction: From Social Organizations to New Social Organizations

Regarding the definition of non-profit organizations, the proposal by Professor Lester Salamon of Johns Hopkins University is typical and representative. He mainly considers what constitutes a "non-profit organization" based on the shared characteristics of non-profit organizations. These five characteristics include: ① Organizational nature; ② Non-governmental nature; ③ Non-profit nature; ④ Autonomy; ⑤ Voluntariness. Among them, non-governmental and non-profit nature are recognized as the basic characteristics of non-profit organizations. However, scholars have proposed different views and supplements on other characteristics of non-profit organizations based on the actual conditions of different countries and regions. In the study of constructing an integrated service model in urban community governance, Japanese scholar Shigetomi Shinichi revised the characteristics of non-profit organizations to six, considering the national conditions of Asian countries: ① Non-governmental nature; ② Non-profit nature; ③ Spontaneity; ④ Continuity/Formality; ⑤ Altruism; ⑥ Charitability. Wang Ming and Jia Xijin believe that defining non-profit organizations in China is important, as they are social organizations that do not aim for profit, have a formal organizational form, belong to the non-governmental system, and possess a certain degree of autonomy and voluntariness, public welfare or mutual benefit, but not all-encompassing, requiring objective and dynamic observation and understanding." This so-called "objective and dynamic observation and understanding" leads to arbitrariness and randomness in defining non-profit organizations, inducing multiple troubles in reality.

From this perspective, scholars generally believe that non-profit organizations mainly refer to social organizations independent of the government and enterprises. In this sense, non-profit organizations are referred to as the "third sector," distinct from the government and enterprises, emphasizing the similar attributes of non-profit organizations. More often, it is explained from the characteristics of social organizations and the comparison with other types of organizations to define what "non-profit organizations" are. This is an inductive refinement, difficult to capture the essence of social organizations, and cannot encompass all the characteristics of social organizations, especially the new characteristics emerging with changes in the social environment. Therefore, there is no consensus in academia on what "non-profit organizations" are, and they have not been defined from the essential perspective of social organizations. Their connotation and extension vary due to different perspectives and regional differences.

As Wang Ming stated, "Under the current historical conditions of a transitional period, a broader definition standard will be more conducive to promoting the development of relevant social organizations." This means that in the third stage of social organization development, such a broad definition is conducive to creating a relatively relaxed and free development atmosphere for social organizations, thus having a certain realistic rationality. However, in the new period of social organization development, with significant changes in the social environment in which social organizations are embedded, such a lack of clear and precise definition will cause much confusion and trouble in reality, which is not conducive to the healthy development of social organizations. Therefore, in this chapter, the author aims to construct a clear new definition of social organizations with explicit connotations and extensions, namely new social organizations.

The so-called new social organizations refer to those different from government-operated non-governmental organizations (GONGOs), community cultural and sports activity teams, and various market entities or market elements with economic rationality as their purpose (such as economic industry associations, law firms, and other profit-making institutions). Instead, they pursue social rationality, providing non-profit social services or social support, and are independent legal entities.

6.3.2 Understanding New Social Organizations

As a new conceptual definition, whether new social organizations can self-justify is a key issue, namely whether they can prove their essential specificity in conceptual connotation to distinguish themselves from "social organizations"; and whether they have their own normative, clear domain and significant characteristics in extension representation, without being confused with social organizations. Therefore, our understanding of new social organizations mainly revolves around these aspects.

1. The Connotation and Extension of New Social Organizations

From its connotation, new social organizations have a completely new reference.

Firstly, "social rationality" is the action logic of new social organizations, which means that the interaction logic between new social organizations and citizens is neither the coercive relationship between the government and citizens in the political field nor the exchange relationship between producers and consumers in the market field. Instead, it is a "trust" relationship based on social members' social recognition of the public welfare concept advocated by new social organizations. It is a resource support and principal-agent relationship based on trust, voluntariness, and public welfare, different from the "economic rationality" of enterprise organizations and the "domination rationality" of government organizations. In a certain sense, it can be understood as another rational mechanism outside the state and market fields. This rational mechanism occupies more and more social space, reshaping, to varying degrees, the habits of life characterized by public consultation and rational dialogue, and embodies an active civic consciousness to pursue the common interest in the "public sphere."

Secondly, public welfare is the soul of new social organizations. This means that the self-positioning of new social organizations is to serve the interests of an unspecified majority or the entire society, completely different from various profit-making organizations and distinct from various "mutual benefit" types of social organizations. The pursuit of public welfare by new social organizations is manifested in practice as voluntary, service-oriented, and non-profit characteristics, meaning that new social organizations aim to provide non-profit social services or social support to society through professional and specialized actions. This is the foundation for new social organizations to stand in society, be placed in the public space, and gain legitimacy and recognition.Finally, the nature of new social organizations is that they are social groups with independent legal person status. New social organizations are formed based on different needs and have a growing self-awareness, self-interest maintenance, self-assertion, autonomous decision-making, and value advocacy, positioning them as equal partners with the government in a "partnership cooperation relationship."

From an extension perspective, the extension of new social organizations is smaller than that of social organizations, referring only to a part of social organizations with the aforementioned connotations. Their organizational types mainly cover three major categories (though the connotations are all contracted). The first is social groups. These are the main body of new social organizations, primarily member-based organizations with non-profit, non-governmental, and social characteristics, with professional social service agencies as the main body. The second is foundations, which mainly refer to various non-member organizations based on donation and public welfare property relations. The third is private non-enterprise units, which refer to entities directly providing various social services, such as various non-profit consulting service organizations. Specifically, the extension of new social organizations includes the following five aspects.

(1) As the main body of social collaborative forces and the main target of government service procurement, new social organizations mainly refer to spontaneously formed organizations that play the most unique role in the reform of the social management system, being the most qualified undertakers after the separation of government functions. However, in reality, the development of such social organizations faces numerous difficulties, not only facing legitimacy issues but also issues of credibility, organizational performance, and other aspects. Moreover, such social organizations are often submerged in the broad category of social organizations and are neglected or abandoned, not receiving the attention and focus they deserve that matches their functions. Therefore, they can be separated from the broad category of social organizations through the "new" category to promote their rapid development.
(2) Extracting various intermediary organizations mainly considers that new social organizations follow social rationality, are "social" rather than "capital," and are social groups with the mission of providing non-profit social services and social support, thus avoiding the infiltration of "economic rationality" and "market

logic.“ This is the key to social organizations gaining credibility and is fundamental to ensuring their role in practicing social justice values, which needs to be identified from a “new” perspective.

(3) Unlike people’s organizations and public institutions, new social organizations have sociality and independence, with their organizational operations and activities less subject to government intervention, having their own independent purposes, norms, and responsibilities, being “social” rather than social organizations under official patronage.

(4) Unlike industry associations and chambers of commerce, the service fields and objects of new social organizations have broader coverage, not limited to specific institutions and groups as their sole service objects, and new social organizations provide more public or semi-public products in the form of social services and social support. In contrast, industry association-type social organizations exist in the economic field as mutual benefit organizations, mostly serving various market entities, with their activities closely linked to enterprises and other profit organizations, being an indispensable part of the existence and development of the market economy. They mainly follow “economic rationality,” being “capital” rather than “social.“

(5) Unlike cultural and sports activity groups and organizations, new social organizations are public welfare and non-profit organizations, while cultural and sports activity types are more mutual benefit organizations, with their logic starting from self-interest rather than social or public welfare considerations, and the functional positioning of cultural and sports activity social organizations is relatively single, lacking positive significance for the development of civil society.

2. Characteristics of New Social Organizations

From the above interpretation of the connotation and extension of new social organizations, it can be seen that they have some basic characteristics different from previous social organizations.

First, a brand-new positioning of the government-society relationship. Unlike the “subordinate partner relationship model” between the government and social organizations, the relationship between new social organizations and the government is a “partnership cooperation relationship” based on the premise of government-society division of labor and cooperation, with both belonging to different “fields” and having their own unique “habits” and action logic. The separation of government and society is the logical premise for the “presence” of new social organizations, and it is also the premise for the reform and development of the social governance system. The division of labor and joint governance between the government and society based on different functional positioning is the result. Clearly, in the new era, these can be effectively undertake. The new social organizations are those that perform social functions and affairs, with their main bodies being specialized and professionalized social work service agencies.

Second, the true meaning of being non-governmental and autonomous. This refers to new social organizations that originate from the grassroots, operate independently, and are self-governing. New social organizations have formal organizational and management structures, written statutes, business scopes, and fixed staff. They are neither government nor affiliated agencies, nor do they represent any government or national stance. Instead, they develop endogenously based on responding to social realities and needs, distinguishing them from the previous "dual nature" of official and civilian, and serving as a prerequisite for practicing public welfare.

Third, an important platform for public welfare and non-profit social services. Unlike profit-oriented services provided by enterprises and other profit-seeking institutions (such as domestic services, legal services, etc.), the social services and support provided by new social organizations are non-profit in nature, belonging to the realm of public welfare and welfare. Some social organizations are constrained by the registration difficulties of the "dual management system" and the imperfect tax legal system, leading to insufficient public welfare, or even the replacement of "non-profit" by "profit". However, the activities of new social organizations must always adhere to public welfare as the criterion and maintain non-profit operations, which is an intrinsic requirement of new social organizations and a core component of their credibility.

Fourth, the organic combination of professionalization and specialization. On one hand, new social organizations place more emphasis on the professionalization and professional development of service personnel; on the other hand, the main bodies of new social organizations are various specialized and professionalized social work service agencies.

Fifth, specialized and differentiated social services. The non-governmental and autonomous nature of new social organizations allows them to maintain high sensitivity and flexibility to social needs and environmental changes, thereby facilitating the provision of various specialized and differentiated social services to meet the increasingly diverse and heterogeneous social needs, compensating for the shortcomings of rigid government management and services.

3. Possible Misunderstandings of New Social Organizations

Misunderstanding one: Equating new social organizations with the "new social organizations" in the "two new organizations". The "new social organizations" in the two new organizations mainly refer to newly emerged types of social organizations, while the new social organizations discussed in this chapter represent a completely new concept. This involves the dialectic of "new" and "old". The "new" discussed in this chapter is not "new" in the ontogenetic sense, i.e., "recently emerged", but "new" understood from the ontological meaning, i.e., new connotations and characteristics, mainly in contrast to government-run organizations and enterprise organizations. Therefore, in terms of form, it can be a previously existing form of social organization, but also includes newly emerged forms of social organizations guided by social rationality. In other words, "new" is mainly understood from the distinction from government-run and profit-oriented organizations.

Misunderstanding two: Equating new social organizations with social organizations. As the above analysis shows, the author believes that new social organizations are different from social organizations, with more restricted connotations and narrower extensions. The reason for proposing the concept of "new social organizations" and making a clear distinction between "new social organizations" and "social organizations" is mainly based on the following considerations. Theoretically, as new social organizations with clear connotations and extensions, they represent the development and improvement of previous social organization theories, a correction of the "top-down" government-run social organization development model, and a rectification of the theoretical community's divergent views on social organizations, with a certain degree of theoretical innovation significance. In practice, due to the ambiguity and broadness of the previous concept of social organizations, the operation of social organizations in reality is mixed, with various "non-governmental non-enterprise units" and "social enterprises" masquerading as "social organizations", rampant in the "social" field. On the one hand, they are "social organizations" that can enjoy national tax and policy benefits for social organizations; on the other hand, they falsely claim to be "non-profit" while actually engaging in profit-making activities, which has "stigmatized" genuine social organizations and severely deteriorated the ecological environment for the development of social organizations, eroding their credibility. Therefore, using the concept of "new social organizations" to theoretically exclude such "social organizations" has significant practical importance. Firstly, it is beneficial for clarifying the relationship between social organizations and the government. GONGOs (Government-Organized Non-Governmental Organizations) will be completely "expunged" from the list of new social organizations, with social organizations and the government belonging to two distinct domains, truly becoming equal entities that follow different operational logics. Second, it helps resolve the trust crisis of social organizations and enhances their credibility. Third, it benefits social organizations by adhering to "social rationality," returning to the social domain, and effectively undertaking the social and public services divested by government transformation.

In summary, new social organizations have more clearly defined their reference in terms of conceptual connotation, more cautiously clarified their content in terms of conceptual extension, and more prominently characterized their identity in terms of features. In institutional practice, they have replaced the operational logic of "dominant rationality" and "instrumental rationality" with "social rationality." In terms of policy implications, it is beneficial to separate "new social organizations" from various types of social organizations for independent policy design and consideration, thereby promoting the unique functions they perform.

6.3.3 New Social Organizations and Social Governance

The proposal of new social organizations is a result of changes in social structure and a product of social transformation and institutional reform. From the long-wave process of global governance and the unique pulse of China's social transformation, the proposal of new social organizations has inherent necessity, external urgency, and practical importance, serving as a crucial link in advancing the modernization of the national governance system and governance methods.

1. Social Governance Innovation: The Practical Basis for Proposing New Social Organizations

After the Third Plenary Session of the 18th Central Committee of the Communist Party of China, the deepening of governance concepts, the shift from "management" to "governance," and the abolition of the "dual management system" have cleared obstacles and laid the foundation for the emergence and development of new social organizations.

(1) The emergence of new social organizations has inherent necessity. Firstly, new social organizations are an inevitable trend in the development of a market economy. The development of a market economy inevitably leads to the growth of civil society, which relies on the development of a third domain independent of the "state" and the "market." Therefore, as an important entity in the third domain, new social organizations inevitably mature with the establishment of a modern market economy system. Secondly, new social organizations are also the only way to promote the modernization of national governance. The modernization of the national governance system and governance methods requires the renewal of governance concepts and the transformation of government functions. The cultivation and functioning of new social organizations are precisely the internal requirements of governance concepts and an important carrier for the transformation of government functions. Therefore, the emergence of new social organizations is a product of social transformation and has inevitability.
(2) The development of new social organizations has external urgency. Firstly, the proposal and cultivation of new social organizations are conducive to fundamentally breaking the constraints and shackles of the "dual management system" under state control thinking, accelerating the formation of a benign social organization management system. Secondly, the growth and expansion of new social organizations, and their role in international affairs, are closely related to the enhancement of China's international status, which is of great significance for enhancing China's international influence. Thirdly, new social organizations are an important component of the modern social organization system. Only by accelerating the formation of a modern social organization system can the capacity of social organizations be continuously improved, thereby enhancing the enthusiasm, initiative, and creativity of society and the state in participating in and developing social organizations. Finally, the positive role and effective undertaking of the historical mission of new social organizations are the realistic responsibilities entrusted to them by the times.

2. Development of New Social Organizations: The Only Way to Modernize Social Governance The process of world modernization shows that the higher the degree of organization in society, the more complete the social services, the stronger the social stability, the greater the social vitality, and the lower the difficulty coefficient of social management. This is also true for China, where in the

new period of reform and development, new social organizations are important carriers for social reorganization, maintaining social stability, and promoting the modernization of social governance.

(1) As new social organizations in the ontological sense, they are important entities in the social governance system. As independent legal entities, new social organizations themselves constitute a "unit" in "pluralistic governance" and are an important force in "social collaboration." The "collaborative" function of new social organizations as entities is mainly reflected in three aspects. Firstly, new social organizations are important tools for delivering social welfare and social policies. On one hand, as a bottom-up organizational form, new social organizations must directly face the diverse needs of social members and can maintain sufficient sensitivity and flexibility to these differentiated needs, thereby having inherent advantages in expressing public opinion, conveying public sentiment, realizing civil rights, and safeguarding people's livelihood. On the other hand, new social organizations pursue social rationality, providing... Non-profit, professional social services or social support are the primary goals and purposes. This positioning allows new social organizations to infuse humanistic and scientific content into social services, distinguishing their service methods from the extensive and empiricist models under traditional systems, effectively compensating for the shortcomings of government "rigid" management and services, while also achieving effective alignment with the needs of social members. Secondly, new social organizations are important carriers for social reorganization and social solidarity. The development of new social organizations is a major initiative to address the challenges of atomization and fragmentation of social structures, achieving social reorganization. Since the reform and opening up, especially since the mid-1990s, with the rapid development of the market economy and the disintegration of the unit system, social stratification has become significant, and "unit people" have gradually moved towards "atomization." The characteristics of atomization, de-organization, and de-support among social members have become prominent, with a large influx of vulnerable groups, increasing social tension, and traditional social management, social welfare, and social support methods have become increasingly ineffective. The lack of organizational care and institutionalized love has resulted in a massive social group that is extremely prone to social instability. However, social organizations, especially new social organizations, can reorganize society at all levels and in all fields of social life, thereby alleviating the "fragmentation" tendency brought about by social atomization. Finally, new social organizations are important platforms for constructing "party-society relations" and "government-society relations" in the new stage, conducive to consolidating and rebuilding the fish-water relationship between the party and the people in the new era, and laying a solid foundation for the ruling party's governance. With the transformation of society, the platform for the party's connection with society—the unit system no longer exists, coupled with the limited role of traditional organizations such as trade unions and women's federations, the party is directly

facing "atomized" and "fragmented" individuals in society, losing an effective platform for organizing and mobilizing the masses. Therefore, to uphold the party's leadership, improve and enhance the party's governance capacity, the party must proactively construct new platforms, vigorously develop new social organizations, and construct a new social service system to reshape new relationships with society. This is a major issue in the transformation of the party-mass work system and the fundamental path to enhance national governance capacity and realize the party's mass line at the current stage.

(2) As a methodological significance, new social organizations are important means to achieve good social governance. The social rationality and governance concepts followed by new social organizations are important rules for realizing the modernization of social governance and effective ideas for constructing cooperation and communication among multiple governance subjects. Firstly, new social organizations are important means to transform government social functions, innovate social management and public service models, and deepen the connotation of social management and public services. The participation of new social organizations in social governance is an important form of humanization and scientification of social management and social services, conducive to improving and promoting the modernization of social governance methods. Secondly, as an effective carrier for citizens to express their wishes and demands and participate in various social affairs in a self-organized manner, new social organizations can enhance citizens' awareness of participation and self-organization, and through the discovery of a series of public issues, form a space for autonomous governance by citizens. Moreover, new social organizations actively practice and advocate universal civic awareness, autonomy concepts, legal concepts, contractual spirit, and public welfare spirit through their operational logic, which is also the historical responsibility and pursuit of new social organizations at the value level, contributing to the development of civil society. Finally, the cultivation and development of new social organizations are key to accelerating the transformation of government functions and the reform of public institutions and people's organizations, a major strategic step as China's reform enters deep waters. The social vitality released by the reform of the social organization system and the development of new social organizations will become a "reverse force," promoting the reform of existing public institutions and people's organizations. At the same time, the development of new social organizations provides important experience templates and practical references for the reform of public institutions and people's organizations, conducive to advancing the reform of public institutions and people's organizations, thereby improving the social governance system.

6.3.4 *Principles for the Development of New Social Organizations*

As a product of social organization development to a new stage, new social organizations are important carriers for deepening reform and innovating social governance. To better promote and facilitate the development of new social organizations, the following principles should be adhered to. First, adhere to the civil, public, and non-profit nature of new social organizations, which is the premise for the development of new social organizations; second, break the myth of government and street administrative omnipotence, fully recognizing the advantages of new social organizations in effectively undertaking the transfer of government functions; third, focus on developing various types of Professional and vocational social service organizations, especially those that are cross-community, de-institutionalized, de-administrative, and autonomous, are the main body of new social organizations. Fourth, promptly establish a modern social work system to guide the development of various social service organizations, social service undertakings, autonomous organizations, and volunteer undertakings, continuously enriching the extension of new social organizations. Fifth, properly handle the relationship between neighborhood committees and new social organizations, strengthen the "three-community linkage" of communities, social workers, and social groups (new social organizations), forming an internal cooperation mechanism to jointly contribute to grassroots social governance. Sixth, vigorously promote the construction of public finance systems and social policies, including government procurement of social service projects, as well as foundation and charitable fundraising methods, and the institutional construction of tax exemptions and free allocation of service venues for new social organizations, to continuously optimize the social environment for the development of new social organizations.

New social organizations, through their operational logic, are also actively practicing and advocating universal civic awareness, autonomy concepts, legal concepts, contract spirit, and public welfare spirit, which endows new social organizations with historical responsibility and pursuit at the value level. This also presupposes the dual mission of new social organizations: one is to play the social governance function as an organizational carrier; the other is to reshape public awareness as a value advocate. How new social organizations, as value carriers, achieve the reshaping of public awareness and the construction of civil society is also an unfinished topic. The efforts made in this book aim to achieve a "perspective transformation," a "connotative function" type of research from a "bottom-up" and "non-official" perspective, aiming to provide theoretical support for the incremental development and functional realization of new social organizations and to contribute to the modernization of social governance.

6.4 Practical Evolution and Realistic Reflection: Structural Limitations and Challenges in the Development of Social Organizations in the New Era

Unlike the consensus on the governance function and reform development of social organizations, social organizations still face a series of new problems and challenges in the new round of "reform and development period." These opportunities and challenges constitute the structural limitations for optimizing the governance function and future development of social organizations.

(1) The precise service capability of social organizations needs further improvement. The main contradiction in Chinese society in the new era has transformed into the contradiction between the people's growing needs for a better life and unbalanced and inadequate development. The development of social organizations also shows obvious imbalances and inadequacies, which, when combined, form a new separation effect. Additionally, the diversity, multi-level nature, and uncertainty of the demand for a better life undoubtedly increase the difficulty for social organizations to achieve precise services.

Surveys show that community social organizations generally report low resident participation and recognition, mainly reflected in the following aspects. First, the participation rate of younger groups is low, and there is a lack of community social organizations and service projects that provide precise services for young people. Second, residents' participation in activities remains superficial, unable to form a mechanism for deep participation, meaning that in various service activities carried out by community social organizations, residents are merely "passive participants," and the deep-seated motivation and mechanism for "active participation" have not been effectively established. Third, residents' understanding of community social organizations is still vague, mostly remaining at the cognitive level of "cultural and entertainment teams." Fourth, the services provided by community organizations are more focused on the disadvantaged groups in the community, lacking a tiered precise response to the diverse needs of residents for a better life.

(2) The phenomenon of "separation of name and reality" in social organizations still exists. There is a serious separation between the "social" name of social organizations and the government "reality" in their actual function. Some social organizations show obvious tendencies of administrative and bureaucratic tendencies in their development, acting as the government's "legs" and "feet" in actual work, almost like a "second government." The relationship between the government and social organizations is still a "partner" relationship rather than the ideal "partner" relationship, and the transformation and development still have a long way to go. Moreover, after the disintegration of the unit system, due to the power vacuum at the grassroots level, the government has promoted the development of community social organizations, forming a transition from the local "ought to be" state to the government-promoted establishment of "actual" facts. Some

community social organizations are still "top-down" social organizations established by government departments extending their functions to the community or approved by higher-level departments to be established, in terms of funding sources, charter formulation, internal operation mechanisms, and organizational functions. They heavily rely on the government, and the autonomy that social organizations should inherently possess is fundamentally lost, turning them into appendages of administrative bodies. Their ability for independent development and self-management is weak.

From the perspective of the external environment for the development of social organizations, firstly, after the founding of the People's Republic of China, the "unit system" communities were established, combining traditional familiar communities formed by kinship ties. Residents formed informal groups within these two typical social organizations, with a strong sense of belonging and identity among people. People habitually resorted to units and the government for their needs rather than social organizations. Residents habitually regarded village committees and neighborhood committees as the legitimate representatives of the government, as extensions of government public function departments in the community. The grassroots and spontaneous nature of community social organizations limited their social mobilization capabilities, and their role in participating in urban and rural community governance and public services was not yet evident, with insufficient influence among community residents. As commercial communities gradually replaced unit system communities, the informal groups within the original social organizations were eroded, and people transitioned from a society of acquaintances to a society of strangers, presenting an atomized state of existence. Relationships between people became indifferent and alienated, and the diversification of values weakened the sense of identity and belonging within groups. People, driven more by individual rationality, had little time to engage in community activities. Secondly, due to the narrow scope of government-purchased services, for registered community social organizations, services are mainly provided to specific groups for stability maintenance. For record-type community social organizations, they are more organized as interest groups for entertainment and leisure, with the main function of organizing residents and attempting to construct a familiar community, thereby identifying some key residents.

From the perspective of the development of community social organizations themselves, firstly, some social organizations lack the ability to integrate various resources within the community, providing low-quality community services that are difficult to meet the actual needs of community residents, failing to truly leverage the professional service advantages of community social organizations. Secondly, the development of related community organizations started relatively late, making it difficult for people to form an objective and comprehensive understanding of such organizations in a short time. People tend to hold a wait-and-see and indifferent attitude towards community organizations and corresponding community activities. Residents lack trust in the authority and legitimacy of community social organizations, with most community residents' understanding and perception of community social organizations still remaining at the level of dance teams, choirs, and other artistic groups within the community. All these reasons reflect that the social recognition of community social organizations is still at a relatively low level during their development process. This recognition, in turn, leads to the stagnation of community social organizations' development, creating a situation where the policy environment suggests a promising development for social organizations, yet the actual situation is that "spring is still far away."

(3) The modern social organization system has not yet formed and effectively played its role. The prerequisites for constructing a modern social organization system, such as "separation of government and society," "clear rights and responsibilities," and "autonomous governance according to law," have not been fully met, leading to the stagnation of the optimization and construction of the modern social organization system. Particularly, the "dual management system" has not yet exited the historical stage. As a legacy of the planned economy, the "dual management system" is a model that emphasizes management over supervision and service, making it difficult to effectively perform functions such as risk identification, incubation, process control, and division of labor and cooperation. Moreover, the existing "dual management system," while avoiding risks, also causes the "reproduction" of risks. For example, the excessively high "threshold" for registration results in a large number of social organizations being unable to obtain legal status and operating in an "illegal" state, outside of supervision, further exacerbating the possibility of risks. Therefore, the key to reform is to strive to form a modern social organization supervision system that aims at organizational development, uses standardized supervision as a means, and takes risk control as the bottom line.

From the situation in Pudong New Area, community social organizations exhibit a dependency on government resources. This resource dependency relationship, on one hand, promotes the development of social organizations, but on the other hand, causes these types of social organizations to lack the "hematopoietic" function in their development process, leading to issues such as a shortage of funds, lack of venues, and insufficient training, with the latter two being chain reactions triggered by the lack of funds. According to statistical results, 42.2% of registered community social organizations and 58.0% of record-type community social organizations reported a lack of funds needed to complete their work. However, the actual situation is that, in terms of funding sources for registered community social organizations, 87.7% of the income of social organizations comes from government financial support and corresponding service purchases, while 41.9% of the funds for record-type community social organizations are directly or indirectly sourced from the government. Subsidy. This high dependency on government funding reduces the flexibility of social organizations themselves, manifesting as strict government control over social organizations and a strong dependency of social organizations on the government. This results in an extremely narrow growth space for various social organizations in our country. To obtain legal status, social organizations must choose to affiliate with the government, which in turn leads to a strong administrative color within the social organizations, resulting in a "path dependency" on the government in urban community governance. Once the government procurement of public services expires, social organizations face the risk of "weaning," with insufficient organizational autonomy. More seriously, excessive reliance on the government may deviate from the true needs of community residents, leading to an administrative path in "top-down" organizational behavior, which may ultimately result in being abandoned by the government due to inadequate response to residents' needs and issues.

Research has found that for registered community social organizations, government regulatory agencies often have strict approval processes at the time of establishment but relax daily supervision, resulting in a situation where permission at the time of establishment and subsequent laissez-faire coexist. In terms of internal supervision, some registered community social organizations have not established good self-regulatory operating mechanisms, such as organizational charters, activity norms, and financial systems. In their development, there are issues such as incomplete organizational structures, imperfect internal governance, irregular organizational behavior, and low social credibility, making it difficult for registered community social organizations to form a complete assessment mechanism. Meanwhile, influenced by traditional concepts, systems, and technologies, the performance evaluation of government departments in our country often relies on top-down "same-body evaluation," leading to a lack of transparency in the evaluation process and low credibility of the evaluation results. Even the limited third-party evaluation services (mostly appearing in government procurement services at the street level) often face the dilemma of "evaluation dominated by the client" and the tension of the "third party" independence in evaluation.

This management system is also reflected in the assessment of social organizations by the government. From statistical data, the assessment forms adopted by the government for projects entrusted to registered community social organizations are obviously imperfect. The acceptance by government departments as the main form of assessment for such organizations accounts for 36.4%, while the acceptance by third-party evaluation agencies accounts for 31.2%, and 27.8% do not adopt any form of assessment, indicating that the assessment mechanism needs further improvement. From the perspective of the role and status between the government and third-party evaluation agencies, the government is in a strong position relative to third-party evaluators, possessing or even monopolizing a large amount of real and effective evaluation information. Information is the basic premise for third-party participation in evaluation. On one hand, the government's monopoly on information makes it difficult for third parties to conduct accurate evaluations due to a lack of information resources. On the other hand, there is currently no unified standard for assessing the effectiveness of social organization services in our country, resulting in considerable arbitrariness and uncertainty in the evaluation of service effectiveness.

(4) Insufficient supply of relevant laws and regulations for social organizations. On one hand, relevant legislation is severely lagging behind the actual development and real needs of social organizations, lacking a legal and regulatory

system that matches the functions of social organizations. On the other hand, the overall level of legislation for social organizations is not high, and its authority is insufficient, with different laws and regulations existing in a fragmented manner across different departments, making it difficult to effectively play a systematic regulatory and collaborative role. Moreover, precise legislation for social organizations in different fields and the macro-level social organization law have not yet been implemented, with issues in operability and matching degree, making it difficult to provide effective legal protection for the development of social organizations. The relationship between community social organizations and grassroots governments can be understood as an asymmetric reciprocal relationship based on mutual resource dependency.

The lack of legislation has left the relationship between grassroots governments and community social organizations in our country unresolved. Some grassroots government and department leaders have not changed their concepts with the rapid development of society, are not very clear about the concept and connotation of community social organizations, and lack sufficient understanding of the role and importance of community social organizations in participating in community governance and public services. There is a lack of effective communication and exchange mechanisms between them. The most intuitive phenomenon is that, on the government side, due to the increasingly complex and uncertain administrative ecology, in the face of a risk society, the social management costs of the government remain high, and management efficiency is increasingly declining. In the pattern of social governance, there is a tendency to award procurement projects to social organizations with which they are more familiar. This situation is reflected in the service field, namely the localization of services. It is evident that a fixed partnership model has formed between the various sectors of the government, making it difficult for external organizations to enter. The exclusionary effect of internal service procurement within the streets and the solidifying hierarchical structure in service procurement are becoming entrenched. As a result, community social organizations find it difficult to achieve governance effects that transcend community boundaries, and the effective governance function is also hard to constructively build the relationship between government and society. There is a lack of institutional cooperation platforms and collaborative governance mechanisms between the government and social organizations, making it difficult to form a governance synergy. Consequently, the relationship between the government and social organizations appears more as a "buddy" relationship rather than a "partner" relationship.

From the statistical data, 39.1% of registered community social organizations believe that the government lacks transparent and fair procurement procedures in the process of purchasing public services, while 16.4% of filed community social organizations think that the imperfect institutional environment and the lack of relevant regulations for cultivation and support are the main issues restricting their development. This shows that the information asymmetry caused by the institutional environment is an important factor restricting the development of community social organizations.

(5) Social organizations need to have professional capabilities that match their mission responsibilities. Social organizations need to further enhance their professional capabilities and governance functions to effectively participate in social governance, poverty governance, and environmental protection battles, and they also need to actively implement the "going out" policy while continuously enhancing their influence, participating in global governance with a more open attitude, and contributing Chinese wisdom. Moreover, although the non-equivalent status in the function transfer process between the government and social organizations hinders the formation of a positive interactive relationship between the two, the improvement of the professional capabilities of social organizations can also generate a "reverse pressure" force to promote the optimization of the government-society relationship. Social organizations should play a greater role in the transfer of government functions, especially in filed community social organizations.

Firstly, the aging and amateurization lead to insufficient service capacity. According to statistical data, 93.3% of the members in filed community social organizations are aged 50 and above, showing a significant aging phenomenon. Due to the insufficient participation of young groups in the community, members of such organizations not only form daily entertainment and interest groups but also take on a large number of roles such as community volunteers and building leaders. They lack professional knowledge in community service, showing high enthusiasm in the process of community service but insufficient professionalization, with obvious amateur characteristics. 46% of filed community social organizations express an urgent need for guidance from professional talents and related training to improve their professional knowledge level. Meanwhile, 91.1% of filed community social organizations indicate a very close relationship with the community neighborhood committee. In field visits to the community, the author found that this close relationship has turned filed community social organizations into highly recognized and cooperative entities with the neighborhood committee, making them execution agencies dispatched by the neighborhood committee, responsible for executing related community affairs, with daily publicity and administrative communication taking up most of their energy, greatly reducing their service capacity and effectiveness. Secondly, the entertainment and looseness lead to limited governance functions, especially the weak linkage mechanism of community issues. The increasing heterogeneity of the community at this stage inevitably leads to a wide variety of community social organizations with complex compositions. Filed community social organizations are mostly spontaneously formed by community residents, with relatively loose organizational structures, integrating community residents with elements such as interests, hobbies, and emotions, attracting community residents to participate in different teams, allowing residents to reach consensus in certain aspects. This is a behavior logic with interest as the link, showing obvious entertainment in organizational goals and looseness in organizational structure, resulting in the inability to form a linkage mechanism for community issues or a weak mechanism. According to statistical data, 77.6% of filed community social organizations are cultural and artistic, sports and fitness, and leisure hobby types, with obvious entertainment, while community public service types only account for 20.5%.

(6) The party building of social organizations still needs to be further deeply promoted. Firstly, the consensus on the party building of social organizations still needs to be further consolidated, and a transformation in understanding needs to be achieved. In past political discourse, the emphasis was usually on the differences and even confrontation between the state and society, focusing on whether there is a public space outside the state system and how it resists public power. "Social organizations" were defined as the "society" end, existing as a form of resistance or even opposition. This has led to the misconception that social organizations and party organizations are incompatible. In practice, this is reflected in the question of whether party building work should be carried out in social organizations. Ambiguity and equivocation. Secondly, it is the active exploration and innovative advancement of party building practices in social organizations. Explore effective ways for party organizations and party members to play their roles in social organizations, fully exert the political leadership, guarantee supervision, and combat fortress roles of party organizations, as well as the exemplary vanguard role of party members. Promote the innovation of mechanisms, carriers, and forms and methods of party building work in different types of social organizations, achieve the organic integration of social organization governance functions and party building, and thereby form a governance synergy.

6.5 Integrated Governance and Systematic Advancement: Imagining and Constructing Paths for Social Organizations to Participate in Social Governance

Innovation Challenges need to be effectively addressed, while differences need to be bridged in development. In the new era and new journey, facing the new changes in the social governance situation in our country and the new problems and challenges emerging in the field of social organizations, we must be guided by Xi Jinping's Thought on Socialism with Chinese Characteristics for a New Era. According to the deployment and requirements of the 19th National Congress of the Communist Party of China, we should strengthen and innovate social governance, implement the new tasks, new requirements, and new measures of social governance and social organization reform into specific work practices, accelerate the separation of government and society, stimulate the vitality of social organizations, and overcome the tendency of social organizations to become administrative. Matters suitable for public service provision and resolution by social organizations should be provided and managed by social organizations according to law. At the same time, strengthen the supervision of various social organizations according to law, promote the standardization, self-discipline, and capacity enhancement of social organizations, and strive to create a social governance pattern of co-construction, co-governance, and sharing, thereby achieving a positive interaction between government governance, social regulation, and residents' autonomy.

6.5.1 *Categorized Policies, Encouragement and Support, and Multiple Measures to Stimulate the Vitality of Social Organizations*

Regarding the issues of lack of funds and weak resource linkage capabilities faced by social organizations, on the one hand, the government needs to adopt multiple measures to actively construct a multi-level policy chain to support social organizations' full participation in grassroots social governance, continuously strengthening financial and tax support for social organizations. Firstly, increase policy support for the development of community social organizations, entrust public services suitable for community social organizations to undertake to them, and support their orderly participation in community governance. Formulate and implement different institutional policies for different community social organizations, creating a policy chain for their cultivation, support, and professional development, especially designing targeted policies for different stages of community social organization development. Secondly, improve and implement financial and tax policies conducive to the development of community social organizations, especially public finance. Research on the Construction of Integrated Service Models in Urban Community Governance At the same time, promote the establishment of a diversified and institutionalized funding guarantee mechanism, encourage and guide social funds to participate in the development of community social organizations, and gradually establish community development foundations and foundation federations in places with conditions, thereby providing funds for urban and rural community social organizations to participate in community governance activities. Thirdly, further improve the purchase of services by municipal and district governments, the autonomy fund projects at the street and town levels, and the internal funding mobilization channels of communities. On this basis, form a support system for the continuous support, institutional support, and regular construction of community social organizations and brand service projects.

On the other hand, moderately encourage community social organizations to carry out some low-cost and paid services. Through government-related funds and tax subsidies to residents, residents can enjoy low-cost services while the self-sustaining "blood-making" function of social organizations is further enhanced, reducing excessive reliance on government resources. Therefore, a competitive mechanism should be moderately introduced to achieve service provision and healthy competition of social organizations in grassroots social fields, which is conducive to enhancing the flexibility of social organizations, stimulating their vitality, improving service levels and specialization in competition, and also conducive to the formation of a service ecological chain of social organizations and the enrichment and diversification of their types and business scopes. Of course, this requires rigorous and systematic in-depth research and design.

In addition, clarify the focus of development, accelerate the development of community social organizations in life services, public welfare and charity, and resident self-help and mutual aid, forming an overall synergy of community social organizations participating in grassroots social governance and services. Urban communities focus on people, enhancing the professionalism and effectiveness of services based on diversified coverage; rural communities focus on fields, achieving organic integration and continuation of social work methods, service concepts, and the incubation and cultivation of community social organizations with the rural governance system.

At the same time, actively explore innovative practices and experiences in cultivating and incubating community organizations at the community level, continuously promote the construction of social organization incubation bases and incubation parks, and help community social organizations solve problems such as workspaces and basic office facilities. For community social organizations with mature conditions, there should be channels to help them. Assist in their timely development into more professional social organizations, thereby better participating in social management and construction.

6.5.2 Demand-Oriented, Service-Led: Enhancing Residents' Recognition of Social Organizations

For the government, the key is to prioritize concepts and institutional design. It is necessary to further deepen the understanding of the importance of cultivating and developing community social organizations, and to promote the inclusion of community social organization development and management into the performance evaluation of grassroots government and the comprehensive evaluation system of social security governance. At the street and town level, formulate and implement community social organization development plans, increase coordination between departments, and improve the operational mechanism, thereby forming a work pattern where all departments jointly support the development of community social organizations. Firstly, focus on cultivating community social organizations. Guided by the needs of people's livelihood, focus on cultivating public welfare, service-oriented, and autonomous community social organizations, enriching the diverse forces of community governance, and achieving full and balanced development. Secondly, categorize and optimize the service cultivation system. Integrate, optimize, and reconstruct the functions of social organization incubation institutions and platforms at all levels to avoid functional duplication, forming a closed loop of social organization ecological development. City and district platforms focus on resource docking, capacity building, and talent cultivation, while streets and communities focus on incubation development, project planning, and brand building, reducing redundant construction. Thirdly, timely adjust and reform evaluation methods. In the new era of community social organization development, the focus should shift to brand building, team enhancement, and institutional construction. Therefore, the evaluation of their development should establish a service-oriented development goal, emphasizing the branding of service projects, public participation, and institutionalization, rather than merely emphasizing the quantity of social organizations. At the same time, cultivate and build a batch of brand social organizations and service projects for community governance, promoting better integration and collaboration between community social organizations, residents' committees, and professional social organizations to achieve collaborative integrated governance. Finally, integrate functions and build a hub-type service coordination platform. Establish district and street community social organization federations and other hub-type organizations, forming a "1 + X + N" service integration model with district hub-type organizations as the main body, street hub-type organizations as the backbone, and community hub-type organizations as a supplement, creating a platform for mobilizing and integrating diverse community forces and advancing social organization party-building work, promoting the orderly and standardized participation of community social organizations in community governance.

6.5.3 Supply-Side Efforts, Comprehensive Development: Forming an Ecological Chain and Aggregation Effect for Social Organization Participation in Services

From a developmental perspective, the growth of social organizations should not rely on the market, nor solely on government funds and policies, but should depend on their own ability to serve the public and reciprocal social mechanisms. Therefore, the reform and optimization of the supply side of community social organizations and the enhancement of their capabilities are crucial.

Firstly, extend and expand the service chain of social organizations to form a virtuous ecological cycle of community governance participation. It is necessary to improve the community social organization system and actively develop community service projects. "To forge iron, one must be strong oneself," starting from the actual situation of the organization, strengthen the construction of the organization's own system, and gradually form a complete organizational system, actively exploring the needs of diverse groups, achieving comprehensive development of community organizations, and thereby creating a comprehensive service system of "care for the elderly, support for the young, assistance for the lonely, help for the disabled, aid for the poor, support for those in difficulty, education for those in need, and supply for those in demand," forming a precise service chain in various stages, levels, and types of resident needs evolution, thereby optimizing the development environment of community social organizations and avoiding falling into a homogeneous vicious competition ecology.

Secondly, the cultivation of social organization capabilities is a critical factor in their growth. Specifically, one is to strengthen and improve the internal management system of social organizations, using the system to regulate members' behavior and cultivate the habit of members adhering to self-established rules. Two is to enhance the recognition and reputation of social organizations by participating in as many public welfare activities as possible. Three is to increase the cultivation of social organizations' ability to undertake government-purchased services, which is an urgent issue currently faced by social organizations. On one hand, strengthen the "hematopoietic" function of social organizations, enhancing their self-development ability to ensure they can undertake the public services transferred by the government. On the other hand, improve the professional service level of social organizations, as most social organizations currently participate in public services in a loose and non-professional manner, and should strengthen the social work committee within social organizations. The input of professional service talents, primarily the backbone, ensures that the public services transferred from the government can be well managed. Fourth, it is necessary to enhance the ability of social organizations to unite social members. Promoting the transformation from "social person" to "community person" and "association person" is an important function of social organizations in social management.

Finally, the development of social organizations should adhere to community-based, demand-oriented, and service-led principles. By adhering to community-based principles, they can fully leverage their organizational advantages of being rooted in the community and close to residents, continuously enhancing their main role and service leadership in community governance based on precise services, and forming good community credibility on the basis of deepening services to residents, thereby integrating into the grassroots social convenience service network. Firstly, community social organizations should fully utilize the "natural connection" and zero distance between community social organizations and residents, effectively exploring and leading various needs of residents, developing refined and targeted service projects based on precise demand positioning, and thereby building their credibility in the community. Secondly, community social organizations should make good use of modern network means such as new media and big data to optimize the channels and methods of service delivery, keeping pace with the times. Thirdly, community social organizations should continuously expand the professionalism, sustainability, and development of service projects, forming a significant brand effect, thereby optimizing their development ecology. Fourthly, community social organizations should also continuously promote their capacity building, especially the professional capacity building of community social organization leaders and key personnel.

Chapter 7
Grid Management and Open Blocks: Two Paradigms of Governance Integration

7.1 Grid Management and Separation of Residence and Station: Logic, Dilemmas, and Reflections[1]

With the establishment of the market economy system, the grassroots social system, which was primarily based on the unit system and supplemented by the street-residence system embedded in the planned economy system, gradually disintegrated. The grassroots social system, which is compatible with the market economy system and primarily based on the community system, emerged. At the interface of the transition period, two management patterns appeared in urban grassroots society. One is that units still play an important role in social management, acting as the main role of actual grassroots managers, and the unit system remains prominent in the post-unit era. The other is that communities have come to the forefront of grassroots social governance, having a foundational position in social governance innovation, becoming the background field for multiple subjects to play roles in grassroots governance, and gradually playing important social governance functions in various types of community forms (unit communities, commercial housing communities, etc.). Units and communities coexist, with units handling major affairs and governance matters, communities handling minor affairs and also major affairs, and more regional matters.

The unit system is neither "dead" nor "rigid," while the community system, although "alive," is not "free," not fully "enjoyable," nor "thriving." This is the pattern and dilemma of urban grassroots social governance in China. Under the inertia of unit system thinking, initial conditions, and the governance orientation of control order, the community system has evolved into a highly administrative organization in grassroots social management practice, becoming the second unit or

[1] Some content has been published in the "Academic Forum" 2014, Issue 12.

L. Hou, *The Integrated Service in Urban Community Governance*, Public Economy and Urban Governance in China, https://doi.org/10.1007/978-981-96-6775-8_7

unit second after the unit, contrary to the government's original intention of developing communities into "self-management, self-education, self-development, and self-restraint" living communities. To correct the trend of community administrativeization and solve the entrenched issues of "excessive administrative integration and insufficient community autonomy" that trouble the construction of grassroots social order, various regions actively explore internal governance structure innovation within the community system framework. In summary, there are two directions and designs, namely "grid management" and "separation of residence and station" reform.

From the scope of practice, grid management may have spread nationwide, while the quasi-marketized "separation of residence and station" exists only in a few pilot cities with limited impact. But what kind of conceptual assumptions exist behind grid management and separation of residence and station reform? What are the differences between the two? What are the foundational premises, internal logic, and real dilemmas of their reform and design? Existing research is still insufficient. In view of this, the research focus of this chapter is positioned on these two directions of community system reform and improvement, and through this, to analyze the integrated innovation approach of community governance and understand the diverse grassroots governance practices. The specific research content includes: first, assessing the internal concepts and operational logic of grid management and separation of residence and station reform; second, analyzing the real dilemmas of grid management and separation of residence and station reform; third, reflecting on the functional myths of grid management and separation of residence and station reform in the process of promoting urban grassroots social governance innovation; fourth, proposing possible paths for grassroots social governance innovation.

7.1.1 Grid Management and Separation of Residence and Station: Conceptual Differences and Logical Divergence

The difference in concepts leads to differences in institutional creation, which in turn guides different development paths in practice. This is also true for grassroots social governance. Grid management and the separation of residence and station reflect two concepts and designs in grassroots social governance, namely the "top-down" and "bottom-up" approaches. In this section, based on sorting out the conceptual assumptions of grid management and the separation of residence and station, the author follows the "process event" analysis approach of "practical sociology" (Sun Liping 2002) to analyze the realistic logic of these two paths, in order to reveal the different logics and reform blueprints of community governance innovation.

1. Conceptual Differences between Grid Management and Separation of Residence and Station

With the deepening of reform, the management form of urban communities has undergone a transformation. Formally, the unit system is gradually giving way to the community system. However, the community system has also exposed the inherent problem of "excessive administrative integration and insufficient community autonomy," which affects the construction of urban grassroots social order. To eliminate this problem, various regions actively explore and experiment with community governance innovation from two paths: strengthening grassroots social governance capabilities and de-administratization of grassroots communities. The first path assumes that district and street government powers are excessive, and grassroots social governance organizations (community committees) lack the capacity to undertake the social tasks transferred from unit organizations. Under this conceptual assumption, this path advocates for the decentralization of state power into community organizations such as community committees, essentially attempting to promote social governance through the optimized reorganization of power within the system. The second path believes that the lack of grassroots community autonomy is caused by excessive state intervention. In other words, it is precisely the state's excessive "overstepping" intervention that leads to the "difficult birth" and "bankruptcy" of community autonomy forces. Adhering to this assumption, this path advocates for the cultivation of civil society to promote the growth of grassroots social autonomy forces, thereby exerting democratic pressure on the survival of grassroots regimes, ultimately achieving self-management of grassroots society. The specific manifestations of these two paths in practice are grid management and the reform of separation of residence and station.

2. Logical Divergence between Grid Management and Separation of Residence and Station Based

on the above conceptual assumptions, grid management and the separation of residence and station have evolved different logical processes in practice, encompassing different innovative implications. The specific logical divergences are as follows.

(1) Governance Practice of Grid Management. In the practice of grassroots social governance innovation, the first path to enhance the capacity of grassroots social organizations is grid management. Grid management refers to "using streets and communities as the basis, dividing unit grids based on certain areas within the management jurisdiction, establishing an urban grid management information platform, managing urban components and events, and achieving a four-level linkage management model and information resource sharing system among city, district, professional disposal departments, and grid supervisors." In simple terms, grid management involves dividing a governed area into several grid-like units according to certain standards, with dedicated personnel providing differentiated, specific, personalized, tracking, and all-time services and management for the demands and issues of residents within the grid. The main idea is to fully utilize modern information technology to break the boundaries

between traditional urban management departments and administrative divisions, mimicking bureaucratic organizational design, and dividing the entire grid management process into six stages: information collection, screening and filing, task dispatch, task handling, result feedback, and evaluation and closure. This achieves timely problem detection, sensitive crisis response, appropriate handling, scientific and efficient management, and specific service delivery within a precisely constructed "grid." The specific practice of grid management in the urban community management system is manifested as follows: First, using streets, communities, and other grassroots management units as the basis, dividing urban social management into several grids through standardized methods; Second, relying on information technology to strengthen communication and information exchange between different grids, establishing an integrated and linked platform for information resource sharing; Third, establishing a unified resource scheduling and coordination mechanism to overcome the problem of "fragmentation," integrating previously scattered management and resources of various departments in an institutionalized manner; Fourth, maintaining the compatibility and openness of the grid system, achieving "multi-grid integration" and dynamic management through mutual compatibility between different grids.

As a management technique, grid management originated from a grid management model pioneered by China's public security system. Patrol technology. As a new model of urban grassroots management, Dongcheng District in Beijing took the lead and was the first to pilot it. In 2004, Dongcheng District explored grid management to improve the efficiency of social management. They used a 10,000 square meter area as the basic grid unit, dividing the entire district into 1,593 grids, and equipped 350 urban management supervisors to implement full-time monitoring across the district. At the same time, with the help of information technology, they electronically encoded six major categories, 54 urban administrative departments, and seven major categories, 33 types of urban issues. The command center in the background used information technology to respond promptly and effectively to various management issues in the jurisdiction, achieving informatized management of urban communities. Subsequently, this model began to be emulated and promoted nationwide, marking the first stage of grid management, the emergence stage. The characteristic of this stage is the goal of digital city construction, focusing on resource integration, information communication, and service enhancement, with an emphasis on establishing a digital technology service platform. The second stage involved model innovation and multiple pilot projects. As the effectiveness of grid management became apparent, in October 2005, the state began promoting Dongcheng District's experience nationwide based on preliminary research and summary, selecting ten cities including Shanghai, Shenzhen, and Wuhan as grid management pilots. Subsequently, typical models such as Shanghai's community "grid" management and Zhoushan,

Zhejiang's "grid management, group service" emerged continuously. The third stage saw the continuous expansion of the field. As a new social governance technology, after 2005, with changes in the social environment, "grid" governance began to undergo new shifts. Grid governance started to combine with the social management goal of "maintaining stability," and as its effects became evident, its application fields continued to expand, with the "grid" also beginning to play a role as an important level of social management. The fourth stage involved reflection and reform. Especially as the unintended negative impacts of grid governance gradually emerged, grid governance entered a new stage of reflection and reform. This chapter can also be seen as an attempt to reflect on this stage.

(2) The practical logic of separating residence and station. In the innovative practice of grassroots social governance, the second path to improve community autonomy is the measure of de-administrativeization of grassroots communities, which is the separation of residence and station. The so-called separation of residence and station refers to the separation of community committees and community workstations in grassroots social management, thereby establishing street administrative service community workstations outside of community party organizations and community committees to undertake administrative management work stripped from the committees. The committees then return to the work of "self-management, self-education, self-service, and self-supervision" of residents, realizing the positioning of their nature as resident self-governing organizations. The main approach of separating residence and station is to set up another organizational structure in the grassroots community field, outside the community committee—a community workstation, which specifically undertakes various administrative affairs delegated by the street, with its work directly responsible to the street office and various government functional departments; while the community committee engages in various affairs related to resident self-organization and self-governance. The two operate independently, coordinate and cooperate with each other, achieving the goal of community co-governance. This results in a certain degree of restructuring of the urban grassroots social management pattern: firstly, a new main organization, the community workstation, is added to the urban grassroots community, independent of the community committee and set up in parallel; secondly, the committee gradually returns to the attributes of a resident self-governing organization, while the community workstation mainly undertakes the administrative functions stripped from the government; thirdly, the community workstation and the committee each perform their duties and responsibilities, differing in nature but supporting and cooperating with each other.

The reform of separating residence and station began in Shenzhen in 2005. After a year of exploration, many urban communities across the country began to imitate and implement the reform of separating residence and station, with different cities trying and innovating in various forms according to their actual situations, developing into various forms such as "one station, multiple residences," "one station, one residence," and "one-stop residence-station separation." These different forms mainly manifest in two directions. The first direction is the increasing administrative nature of community workstations and the further marginalization of committees. Due to the emptiness of urban communities and residents' lack of enthusiasm for community affairs, after extracting the administrative tasks assigned by the government, the committees have nothing to do, becoming mere decorations, with self-governance affairs being as intangible and elusive as a balloon, visible but untouchable, leading to the weakening, marginalization, and even hollowing out of the committees. In other words, the separation of residence and station, by transferring the administrative affairs of the committees to the community workstations, has resulted in dual practical outcomes: on one hand, the community workstations have actually evolved... As a subordinate execution agency of the street office, the trend towards instrumentalization is evident; on the other hand, the residents' committee is once again marginalized due to the separation of administrative affairs and limited self-governance capabilities. The second trend is quasi-marketization, where a new type of contractual cooperative relationship is formed between the government and social organizations (community workstations), laying the foundation for de-administrative urban grassroots social management. It is important to note that in this trend of separation between the residents' committee and the workstation, the community workstation does not act as an extension tool of the street office, nor does it simply take over the administrative functions stripped from the residents' committee. Instead, it participates in community governance as an independent non-profit civil organization alongside the community party branch and the residents' committee. The relationship between the residents' committee and the workstation is no longer one of mutual substitution but one of mutual cooperation and complementarity. After the separation, the community needs to properly handle the relationship between the residents' committee and the homeowners' committee, both of which are resident self-governing organizations with different functions. Generally speaking, the residents' committee mainly handles community political, cultural, and social self-governance affairs and is an authoritative organization designated by the government that can guide the work of the homeowners' committee. The homeowners' committee mainly deals with economic interests related to property rights or social conflicts arising from economic interests. Their functions differ, and they should each perform their duties and complement each other to achieve community co-governance. From the reform experiences across various regions, the quasi-marketization trend is more likely to gain the cooperation of grassroots social management participants, whereas the first trend is prone to resistance from residents' committee members, affecting the actual effectiveness of the separation reform. The separation reform of the residents' committee and the workstation initially clarified the relationships between community governance entities, bringing community organizations back to a positive track of interactive collaboration, with significant advantages. Firstly, the separation is conducive to reducing the burden on the residents' committee.

Through the reform of the community residents' committee and the establishment of community workstations, administrative work that does not fall within the responsibilities of the residents' committee is stripped away and transferred to the community workstation, allowing the community residents' committee to break free from administrative affairs and have the capacity and energy to manage and serve community self-governance, potentially restoring its autonomous status. After the "separation," the residents' committee is directly responsible to the community residents, achieving a transformation in identity, from being the "legs" of the government to the "head" of the community residents, potentially solving the long-standing issue of the administrative tendency of grassroots community residents' committees. Secondly, the "separation" promotes the "separation of deliberation and execution," which helps optimize the community governance structure and professionalize and professionalize community service work. On one hand, the community residents' committee, elected by residents, becomes the community's deliberative body, focusing on community public affairs, building community consensus, and promoting community self-governance. On the other hand, the community workstation can exist as a professional execution agency, with its staff recruited openly from society, composed of professional and vocational social workers, whose mission is to provide professional and vocational public services to community residents. Thirdly, the separation is conducive to expanding grassroots democracy. Through the separation and functional division, on one hand, various government tasks are handed over to professional service agencies, namely community workstations, for better implementation, facilitating the real shift of the work focus downward; on the other hand, after the separation of community transactional and administrative work from the residents' committee, the residents' committee has more time and energy to engage in self-governance work, strengthening the grassroots democratic self-governance function.

7.1.2 *Trapped Governance: Realistic Representation and Development Reflection*[2]

Grid management and the separation reform of the residents' committee and workstation have improved and perfected the grassroots social governance system, advancing the process of social governance innovation to a certain extent. However, with the technical inclination of grid management and the prominent institutional obstacles of the separation reform, both paths have encountered dilemmas and paradoxes in reality and development.

1. The Dilemma and Breakthrough of Grid Management

From practice, the strong administrative color inherent in grid management, which focuses on social control, weakens the generation of community self-organized governance systems, which is not conducive to community self-governance.

From the actual operation process of grid management, its negative impact on community self-governance mainly includes four points.

Firstly, "grid management" has brought about "segmentation." In an ideal sense, the community, as a living community formed by people in a certain area, is the unfolding of various social relationships of community members in a certain spatial structure, a space for members to autonomously choose their lives and plan public practices, and a space for members to… In the pursuit of their own rights and interests, through daily life practices, a community "public sphere" that transcends the individual gradually forms. However, grid management artificially constructs "boundaries" that fragment and divide complete life practices. While this approach

---

[2] Since the practice of "separation of residence and station" began in Yantian District, Shenzhen in 2005, the academic community has engaged in creative discussions around this concept. These discussions primarily place it within the context of grassroots government construction, social governance systems, community building, and community autonomy. Comprehensive and systematic research has been conducted on the institutional design, practical logic, operational outcomes (both positive and negative), and institutional variations of "separation of residence and station." Therefore, this section provides a descriptive overview of the research on "separation of residence and station," serving as a reference for comparative studies with "grid management " in the field of grassroots social governance. Similarly, academic research on "grid management" also places it within the context of grassroots government construction, social governance systems, community building, and community autonomy. However, the focus is on the positive impact and functions of grid management's institutional design on grassroots social governance, presenting a one-sided view. There are abundant related achievements, especially the series of papers included in the academic seminar "Urban Social Management: Grid Model and Grassroots Order Construction" organized by the journal "Learning and Exploration" in 2012, which are typical representatives. However, there is relatively little research on the unintended consequences of grid management, especially its unintended negative functions. In the article "Grid Social Management and Its Unintended Consequences—A Case Study of Q District in N City" by Liu An, the unintended consequences of grid management are discussed from aspects such as "technological" governance, "bureaucratic" organizational structure, "administrative" governance, and "selective execution," showing a certain degree of innovation. This section's research on the unintended consequences of grid management mainly conducts institutional analysis from the aspects of the design essence, operational logic, and actual effects of grid management.

helps embed governmental power within the community, ensuring the effectiveness of administrative execution and achieving the effect of "divide and conquer," it inevitably damages the community ties that have been established over a long period, affecting the organic connections among community residents and inhibiting the generation of internal community autonomy. In urban community governance, the construction of an integrated service model generates internal community autonomy.

Secondly, "technological" leads to "hierarchical." Grid management is a city management method based on digital information technology, attempting to establish an organic integration relationship between technology, resources, and public management and services. Through a digital technology service platform, it establishes an efficient problem prevention and resolution mechanism in the urban grassroots society. Grid management requires "a network in the community, a grid in the network, people assigned in the grid, and responsibilities borne by people," which results in "panoptic monitoring" and control of grassroots workers, bringing considerable pressure. Additionally, the introduction of information technology into grid management is also a complex micro "political process" within and between grid levels, continuing the previous power struggles between different management levels by setting the way technology functions. This implies that there is a strengthened hierarchical control concept behind grid management, which itself is a pressure transmission mechanism. The combination of technology and hierarchy leads to a system design that exceeds the "technological threshold" it can bear, resulting in numerous unintended consequences, reminiscent of Foucault's depiction of the "panopticon" prison.

Thirdly, "bureaucratization" leads to "shrinkage." From a governance perspective, community governance should be a multi-centered governance process where stakeholders within the field implement cooperation, consultation, and bargaining around public issues according to certain rules. This process helps promote participation and interaction among subjects, enhancing community autonomy, and gradually transforming the community from a traditional mutual aid living community role into an important civic force participating in urban governance and government decision-making. However, in "grid management," the grid levels, with responsibilities and powers granted from higher authorities, have clear internal divisions of labor and a well-established organizational structure (with grid leaders, grid administrators, grid assistants, and grid supervisors within the grid), forming a structurally complete administrative work system, which is an important tool for government control of society. Therefore, the grid inherently continues the logic and habits of the four-level bureaucratic management structure composed of "city, district, street, and community." Consequently, under the "iron cage" of the certainty, stability, discipline, and reliability of the bureaucratic operational structure, the community will inevitably form a social coercive structure within the field, and the inherent institutional pressure of the social coercive structure will inevitably cause the community's self-organizing ability to shrink inversely.

Fourth, "administratization" leads to "marginalization." The community serves as a link between the government and residents. A strong community does not necessarily lead to a strong nation, but a weak community will certainly lead to a weak nation. As Merton (2001) stated, "In a social system, structural inadequacies or partial interruptions in communication channels between people can also lead to social disorganization. People in certain social relationships, local communities, or national societies must be able to communicate because they depend on each other to meet societal expectations and their personal goals." Furthermore, Durkheim (2000) in "The Division of Labor in Society" also revealed the risk of increasing distance between the state and individuals, "If there is no series of intermediate groups between the government and individuals, then the state cannot continue to exist. If these intermediate groups have very close ties with individuals, they will strongly absorb individuals into group activities, thereby integrating them into the mainstream of social life." According to Durkheim, if a series of intermediary organizations between the state and individuals is lost, "the distance between the state and individuals becomes greater, their relationship becomes more superficial and intermittent, and the state cannot penetrate deeply into individuals' consciousness to unite them." Therefore, the community, as a key linking organization between the state and individuals, must not be marginalized in local governance. Otherwise, not only will community autonomy be unattainable, but national governance will also face crises and difficulties due to social disorganization.

Under the grid management, residents become objects of power management and surveillance, and the community transforms into a space where administrative power exercises its will and extracts resources, rather than a living community integrating stakeholders within the community. Therefore, how to dilute the administrative color of "grid management," achieve effective collaboration between community autonomy and government administrative power, eliminate the technical limitations of "grid management," optimize the relationship between technological progress and social governance, and find the intersection between grid management and community autonomy to achieve mutual construction and mutual strengthening for a win–win outcome, is the direction and challenge for future community construction, community system reform, and social governance innovation. The author believes that community service grid management and community management democratization, linking grid management with community autonomy through community services, is the only way to achieve the aforementioned goals.

Firstly, the state and society are not oppositional; rather, they are in a mutually interactive and co-constructive relationship. Zheng Yongnian (2011) believes that "China needs a society with self-organizing capabilities. Without society, the regime has no foundation; if society is fragile, the government will inevitably be fragile." In terms of community governance, an interactive mechanism between community autonomy and government management must be formed. On one hand, the government should govern the country and society according to the law, acting within its authority and refraining from unauthorized actions, especially in market areas involving private interests, while taking responsibility in areas involving public interests (such as safety, health, education, and healthcare) and providing institutional guarantees for community autonomy. On the other hand, through social autonomy and services, the mechanism for expressing residents' rights and realizing their interests should be continuously improved, cultivating residents' "publicness" and the community's "social capital" through public issues, thereby rebuilding horizontal social connections. In urban community governance, constructing an integrated service model promotes the regeneration of community spirit and consolidates the community governance order based on social capital as a value foundation. Although "grid management" achieves the connection between the state and community individuals through administrative power, it cannot rebuild internal community links and horizontal integration through administrative power. Therefore, only through the interaction between the state and society, achieving mutual construction and transformation between grid governance and social autonomy, can true good governance of society be realized.

Secondly, positioning "grid" with "service," promoting "autonomy" with "grid," and promoting "service" with "autonomy" form a trinity system. Community service is both a material process where multiple subjects in the community field provide various specific social services to community members to meet residents' needs, and a spiritual process where residents participate in co-constructing community culture and values, shaping a sense of identity and belonging. Community service includes public services provided by the government, mutual assistance services among residents, and interactions between the government and the community. At the community service level, the administrative management of "grid management" and the autonomous management of the community intersect. Therefore, by positioning the grid in service, the original "management" relying solely on administrative power is transformed into "governance" relying on multi-participation, shifting from the original "rigid control" focusing on social order and stability to "soft constraint" focusing on meeting community needs and promoting internal harmony, essentially turning the grid into… A service platform that is not aimed at control, but purely serves the residents in a flattened manner. Through the provision of community services within the grid, it not only eradicates the sense of a stranger world brought about by modernization, urbanization, and industrialization, characterized by interpersonal alienation and social atomization in urban society, but also enables the reconstruction of neighborly relations and community culture of mutual help and friendliness through the common actions and participation of community residents themselves, making the community once again an autonomous and living community with a sense of identity and belonging as core elements. A living community that reaches a certain level of autonomy establishes a new appropriate relationship with the government externally, reintegrates structure and resources internally, and provides higher quality community services with a higher degree of community autonomy.

2. The Paradox and Way Out of the Separation of Residence and Station Reform

From practice, the separation of residence and station reform also presents insurmountable paradoxes. The separation of residence and station starts from the entrenched issues of "administrativization" and "involution" of community residents' committees, aiming to achieve the effective return of the autonomous status of residents' committees through the de-administrativization burden reduction, thereby realizing community autonomy. However, from the development model of the separation of residence and station mentioned above, in the first model, the community workstation replaces the community residents' committee and becomes a subordinate institution and administrative tool of the sub-district office. The residents' committee responsible for community autonomy affairs is marginalized again due to the lack of resources and inability to gain residents' recognition under the current institutional scenario, making community autonomy unachievable and even facing its own identity crisis. In the second model, the quasi-marketization of community workstations, although it may form a new contractual cooperative relationship between the government and social organizations through government procurement and the service provision by community workstations, constructing a so-called "government-driven, civil operation" grassroots social service system. However, the lag in the development of professional social work institutions makes the theoretical design of the separation of residence and station model lack sufficient social force support in practice, making it difficult to unfold; moreover, in the process of the residents' committee transforming from a responsibility-oriented participant to a livelihood-oriented participant,[3] the related interest conflicts caused by role transformation continue, all of which lead to the limited effect of the separation of residence and station.

Therefore, from the actual operation of the separation of residence and station, its institutional design is basically carried out by following the expansion and transfer of bureaucratic administrative power at the grassroots level, which is a form of innovation guided by the sub-district office, and does not touch the social system itself of "indistinguishable government and society" and "confusion of government and society," thus it has not surpassed the institutional barriers produced by the traditional vertical integration of urban grassroots community administrativization, and there are insurmountable structural defects.

From the process of community autonomy, there are three points that need further consideration after the separation of residence and station. First, how to ensure the autonomous attributes and status of community workstations and community residents' committees, and how to prevent the administrative substitution and excessive marketization of community workstations; second, how to properly handle the relationship between community workstations and residents' committees, and establish an effective role coordination and interest integration mechanism; third, how to avoid the potential community autonomy crisis that may result from the withdrawal of the administrative functions of the residents' committee, and also to prevent a series of issues such as conflicts and contradictions that may occur between the residents' committee and the owners' committee during the role transformation process.

[3] Here, the reference is primarily to Wang Xing's formulation. Wang Xing (2012) refers to livelihood-oriented participants as individuals and organizations whose interests are directly embedded in grassroots society, mainly including community residents, homeowners' associations, and community property management companies; whereas responsibility-oriented participants are actors involved in grassroots community management based on professional division of labor, mainly including government functional departments at various levels and public utility maintenance departments.

7.1.3 Imagining the Way Out: Logical Premises and Development Phases

Whether it is the grid management led by administration or the quasi-marketization separation of residence and station with community and government cooperative governance, the key issue lies in the "separation of government and society" and the division and cooperation between government and social organizations on this basis, which is the fundamental prerequisite for community governance innovation, and is the key to the positive functional dominance of grid management, the avoidance of unintended negative effects, and the smooth realization of the original intention of the separation of residence and station. The Fourth Plenary Session of the 19th Central Committee of the Communist Party of China proposed a new pattern of social governance system of "Party leadership, government responsibility, democratic consultation, social coordination, public participation, legal protection, and technological support," which contains the functional division and role positioning of government, market, and society (community) in social governance innovation. In short, first, the Party and government must accurately position themselves, neither absent nor overstepping, and must be in place, and the responsibilities they undertake cannot be shirked to the market and society, nor should they handle things that are not within their scope of responsibility or not suitable for them to do. or tasks that one cannot do well, one should never overstep one's bounds; secondly, the market provides private products or, through government bidding, provides part of the public products entrusted by the government according to contract requirements; thirdly, society (community) provides semi-public products or, through government service purchase contracts, provides part of the public products entrusted by the government; finally, all governance entities must act according to the law, using the law as the criterion. A healthy society should be a three-dimensional structure composed of government, market, and society (community), where each cooperates with a division of labor, complements each other's strengths, fills in gaps, and jointly completes the task of social governance. Only grassroots social governance innovation carried out under such premises and foundations can better mobilize the enthusiasm and initiative of all parties in the community, jointly participate in the practice of community governance, and achieve the community's development goals.

Of course, the reform of the community governance system is a systematic project, a process of multi-party coordination and joint advancement. From the current conditions and environment, the promotion of the new pattern of grassroots social governance innovation in our country can generally be achieved in three steps. The first step is government-led (party committee leadership, government responsibility), relying on the push and pull of administrative power, to do a good job in top-level design of the system and strong support of resources, setting an ideal type, and cultivating citizens' community awareness and self-governance ability (shallow social coordination, public participation). The second step is for the government to "release" while "collecting"; "release" means to guide well, support well, and cultivate well, and what should be done must still be done; "collect" means not to manage what can be left unmanaged, not to do what can be left undone, and not to ask what can be left unasked, aiming to exercise the community's self-organization ability, allowing top-down administrative power and bottom-up self-governance power to interact and collaborate, with administrative power preparing to orderly fade out and self-governance power preparing to gradually take the stage, achieving a balance between administrative power and self-governance power. The third step is for the government to govern by non-interference, with all administrative power detrimental to community self-governance development withdrawing, doing strategic work such as public goods production, planning and design, financial support, supervision and evaluation, and coordination outside the field, while the community, including social organizations, fully engages to produce high-quality, efficient, and sufficient community material and spiritual products, with civil self-governance power maturing, complementing the mature administrative power, and jointly building a harmonious and prosperous living community. At the current stage, the administrative color of grid management should be diluted, cultivating the community's self-governance power, organically combining weak grid management and quasi-market separation of residence and station, or embedding quasi-market separation of residence and station into grid management, with the government's top-down administrative power and the community's bottom-up self-governance power achieving integration at the community service interface, which may be a relatively appropriate path to promote the reform and improvement of China's community governance system.

7.2 Open Block Space and Its Governance: Community Space Privatization and Its Breakthrough Gated Community[4]

Also known as isolated community or gated community, is a defensible residential model that emerged in urban spaces in Western countries under the background of neoliberal globalization. American scholar Blakely et al. (1997) first proposed the concept of a gated community in their monograph "Fortress America: Gated Communities in the United States," which refers to residential areas enclosed by walls and fences to achieve the privatization of public space and restrict access. From the representation of physical space, gates, walls, fences, and other defensive measures are its common landscape, while tight security, spatial segmentation, internal privacy, and external exclusion are its external representations. The spread of gated communities has greatly promoted the privatization of urban space and has derived various symbolic values and imagery attached to spatial carriers, leading to the involvement and research of many disciplines such as architecture, planning, urban geography, sociology, economics, and political science, achieving fruitful research results. In terms of practice, the spread and accumulation of gated communities have had a profound impact on the socio-economic environment, ecological travel, and social

[4] Part of the content has been published in "Learning and Practice" Issue 5, 2016.

structure of cities, becoming a key consideration and interest concern in urban planning and social management, prompting active responses and governance practices by governments worldwide.

7.2.1 *Historical Origins: The Emergence and Evolution of Gated Communities*

Gated communities first appeared in the United States as a result of the affluent class seeking to separate themselves from the chaotic industrialized city (blocks) (Blakely et al. 1997), and some gated communities were tourist resorts providing hunting and fishing environments and facilities for the wealthy, such as Tuxedo Park in New York City, which is surrounded by an 8-foot-high[5] and 24-mile-long[6] wire fence. Scenic Spot. In the early twentieth century, some aristocrats on the East Coast of the United States and Hollywood elites began to build and move into gated communities in large numbers based on considerations of privacy, security, and prestige. Since the 1970s, these defensible residential models, which first appeared in the sunny regions of the West Coast of the United States due to safety concerns, have gradually shown two distinct development trends in multi-racial, multicultural, high-crime, and densely populated urban spaces. First, the privatization (commercialization) of cities and the diversification of gated communities based on clan, class, and territorial use; second, the cross-class and universalization of gated communities, meaning they are no longer the exclusive domain of the upper class, as a large number of middle-class and minority groups have also begun to move into gated communities (Grant et al. 2004; Sanchez et al. 2005), thus forming gated communities in the United States.

Since the 1970s, with the massive construction of gated communities, developers and society's artificial construction and awareness promotion of factors such as resident safety and identity segregation have gradually made gated communities the dominant architectural model for new residential areas (Blakely et al. 1997), appearing in urban spaces worldwide under the wave of globalization. Its ecological evolution and development can be roughly divided into four stages (Coy 2006).

First, the preparatory stage before the 1970s. With the transformation of traditional societies worldwide and the continuous advancement of urbanization and modernization, the development of gated communities in the United States and Europe began to spread globally, causing changes in urban spaces. This includes the inner-city movement marked by exclusive residential areas, the emergence of urban apartment buildings with limited, simple security facilities, the blurring and indistinct boundaries between public and private spaces, the decline and overcrowding of high-end residential areas, and the modernization of traditional lifestyles. This is a process where residential areas with the characteristics and nature of gated communities gradually increased.

[5] 1 foot = 0.3048 m.

[6] 1 mile = 1.609344 km.

Second, the innovation stage from the mid-1970s to the early 1980s. During this stage, gated communities began to appear in urban spaces in new forms and carriers. The most typical is the emergence of large-scale gated community developers in line with the marketization process in major city construction processes. The development of these large projects and the construction of marketing concepts played an important role in demonstration and promotion. Especially the emergence of urban violence and crime issues during the urbanization process provided a huge market space for gated communities. Additionally, the emergence of commercial centers not only changed the consumption habits of the urban upper and middle classes but also caused a repositioning and change in social space. Suburban areas of cities also began to see the emergence of gated communities.

Third, the expansion stage from the mid-1980s to the early 1990s. This stage was accompanied by the retreat of national power and the surge of market forces under the background of neoliberal globalization, resulting in two consequences. First, the deepening of the national fiscal crisis and the continuous decline in urban governance capabilities, highlighting issues such as urban employment and violence; second, numerous profit-oriented developers joined the construction of gated communities, increasingly adopting more secure facilities to meet people's considerations for a safer living environment, leading to gated communities breaking through the geographical boundaries of metropolises and entering the spaces of small and medium-sized cities, becoming an important iconic architectural landscape of urban society.

Fourth, the new development stage since the mid-1990s. The important hallmark of this new development stage is the questioning of the security and cultural identity of gated communities, leading to reform and innovation. This process stems from the continuous expansion of gated communities in the previous stage, where not only the middle class but also groups with relatively low social status in cities began to enter gated community spaces, causing the exclusivity, segregation, and identity superiority of gated communities to begin to erode. Moreover, with the intensification of urbanization, a series of urban problems,Issues such as traffic congestion and long commuting times have begun to affect the lives of residents in gated communities. Another significant indicator is that with the spread and expansion of gated communities, the privatization of space has led to the fragmentation of urban architectural spaces and the deepening social psychological and class structure divisions and isolation, which are guiding a new wave of reform and governance targeting gated communities. Amid these doubts and debates, the construction standards for gated communities have been changed and adjusted, especially considering the unique needs of their target groups. The result is the emergence of new forms of gated communities that meet the needs of the middle class and the formation of small gated communities in urban upper-class areas.

Thus, it can be seen that the emergence and evolution of gated communities are the result of a combination of multiple factors. On one hand, it is the result of the "collusion" between local governments and real estate developers forming an Urban Growth Coalition under the macro drive of neoliberalism during the housing marketization and urbanization process. On the other hand, it is also the inevitable competitive consumption of symbolic signs such as identity status, privatization, and security under the lifestyle shaped by the social upper class and economic globalization. It is this complex intertwining of factors and positional games that have led to the "privatization" and "enclosure" of urban social space organization methods since the 1970s, as well as the generation, expansion, spread, questioning, and reform of gated communities, i.e., the ecological evolution process of enclosed (isolated) communities.

7.2.2 *Diverse Practices: Global Patterns of Gated Communities*

The emergence, expansion, and spread of gated communities since the 1970s have made them a global urban landscape, and research on gated communities has also proliferated. Existing studies show that due to different cultural, economic, and social background factors, the types, characteristics, spatial distribution, and scale management of gated communities also exhibit significant differences. Next, the author will conduct a comparative analysis of gated communities in the United States, the United Kingdom, Latin American countries, and China to clarify the diverse patterns of their development.

1. Citizen-Driven Path: The Practice of Gated Communities in the United States

The formation and evolution of gated communities in the United States highlight that their construction path is a bottom-up, citizen-driven, and conscious process. Their formation and development have the following characteristics. First, there is a diversity of gated community types. Blakely and Snyder, after an in-depth investigation of American gated communities in 1997, proposed an influential ideal type classification of gated communities. They divided American gated communities into three main types: Lifestyle Zone, Prestige Zone, and Security Zone, and provided a detailed analysis of the characteristics, subtypes, and features of each community type. Second, the development scale of gated communities is enormous. Blakely and Snyder's research further pointed out that in 1997, there were about 20,000 gated communities in the United States, including 9 million residents in 3 million dwelling units. Another study indicated that by 2002, about 7 million households[7] (5.9% of the total number of American households) lived in gated communities, with about 4 million households (3.4% of the total number of American households) residing in communities with access control facilities (requiring a password, key, or card to enter). By 2007, 11.1% of residents in the western United States, 6.8% in the southern United States, 3.1% in the northern United States, and 2.1% in the Midwest lived in gated communities. Third, the residents of gated communities are diverse. As gated communities continue to develop, the residents are no longer limited to the affluent class but have spread across all social classes. A 2003 survey of 219 gated

[7] Data source: American Housing Survey (AHS).

communities in Los Angeles showed that only half of the communities were located in wealthy areas, one-third were middle-class white residential areas, and one-fifth were middle to low-income Hispanic and Asian residential areas.

2. Native Evolutionary Path: The Construction of Gated Communities in the United Kingdom

In the United Kingdom, the development of gated communities began with the innovation of housing products by developers and matured with consumer acceptance, market stability, government support, institutional changes, and the support of related policies.The result is a joint effort by the market, government, and society. Blandy believes that the development of gated communities in the UK is a process of historical change and original evolution. It has the following three characteristics. First, in terms of the types of gated communities, Blandy and Parsons categorize UK gated communities from the dimensions of architectural form and intent into three types: "Infill," "Heritage Conversion," and "Village." Infill communities are located in the "space" zones between cities and towns, mainly built for young people and the avant-garde middle class, generally smaller in scale and more avant-garde in design; Heritage Conversion communities are mainly redeveloped from existing sites such as military bases, prisons, or mental hospitals, primarily meeting the housing needs of the urban lower class, scattered in rural and urban areas; Village communities are located in rural areas, larger in scale, serving the upper-middle class (nobility), and are a traditional British lifestyle architectural type. Second, the development scale of gated communities. A study shows that by 2005, at least 12% of the UK population lived in gated communities, with over 1,000 gated communities in England alone. In terms of building scale, UK gated communities are generally small, with small communities of fewer than 50 households accounting for 35% of the total number of gated communities, while gated communities with more than 300 households account for only 4%. Third, the spatial distribution of gated communities. Research by Blandy et al. found that 50% of the UK's gated communities are located in suburban areas, 30% are built in city center areas, and the remaining 20% are scattered in rural areas. It is particularly noteworthy that the cultural and political background of the UK leads to a special emphasis on the social isolation function of gated communities in various aspects (Webster 2001; Atkinson and Flint 2004), which is a significant difference from American gated communities.

3. Capital-driven market path: Development of gated communities in Latin American countries

The development of gated communities in Latin American countries directly stems from their market-oriented reforms and neoliberal policies, driven by capital and the market. Its development characteristics include three points. First, the uncontrolled development of gated communities. Since the mid-1970s, gated communities have become prevalent in Latin America, and by the twenty-first century, different types of gated communities have become an important component of urban areas in Latin America, becoming a significant part of the increasing urban spatial segregation and privatization process. Although there is a lack of data on the development scale of

Latin American gated communities as a whole, data from different countries and cities have shown the wide distribution of gated communities. For example, a study shows that in the 1990s alone,gated communities were built in Buenos Aires, housing nearly 500,000 residents (Janoschka 2002); Mexico City also saw the emergence of over 700 gated communities at the same time, accommodating about 50,000 families; particularly in São Paulo, Brazil, the largest gated community in Alphaville houses about 40,000 residents, and Alphaville is essentially divided by 14 independent gated communities (Coy 2006). Currently, gated communities are spreading uncontrollably across all cities in Latin American countries. At the same time, due to the lack of a relatively complete tax system like those in the US and UK, there is inevitably a lack of planning control and disorder in land use. Second, the fragmentation of cities and gated communities. Most gated communities in Latin America are large real estate projects built with unified planning, managed by privatized property companies. With the emergence of a large number of urban gated communities, coupled with a lack of scientific planning, urban spaces in Latin America are gradually being fragmented by gated communities, showing a fragmented state and severe social spatial segregation. Third, urban violence and the prosperity of gated communities. Numerous studies show that a very important and significant factor in the emergence of gated communities in Latin America is the continuous increase in urban violence, leading to a demand for security that exceeds the range public goods can provide, evolving into a "private good" that requires payment, thereby causing the emergence of a large number of gated communities.

4. The Dual Path of Market and Power: The Construction of Gated Communities in China

The emergence of gated communities in China is a process where the government strengthens its control and penetration into society, with communities existing more as "grassroots governance units". The development and expansion of gated communities since the 1990s have been driven by market forces, resulting from capital-driven dynamics in the market field. There are four characteristics of their development.

(1) The layout and scale of gated communities. Gated communities in China have become the basic organizational and construction method for urban housing today. Whether it is newly built commercial housing communities or old communities in urban renewal, the form of gated communities is adopted. Besides luxurious villa residential areas, affordable housing and low-rent housing communities also adopt the management and form of gated communities. From a trend perspective, the more closed a community is, the more its "security" is guaranteed, and consequently, the higher its housing prices.
(2) Unique development evolution path. The development of gated communities in China is generally consistent with the global development process of gated communities. However, due to its unique national conditions and urbanization advancement methods, it has its own unique evolutionary trajectory. There are two distinct peaks in the development of gated communities in China. First, the construction of "work unit compounds" and "closed generation" during

the planned economy period. As the name suggests, a work unit compound is a large courtyard centered around a "work unit," integrating office production, residence, logistics, and various life and welfare services, providing all social services to employees of the unit, hence also called "unit society." It is primarily a production space, a residential space segregated by identity, and a closed space where production and life overlap. Its services are limited to unit employees, and outsiders cannot enter or exit freely, achieving internal identity and external exclusion through unit identity and gates and fences. It rose in the 1950s and declined in the 1990s. The urban space construction relying on work units and work unit compounds has profoundly influenced residents' living habits, thinking patterns, and urban management and operation. Even now, work unit compounds (communities) remain a spatial organization method in many cities. Second, the development of "gated commercial housing communities" and "closed expansion" during the transition period. This is a type of residential community segregated by income. With the complete collapse of the unit housing allocation system in the 1990s and the advancement of market-oriented housing system reforms, residential housing has become monetized and privatized. Most commercial housing communities implement closed management, achieving physical management of people entering and exiting the community and property segregation based on money through gates, high walls, and modern electronic surveillance equipment like cameras. After 1998, amidst the wave of neoliberal globalization, "gated communities spread," and gated commercial housing communities became the mainstream residential mode for urban residents. Moreover, the higher the end of the residential area, the higher the housing prices, and the stronger the closure.

(3) The motivation for moving into gated communities is primarily to obtain high-end infrastructure, community environment, and services, mainly driven by the pursuit of derivative needs beyond "security." Although it has significantly impacted urban segregation and traffic planning, it has not yet deepened to the level of cultural, value, and class differentiation social isolation. However, this requires extreme vigilance, especially as the continuous surge in housing prices in recent years has far exceeded people's psychological expectations, and real estate developers, in pursuit of higher profits, are continuously pushing the economic interest segregation towards class (layer) differentiation in the creation of high-end communities.
(4) Power penetration in the construction of gated communities. This is mainly reflected in the penetration of government will in community management and the participation of urban residents' committees, as permanent institutions acting as government agents, in community management and services. This is also an important feature that significantly distinguishes Chinese gated community practices from those abroad. Research on the Construction of Integrated Service Models in Urban Community Governance.

7.2.3 Theoretical Debate: The Pros and Cons of Gated

Communities Since the 1990s, the privatization and isolation effects of urban space caused by community closure have begun to emerge, greatly impacting urban planning and social management. Especially as "urban diseases" (traffic congestion, environmental pollution, etc.) become increasingly severe, the negative effects of gated communities also… Increasingly emerging, it has further sparked a series of debates about gated communities. The core debates mainly revolve around two themes. First, whether the promise of security in gated communities is genuinely attainable; second, whether the development of gated communities leads to residential segregation and social polarization.

1. Security in Gated Communities: Real or Illusory Gated

Communities promise higher security. Developers use a series of enclosure methods (gated access, high walls, modern electronic surveillance equipment, etc.) and employ media and various marketing strategies to create a "reality" of greater security in gated communities. Existing research shows that security is the primary consideration for residents moving into gated communities. The study by Blakely and Snyder (1997) indicates that over 70% of American respondents consider a sense of security an important reason for choosing isolated communities. Song Weixuan (2010), in reviewing literature on gated communities, also found that in the United States, Latin America, and South Africa, the growing fear of insecurity and the demand for safety in urban environments of violent crime are significant reasons for the rise of gated communities. The research by Xu et al. (2009) also points out that in China, over one-third of residents consider security the primary factor for moving into gated communities.

However, is the "security" promised by gated communities genuinely attainable? Some research holds a negative view. Jane Jacobs (1961), in "The Death and Life of Great American Cities," pointed out that "gated communities do not necessarily bring security" and that "metal fences are not more effective than 'neighborhood watch' in ensuring residents' safety." Other studies suggest that while gated communities ensure internal security, they make the surrounding streets more vulnerable to attacks, posing a threat to the safety of residents in a broader area. In other words, the security of gated communities comes at the expense of the insecurity of surrounding communities (Blakely et al. 1997). In gated communities, people transfer the responsibility of community security control to hired security organizations or electronic surveillance systems, leading to less attention to suspicious individuals or activities within the community, ironically making gated communities less secure (Blakely et al. 1997). Furthermore, the sense of community belonging and security promoted and constructed by gated communities may be more of an illusion rather than reality (Wilson 2000). Developers' focus on community enclosure and security behind marketing strategies is merely a form of "impression management." Helsley and Strange (1999), based on long-term tracking of crime rate data in gated communities, found that the crime prevention effect of gated communities is very limited and shows a certain cyclical evolution pattern, with crime rates decreasing in the first year after the community is built, but aligning with non-gated communities after a year. Handel (2014) also confirmed how gated communities transform from fortresses to exclusive spaces and the dissipation of their security.

Thus, with urbanization, the issues of violence and crime become prominent, prompting further consideration of residential safety. Developers have created a "safe" community atmosphere through the construction of gated communities, leading to their rapid development in the process of "meeting demand." However, the "security promise" of gated communities has encountered a "Waterloo" in empirical testing. Especially with the generalization and normalization of gated communities and the emergence of new urban issues, on one hand, the urgency and nature of residents' "security" needs may have changed; on the other hand, developers' false fulfillment, partial fulfillment, or non-fulfillment of "security" promises have already caused the "security" provided by gated communities to lose its uniqueness as a "private good," making its questioning and criticism inevitable.

2. Spatial Effects of Gated Communities: Spatial Privatization and Social Isolation

The construction of gated communities has objectively led to the privatization and fragmentation of urban space, a "mosaic patchwork" process. However, whether this fragmentation process has a positive or negative impact on urban development is a subject of serious disagreement in existing research.

Scholars supporting the development of gated communities believe that they are a positive form of social spatial organization, conducive to achieving community integration. This "integration" can be understood from two aspects. First, The role in promoting internal integration within the community. Closed communities lead to the homogenization of internal communities, which helps generate a sense of community identity and common community awareness, reducing the likelihood of internal conflicts. Moreover, the internal closure process is also a process of isolation from different types of external communities, which can eliminate the possibility of conflicts arising from differences in life values and cultural orientations. Wilson (2000) believes that closed communities are a spatial organization method with positive significance. They can enhance the homogeneity of residents, catalyze the generation of common community awareness, and protect internal community residents from violence and potential dangers from open urban spaces. Some scholars also believe that closed communities help preserve traditional customs and the diversity of residents' lifestyles, achieving the effect of strengthening personal community identity through a well-developed community infrastructure system, thus being a positive spatial social phenomenon. Secondly, the linking role in external community integration. From the spatial perspective between communities, since the "walls" of closed communities are not impermeable, there is a possibility of functional complementarity and symbiosis between the community and surrounding neighborhoods, which helps achieve connections between adjacent communities. This means that the existence of "walls" creates opportunity spaces for the coexistence of different types and classes of residential areas, allowing for social integration at a higher level. For example, empirical research on closed communities built in two adjacent poor areas in London found that the "walls" of closed communities strengthened the mixed residence of the rich and the poor in the same area to some extent, thereby alleviating social spatial differentiation caused by identity differences (Manzi and Smith-Bowers 2005). Asiedu and Arku (2009) also found through the experience of closed community construction in Ghana that there is economic complementarity and symbiosis between the community and surrounding neighborhoods, creating employment opportunities for the local low-income groups, thus providing an opportunity for integration between them. Additionally, some scholars propose from a more macro perspective that the development of closed communities in urban suburbs is conducive to increasing land transfer fees in the area, thereby promoting the urbanization process.

However, most scholars believe that closed communities will lead to the privatization of urban space and social isolation, potentially triggering a series of serious social issues. Scholars holding this view generally believe that the exclusive space created by community closure will, to some extent, exacerbate residential space isolation and, in the process of continuous isolation, lead to social isolation and social inequality, thus receiving criticism from many scholars (Blakely et al. 1997; Thuillier 2005; Vesselinov et al. 2007). Existing research mainly involves the following aspects.

Firstly, closed communities and residential isolation. Mike pointed out that as a means of spatial closure, the "walls" of closed communities achieve spatial isolation between different groups, widening social distances between people, increasing the difficulty of neighborhood interactions, and enhancing people's social perception of "difference," forming psychological barriers. Falk also found that the process of transforming urban public space into private space by closed communities is one-way and thus difficult to reverse. With the reduction of public space, experience sharing and social connections between individuals become more difficult, and social isolation gradually reproduces. Goix (2005) used geographic information system technology to analyze survey data from over 200 closed communities within 2,000 survey areas in Los Angeles and found that the spread of closed communities exacerbated residential isolation with surrounding neighborhood communities. Lemanski (2006) conducted a comparative study of closed communities and their adjacent non-closed communities in South African urban areas and found that residents of different communities perceive each other as "the other," with decreasing tolerance and social interaction, leading to cognitive isolation between internal and external community groups through spatial isolation, increasing the socio-economic status differences in South Africa's racial segregation.

Secondly, closed communities and urban fragmentation. For the city itself, the development of closed communities also has two negative impacts. Firstly, the fragmentation of urban space. The emergence of a large number of closed communities inevitably reduces the density and accessibility of the urban road network, not only causing the utilization of urban space to… inefficiencies and the blurring of accessibility further exacerbate and intensify the difficulty of managing urban issues such as traffic congestion and environmental degradation, severely affecting the effectiveness of urban management and governance. Secondly, the fragmentation of urban culture and psychology. In the process of blocking resident interactions and residential segregation, gated communities reduce the overall integration level of the city. Over time, urban culture will be difficult to integrate, urban inclusiveness will be hard to extend, and the city will simultaneously complete social, psychological, and cultural fragmentation in spatial fragmentation.

Thirdly, gated communities and social inequality. In the process of privatizing urban space through identity recognition and capability differences (mainly economic income), gated communities also generate and accompany more social inequalities. Gated communities may cause severe social exclusion, where social exclusion and spatial segregation influence each other, leading to a series of cultural, economic, and spatial segregation and exclusion overlaps, creating a chain reaction that inevitably triggers large-scale social crises (Madanipour 2006). Some scholars, using the social spatial distance analysis method, analyzed the census data of the southwestern metropolitan area of the United States from 2000 to 2010 and found that gated communities have a significant effect on local-level social segregation, producing social inequality. In fact, from the evolution of gated communities, social inequality is the cause of the emergence of gated communities. However, once gated communities are established, they in turn become a reason for the reproduction of social inequality.

3. Research on the Debate of Gated Communities in China

From the perspective of Chinese research, the debate surrounding gated communities has its particularities. Walls and gates have been symbols of "boundaries" in China since ancient times, and people are accustomed to and psychologically understand this. Therefore, compared to the Western criticism and concern about gated communities exacerbating social segregation, China seems to have not generated much concern. There is a small amount of research on whether the spatial division of gated communities will cause or exacerbate social segregation and inequality (Song and Zhu 2009; Feng Dan et al. 2011). Instead, more scholars in the fields of urban planning and architectural design have conducted a series of studies on the impact of gated communities on urban spatial structure and planning design. Firstly, research on the negative impacts of gated communities. For example, the large emergence of gated communities can block urban road networks, affecting their accessibility (Qin Ruiying et al. 2008), and impact the functional layout of urban land use (Xu Di et al. 2009), exacerbating urban deprivation of farmers' land. Secondly, exploring the planning and design solutions for gated communities. Some scholars have studied the challenges and overall response strategies of gated communities to urban planning and design (Xu Miao and Yang 2008; Yu Kanhua et al. 2009), proposing many valuable planning and design schemes, such as the "dual-level model" (Zhong Botao 2003), "neighborhood residential strategy" (Sun Kefeng 2004), "continuous space organization" (Jing Ziyang and Zhang 2006), and the call to retrieve "new urbanism" (Dou Yide 2004), among others.

Overall, current domestic research on gated communities is mainly in disciplines such as urban planning and construction design, focusing on sorting and introducing Western academic achievements. The research focus is concentrated on the formation mechanisms, positive and negative impacts, governance methods, and social spatial effects of gated communities (Wu Qiyan and Cui 1999; Dou Yide 2004; Su Zhenmin and LIn 2007; Xu Miao and Yang 2008; Qin Ruiying et al. 2008; Sun Bindong and Wu 2009; Song Weixuan 2010). In contrast, sociology, which is the mainstream field in Western research on gated communities, is absent in the Chinese context.

It is evident that the emergence of gated communities has led to the privatization of urban space. However, whether the process of privatization has caused residential segregation and social inequality remains an unresolved debate. It will inevitably become more in-depth, comprehensive, and diverse with more practical exploration and theoretical reflection. It is important to note that the aforementioned debates are based on case studies by scholars from different fields under different political, economic, and cultural backgrounds, and the inconsistent or even contradictory conclusions drawn are understandable. These The existence of debates itself also verifies the diversity of the development of closed communities worldwide. However, the differentiated practices also imply some convergent issues, namely the changes and challenges brought to urban social management by the community space segmentation effect caused by the development and spread of closed communities.

7.3 Realistic Challenges: The Predicament of Closed Communities Under the New Normal of Social Governance Closed

Communities construct an illusory territorial community, a constructed closure within the collective state, attempting to fulfill promises of privacy and security. This promise from the supply side caters to urban residents' psychological expectations for safety, privacy, and being undisturbed, thus gaining recognition from the consumer side and gradually becoming the basic organizational form of urban space worldwide. This territorial community uses artificially constructed separators (usually walls, fences, and access control facilities) as tools to mechanically divide the physical boundaries of living areas. However, due to the lack of community residents' participation in the construction of these separators, which are mostly subjective constructions by developers and urban planners, the "boundaries" presented by this entanglement of barriers and interests obscure public awareness and segment public participation, turning residents into "irrelevant neighbors" and "silent majorities," and transforming the community into a profit-making space for developers and a basic unit of urban management. Clearly, this does not align with the social governance trends of the new era. This is specifically manifested in the following five aspects of tension.

(1) The tension between the pluralistic and inclusive governance philosophy and the closed segregation of communities

The essence of governance is based on resident participation, with pluralistic interaction as the rule, democratic consultation as the path, and cooperative co-governance as the orientation. Its fundamental philosophy is pluralistic inclusion, essentially a practice of cooperative co-governance based on democratic consultation among multiple subjects. However, numerous foreign studies have found that community closure signifies external isolation, exclusion, and internal privatization and indifference, thereby creating an exclusive space, further exacerbating residential space segregation, and moving towards social isolation in the continuous process of segregation, resulting in social inequality. On one hand, after community closure, the rejection of external forces (subjects, organizations, and resources) from participating in community construction turns community building into a purely internal affair. However, once the exchange of information and energy with the larger field is interrupted and isolated, such community governance becomes unimaginable; moreover, the physical barriers artificially constructed can easily evolve into psychological barriers, further causing a unification and resonance between the internal psychological construction of social inequality and external physical representation, with the potential to trigger greater inter-class contradictions and conflicts. On the other hand, the privatized space created by community closure will increase residents' private consciousness, thereby increasing the difficulty of pluralistic co-governance based on democratic consultation. Additionally, in a physical sense, the segmentation of urban community space also results in the loss of the possibility for residents to organize and carry out collective actions and strive for public interests on a larger scale. Thus, it is evident that there is significant tension between the pluralistic inclusion inherent in community governance and the spatial isolation of closed communities.

(2) The tension between the anti-ecological "panopticon" induced by closed communities and the liberation of human freedom

The closure of communities is mainly achieved through tangible materials such as walls and fences, as well as modern electronic surveillance equipment, creating a bodily management scenario that achieves high-precision positioning and identification of the identity, physical characteristics, and spatiotemporal aspects of people entering and leaving the community. Although it can monitor people entering and leaving the community, it also controls residents' communication and activities in the community's public space. This method is often utilized by property companies and developers, placing them in an advantageous position of information control in the interest game with community residents. Residents' freedom, especially the freedom to carry out collective activities around public interests, is restricted by interest groups, resulting in a disadvantage in the interest game. Furthermore, such cold surveillance facilities may also cause residents to have a heightened defensive mentality, which in turn further hinders interpersonal interactions between residents and community service personnel (such as property staff), deepening the gap in understanding and communication between them.

(3) The tension between the expectations of cross-community boundary interactions generated by the prosperous development of social organizations and the closure of communities

The tension between the expectation of cross-community boundary interactions generated by the prosperous development of social organizations and the closed nature of communities is essentially the tension between the functional boundaries of social organizations and the physical boundaries of closed communities. The new normal of social governance requires orderly division and cooperation between government and society, enabling professional social work services to effectively land and actively intervene in communities. The development and role of social organizations, as important carriers of social work, have become significant governance variables in grassroots community spaces (Huang Xiaoxing 2011, 2013; He Xuesong 2016). The notable characteristic of social organizations is their professionalism and vocational nature, allowing them to practice services across community boundaries. Their open practice orientation inevitably requires cross-community functionality and open service boundaries. However, the territorial segregation caused by the closed nature of communities hinders the extension of functional boundaries in the service delivery of social organizations, making it difficult for their functions to be fully realized on a larger scale, significantly limiting their leading role in social governance innovation. Therefore, how to create more space in social governance for social organizations to no longer be "confined to a corner," and how to conduct cross-boundary interactions and service practices in community fields, allowing the functional boundaries of social organizations to no longer be "bounded by the community," should become an important policy issue under the new normal of social governance.

(4) The tension between the closure of social physical boundaries and the psychological distance segregation of residents, and social integration

The tension between the closure of social physical boundaries and the psychological distance segregation of residents, specifically refers to the coupling and overlay of community physical boundary closure and residents' psychological distance segregation, which exacerbates the risk of social integration caused by the de-support and atomization of society. In the new era of social governance, the trend of de-support and atomization in society is evident, especially with the deep disintegration of the unit system and the decline of traditional social group functions, society generally presents a de-support trend, with the atomization and fragmentation characteristics of social members being prominent. The spread of closed communities in modern urban spaces undoubtedly increases the difficulty of social reorganization. Consistent with the overall de-support of society, the atomization within closed communities is also intensifying, and a psychological sense of common belonging is not formed due to geographical co-presence. Instead, the diverse heterogeneity of community residents and the amplification of defensive psychology manifest as mutual silence and segregation. This means that geographical co-presence is not a sufficient condition for forming community cohesion, and the defense caused by community boundary closure and the interaction obstruction caused by residents' heterogeneous diversity may become new inducements for social conflict in limited community spaces, with the risk of social integration being amplified by the overlay of these two effects.

(5) The tension between the uniformity in policy implementation and the diversity in the reality of breaking walls and opening enclosures

The tension between the uniformity in policy implementation and the diversity in the reality of breaking walls and opening enclosures is essentially the crisis of governance paradigms hidden behind policy tools and the obstacles in the reality of breaking walls and opening enclosures as reflected in the "Opinions of the Central Committee of the Communist Party of China and the State Council on Further Strengthening Urban Planning, Construction, and Management" (hereinafter referred to as the "Opinions"). The "Opinions" state, "New residential areas should promote the block system, and in principle, no more closed residential communities will be built. Existing residential communities and unit compounds should gradually open up to achieve the publicization of internal roads, solve the problem of traffic network layout, and promote the economical use of land," which is the uniformity in policy requirements. However, in reality, whether it is the openness of new constructions or the breaking of walls in existing communities, there are complex interest entanglements and entrenched psychological stereotypes, and different communities also have a high degree of heterogeneous diversity due to their different positions in the traffic network structure and the actual situation of residents. This means a non-synchronous diversity in the process of "breaking walls and opening enclosures." This tension inevitably causes unsmooth policy execution and less than ideal progress in the reality of breaking walls and opening enclosures.

The existence of the aforementioned tensions genuinely marks the difficulties faced by closed communities under the new normal of social governance, while also indicating the policy space for reform and adjustment and the future open space.

7.4 Breaking Walls and Opening Enclosures: The Current Fate and Response of Closed Communities

Since the beginning of the twenty-first century, the aforementioned crisis of gated communities has been continuously amplified during its spread, and the debate over its pros and cons has gradually shown an "imbalance"—the negative impacts of gated communities have been increasingly discussed by scholars. The large-scale expansion of gated communities has had a significant impact on the physical spatial structure of cities, leading to the privatization and segregation of urban spaces, which in turn has brought about important changes to urban planning, transportation networks, and the accessibility of public resources. It has also caused changes in people's social psychological structures, resulting in urban social indifference and increased psychological distance, which greatly hinders urban cultural integration and psychological structures. At the same time, the superimposition and resonance of these impacts have generated a significant "compound effect," bringing irreversible crises and challenges to urban social management and inclusive city construction. Therefore, how to address the challenges brought by the spatial segmentation effect of gated communities on urban spatial planning, and how to reduce the pressure on urban social management caused by the social exclusion and exacerbation of social inequality due to the privatization of space in the construction and expansion of gated communities, has led various countries to reform and explore ways to eliminate the "closed effect" of gated communities. From the governance experience of the West, the current governance of gated communities can be summarized into three paths.

(1) The government uses administrative means to introduce relevant policies to curb the construction of gated communities, mainly represented by the United States. To address the negative impacts of gated communities, since 2000, many states in the United States have formulated relevant self-governance acts to curb the construction of gated communities. For example, two towns in North Carolina—Caro and Carrboro—have issued ordinances to limit the existence of gated communities because these communities are highly exclusive and restrict the entry of emergency vehicles. In other states, such as some cities in Oregon, although there are no ordinances and regulations to restrict community closure, they consistently reject the planning and construction of gated communities. Particularly, the regional planning management and development of New York City do not allow the emergence of community closures. In summary, although there is no unified policy or regulation in the United States to restrict gated communities, there are some practices and unwritten rules that can limit gated communities through planning control.

However, these precedents of restricting community closures in the United States are not applicable in Canada and the United Kingdom. This is mainly because the planning systems of the two countries, which focus on development planning and development control, differ significantly from those in the United States. In the United States, planning rights and control restriction rights are consistent, and localities have a high degree of autonomy. In Canada and the United Kingdom, it is different; the planning systems do not have consistent planning and prohibition rights, nor are they as standardized, and they are easily subject to changes due to economic interests. Moreover, in Canada and the United Kingdom, the federal government also has greater authority. This is an important reason why they adopt the second path, which is planning guidance.

(2) Planning guidance for gated communities in urban planning. Taking Canada as an example, Canada's planning guidance for gated communities in urban planning is mainly reflected in four points. First, strictly regulate the architectural style of gated communities. In urban planning and construction, corresponding regulations have been made on the height, color, sightlines, connections, corners, and repairs of walls, fences, or plants used for community closure, and it is required that walls be conspicuous, but gates cannot be built in prominent positions in the neighborhood. Second, limit the scale of development. Planners suggest that local governments develop more small-scale gated community

projects (less than 10 hectares[8]) to ensure street connectivity. If a project affects urban travel and transportation, the government should consider the convenience of walking and public transportation. Third, ensure the accessibility of emergency vehicles in gated communities. Ensure the connectivity of roads and public transportation within the community, especially emphasizing the accessibility of emergency passages such as fire, ambulance, and police. Locking gated communities is prohibited, especially in neighborhoods with public transportation. Fourth, stipulate the ancillary public responsibilities of developers. Developers should optimize the community environment, increase the openness of space, and enhance the guarantee and optimization of the spillover effects of public infrastructure (such as water, electricity, roads, etc.) and public spaces.

(3) Emphasis and attention on urban public spaces. Public spaces are important carriers for residents to step out of private domains for communication and interaction, and they are also important means for residents to dialogue, negotiate public issue resolutions, and form a sense of community belonging and cohesion. Therefore, Western countries particularly emphasize their role in eliminating the closed effects of gated communities.The positive construction function in terms of the negative impact of the district. It should be noted that although the author analyzes it as a separate path here, from the planning practices of countries around the world, the emphasis on public interaction and communication spaces in urban planning and construction is nested and matched with the aforementioned two paths.

As for the governance of closed communities in China, it is basically a comprehensive application of the aforementioned paths. It is primarily administrative, with the participation of urban planning as a supplement, and is mostly carried out as experimental attempts through local planning innovations. This shows that the specific paths in the reform practices and planning of different countries point to a policy expectation that closed communities should gradually open up, and community construction is a process towards more open block spaces.

7.5 Future Path: How is the Block System Possible? How Can It Be Achieved?

7.5.1 Moving Towards Open Block Spaces

From the analysis of the origins, advantages and disadvantages, and opportunities and challenges of closed communities mentioned above, it can be found that the emergence of closed communities worldwide is the result of multiple factors intertwined and superimposed under the shaping of neoliberal globalization. Although practices and characteristics vary, the functional logic and development expectations

[8] 1 hectare = 10,000 square meters.

behind them are similar. The governance practices of different countries indicate that closed communities will eventually disappear in the process of moving towards more open block spaces.

However, the process of their demise must be a socially proactive and positively constructed process. The existence and spread of closed communities have a deep real foundation, psychological foundation, and cultural (segregation) foundation. From this perspective, the "opening" of closed communities is by no means as simple as "tearing down walls." The social psychological needs and identity symbol construction behind closed communities should not be ignored. Therefore, the spatial division and privatization of closed communities, which cause spatial and social issues, are only external inducements and motivating factors for the governance of closed communities. Only by eliminating the real demand and functional consumption for closed communities in reality can the open block system be naturally achieved.

On February 6, 2016, the Central Committee of the Communist Party of China and the State Council issued the "Several Opinions on Further Strengthening Urban Planning and Construction Management" (hereinafter referred to as the "Opinions"), which pointed out that "new residential areas should promote the block system, and in principle, no more closed residential communities should be built. Existing residential communities and unit compounds should gradually open up to realize the publicization of internal roads and solve the layout problems of the traffic road network, promoting the economical use of land." Its policy implications are twofold. First, to conduct urban planning and construction with the goal of building livable blocks and promoting the block system; second, to open closed communities by relying on optimizing the block road network structure.

Regarding the former policy implication, the "construction" of the open block system is its construction goal. Open living spaces are the main body of its construction and are also the key to fundamentally eliminating the demand for closed communities. This involves the following three issues that need clarification.

(1) How to understand "open." Of course, "open" is relative to "closed," referring to the dismantling of a series of "walls" that closed communities rely on, thereby achieving "accessibility," which is only an instrumental understanding. A deeper understanding should be made from a value perspective, referring to three levels. First, openness is the process of moving out of the private domain and into public space. In this context, how to bring community residents out of private living spaces and into public discourse spaces is its main concern. Therefore, in urban planning and construction (including the process of demolishing walls and opening communities), the construction of neighborhood spaces, public platforms, and carriers is particularly important. It is especially important to note that the radiation range of public spaces (platforms, topics, awareness, etc.) should become the functional boundary of the block system. It can be vague, flexible, and permeable, but it must exist. In other words, openness does not mean "no boundaries." Second, openness is the process of moving out of the individual and integrating into the organization, essentially a reorganization process of fragmented individuals after community opening. The space released

after the "opening" of closed communities is an important institutional space and opportunity space for social organizations to interact across boundaries and play roles. From this perspective, the construction of social organizations is particularly important. Social organizations can provide professional services that cross "community" boundaries and will inevitably become important governance entities in open blocks in the future. One construction standard is that the professional services of social organizations should achieve residents The high satisfaction of needs for safety, neighborhood belonging, and neighborhood culture is also an important opportunity and mission for the development of social organizations in the new era. Thirdly, openness is the process of moving out of segregation and towards inclusiveness. After more than 60 years of development, the private consciousness of spatial division in closed communities has evolved into the living habits of residents. Therefore, to completely eliminate the constructive function of closed communities, it is necessary to break the "closed consciousness" and reconstruct the habit of "inclusive sharing." In this sense, openness is also a cultural construction that needs to be gradually acquired in the process of socialization, and thus it is inevitably a long process.

(2) The true meaning of a living community. The goal of urban planning and construction is the construction of livable neighborhoods, with standards of "openness and convenience, appropriate scale, complete facilities, and harmonious neighborhoods." In community governance, there has always been a theoretical and practical paradox between "the community as a basic governance unit" and "the community as a living community," which was pioneered by Tönnies in "Community and Society." As a basic governance unit, the community is an important component of the modern social grassroots management system, while as a living community, it is the true weaving of life in traditional society. In terms of construction standards, "openness and convenience, harmonious neighborhoods" are for the construction of "livability," while "appropriate scale, complete facilities" also consider "service governance." Thus, the proposed block system construction in the "Opinion" is an inclusive system that balances life and service, construction and management.

(3) What is the block system? This is a new term[9] and inevitably an unfinished research topic. From the academic tradition of sociology, whether it can be studied as a management innovation of urban grassroots society following the "street residence system" and "community system" still requires further advancement of reforms in practice and in-depth research by scholars in related fields.

[9] Existing academic research on the "block system" is limited to interpretations of the discourse in the "Opinions," and has not yet emerged as an academic concept in scholarly texts. Additionally, the explanation of the "block system" in Baidu's encyclopedia is an entry that appeared after the "Opinions." The "newness" of the "block system" also suggests its immense academic value as an academic "virgin land." Of course, this requires summarization, refinement, and conclusion in conjunction with the practice of the "block system.".

In terms of policy implications, the "openness" of closed communities is the object of its deconstruction. The "demolition of walls" in closed communities is a direct response to the privatization of urban space and a practical countermeasure to address the negative impact of community closure on urban spatial structure. Similarly, there are two issues that need to be addressed.

(1) How to open? That is, how to carry out and implement the "openness" of closed communities. This involves two levels of issues. First, the method of opening, which includes both stock reform and incremental planning. For the former, it refers to the "deconstruction" of already built and used closed communities, with the basic requirement of "no more construction of closed communities," and the principle of "reform," which means changing their "closed" attributes and optimizing the spatial layout of neighborhoods. For the latter, it refers to the "construction" of new communities, with the basic requirement of "promoting the block system for new residential buildings," and the principle of "planning," which means reasonably planning their "open" attributes to ensure the accessibility of the neighborhood road network. In short, the "openness" process of closed communities should fully utilize the constructive role of policies, regulations, and urban planning, which is also the basic experience of global closed community governance.
(2) After opening, what then? That is, the impact assessment of the potential effects on social governance after the "demolition of walls" in closed communities. It is particularly necessary to consider the impact on community governance structure and social management innovation after opening up neighborhoods. There are two possible directions for consideration. First, the residents' committee as a grassroots social… The return of the principal status of important carriers in governance. The operation within closed communities centers on home ownership (property rights), revolving around economic interests. The scope of property services defines the boundaries of the "community" recognized by residents, leading to a highly privatized community space. The accessibility of public services is also very limited due to the isolation between residential complexes and communities (here referring to residents' committees), marginalizing the residents' committees in the segmentation of urban space. However, as closed communities open up, the boundaries of the "community" begin to extend beyond the confines of "closed complexes," achieving connectivity on a larger scale. This, in turn, transforms the logic and domain of governance, with the function of the residents' committee (usually representing the government in providing public management and services) beginning to enter the interior of open communities, making the residents' committee one of the important governance entities. However, the return of this principal status is misaligned with the administrative dilemma of the residents' committee, and there are continuity issues between the residents' committee as a governance unit and the residential complex as a property unit. Therefore, the transformation and adjustment of the status, role, and function of the residents' committee is a larger research

topic that requires further consideration. Secondly, the change in the relationship between the state and society. The opening of closed communities, the transformation of block spaces, the return of the principal status of residents' committees, and the respective changes in state and social forces (mainly their agents) will inevitably lead to new changes in the relationship between the state and society. This change, in turn, will act as an important structural constraint force further regulating the direction of block spaces. This is a research direction that needs further refinement and deepening.

In summary, the construction of the block system and the opening of closed communities are complementary and mutually progressive. The former is an intrinsic component and key force aimed at deconstructing residents' security needs, symbolic consumption, and closed mentality towards closed communities, while constructing an open and inclusive social interaction psychological habitus. The latter is an external inducement and motivating factor aimed at breaking the privatization of urban space and addressing social isolation and its spatial effects. The combination and integration of the two is the "dual-wheel drive" towards open block spaces, and only in this way can the replacement of closed communities by open blocks truly come to fruition.

7.5.2 Construction of the Block System

Against this backdrop, the "Opinions" mark the beginning of the government using administrative means to introduce relevant policies to curb the construction of closed communities,[10] also representing a reform attempt from the supply-side dimension. However, "breaking walls and opening enclosures" cannot be effectively achieved by the government's unilateral actions alone. Not starting from the consumption side (residents' social psychological needs and identity symbol construction) and not respecting the community's subject and reality, mechanical "wall demolition" may induce new community governance crises. This aspect has been addressed by the author in "Towards Open Block Spaces: The Privatization of Community Space and Its Breakthrough." However, how is the block system possible? How can it be feasible? In what dimensions does it facilitate the promotion of grassroots social governance innovation? These are more pressing practical issues, and solving these issues involves a systematic project of collaborative advancement of dual-side reforms on both the consumption and supply sides. The author believes the following aspects need consideration.

[10] The author previously pointed out in "Towards Open Block Spaces: The Privatization of Community Space and Its Breakthrough" that, from the governance experience of the West, the governance of closed communities can be summarized into three approaches: the government introducing relevant policies through administrative means to curb the construction of closed communities, planning guidance for closed communities in urban planning, and emphasizing and valuing urban public spaces.

1. How is the Block System Possible

In the author's view, the block system can be a construction of a living entity, an arrangement of institutional settings, or an advocacy of conceptual values. As a living entity, the block system is an important spatial carrier in urban planning and construction. It is important to note that its construction subjects are not only urban managers and planning experts but also residents living in the blocks and social organizations embedded within functional boundaries. This is a process of linkage construction from the internal physical space to the peripheral related subjects, and only in this way does the block system as a living entity have true meaning. As an institutional setting, the block system is an institutional arrangement for urban grassroots social management and services. Of course, to what extent it can be studied and analyzed as a management system for urban grassroots society following the "street-residence system" and "community system" still requires further in-depth reform in practice and scholarly exploration. As an institutional arrangement, how the block system will handle the relationship issues with the original property companies,[11] homeowners' committees,[12] and the community residents' committees whose status may return due to the demolition of walls in residential complexes in future development is a question that needs to be addressed. Especially after obtaining the special legal person status, the residents' committee,[13] with its identity clarification, faces the challenge of precisely defining service boundaries and business scope to effectively connect with the flexible space created after the opening of neighborhoods. This is an unresolved issue that urgently requires an answer. As an institutional setup, its advancement also requires balancing interests between spatial justice and benefit considerations,[14] knowing that the neighborhood system is a reform attempt based on addressing the spatial privatization and social inequality issues caused by closed communities. As a conceptual value, the neighborhood system emphasizes the creation and advocacy of concepts like "openness" and "inclusiveness," embedding them as the soul in the construction of living entities and institutional arrangements, becoming the core distinction of the neighborhood system from closed communities.

2. How the Neighborhood System Can Be

---

[11] I believe that the opening of communities does not mean the complete withdrawal of the original property management companies. As one of the management and service entities of the community, property companies will undergo certain changes and adjustments, but only in terms of the boundaries of their functions and the specific content and form of services.

[12] The homeowners' committee is a type of organization generated by shared property rights, and its function and role must be mediated by public interests and common issues faced, which are also embedded in specific spatial fields. Therefore, after the "demolition of walls" in the community, how this mediation is generated and cultivated is also a topic that requires further consideration.

[13] "Huang Shuxian issued the first national unified social credit code certificate for grassroots mass self-governing organizations and investigated community work," http://www.mca.gov.cn/article/xw/mzyw/201711/20171115006588.shtml.

[14] For research on "breaking down walls and opening up and spatial justice," refer to the series of articles in "Exploration and Free Views," Issue 4, 2016.

Implemented Breaking down walls and opening up refers to two aspects of opening from the closed community itself. Firstly, "new residential areas should promote the neighborhood system," which is an incremental opening; secondly, "already built residential areas and unit compounds should gradually open up," which is a reform of the stock. I am in favor of the former but hold reservations about the latter.

For the former, moving towards open neighborhood spaces is a basic experience and universal path for governing closed communities worldwide, and it is also an inevitable choice under the pressure of traffic network accessibility in China's reality. This means that promoting the neighborhood system in new residential areas is both a governance reference from Western universal experience and a necessity forced by the current situation of urban space governance. However, for the latter, the "opening" of closed communities should be treated differently and advanced gradually. On one hand, not all closed communities need to be opened; on the other hand, the stock reform of closed communities should emphasize methods, progressing step by step, not simply "demolishing walls," but conducting deep reforms with the goal of "enclosed but not closed, separated but not isolated" based on scientific demonstration.In the process of promoting this, there should be specific institutional channels to incorporate residents, homeowners, property management, developers, and other related interest groups into the process of policy demonstration, formulation, and implementation of "breaking down walls and opening up," with particular emphasis on respecting and protecting the interests of homeowners.[15]

Moreover, since the "breaking down walls and opening up" policy is very extensive (estimated to involve over 700 million urban residents) and highly disruptive, its advancement must not be "one-size-fits-all." A more appropriate approach is to gradually achieve reform optimization according to the principles of "pilot first, model demonstration, policy support, and classified advancement." The so-called "pilot first, model demonstration" involves two aspects. One is the pilot of small-scale open neighborhoods. For example, the Pujiang Overseas Chinese Town community in Minhang District, Shanghai, has piloted various models and operates well, and efforts should be made to summarize and refine its operational rules and management norms. The second is the pilot opening of specific types of closed communities. Specific types mainly refer to those with relatively singular and clear property ownership, such as collective or state-owned property units. Government agency compounds, higher

[15] Particularly, Article 73 of the "Property Law of the People's Republic of China" stipulates: "Roads within a building area are owned by the owners, except for urban public roads. Green spaces within a building area are owned by the owners, except for urban public green spaces or those explicitly belonging to individuals. Other public places, public facilities, and property service rooms within a building area are owned by the owners." This means that roads, green spaces, etc., within a closed community are owned by the community's owners, and "breaking walls and opening enclosures" cannot be promoted solely through government administrative intervention. It must also be negotiated and promoted based on compliance with the relevant provisions of the "Property Law of the People's Republic of China" and certain compensation to residents. Zhang Peng (2016) proposed from the perspective of property rights that "breaking walls and opening enclosures" should minimize negative impacts on stakeholders, strengthen the construction of democratic participation procedures in the plan formulation process, and improve damage relief channels.

education institutions, etc., can take the lead in setting an example by opening their public facilities, internal spaces, and resources to the public. These two aspects of the pilot can produce positive demonstration effects. "Policy support, classified advancement" means that "breaking down walls and opening up" is a complex policy agenda with entangled interests, and its practical advancement inevitably requires the assistance and support of various policies, such as policies for classified disposal, compensation and relocation policies, judicial relief, and public participation systems. One of the classification principles here is the nature of property rights, as analyzed above for property units with relatively singular and clear ownership. Property units of a public nature can initially pilot "breaking walls and opening enclosures," while for private property communities with more complex, diverse, and ambiguous ownership, especially those with various entangled interests and historical issues, reforms should be gradually optimized based on thorough argumentation, repeated games, and multi-party participation.

3. Block System and Innovative Social Governance

In fact, the "Opinions" are intended to address the various segregations that occur in closed societies in reality. The effects and inequalities, as well as the negative impacts on urban macro planning, further deepen and promote grassroots social governance innovation. From the original meaning, the block system is a form of urban spatial organization relative to closed communities, with openness as its significant feature; from the value meaning, the block system is an expansion and development of the previous community system and street-residence system, with diversity and governance as its basic value pursuits. This determines the coupling between the open block system and innovative grassroots social governance.

Openness is the process of stepping out of the private domain and into public space. On one hand, the openness of blocks helps break the artificial segregation caused by physical boundaries, facilitates the integration of resources across community boundaries, and promotes interaction and communication among people. It is also an important premise for the development of neighborhood space, public space, and carriers, further encouraging residents to step out of the private domain for exchange and communication, achieving dialogue, consultation, and the resolution of public issues. On the other hand, the openness of blocks breaks the tendency of closure in community public and administrative affairs, facilitating the intensive provision of administrative resources and services, creating possibilities for social organizations to design and provide specialized services at a higher level. This helps bridge the tension between the expectations of social organizations for cross-community boundary interaction and community closure, creating opportunity space for the domain operation and linkage of professional social services and community endogenous organizational activities, overcoming the difficulties of professional social organizations landing, avoiding homogeneous competition with endogenous organizations, and the embarrassment of professional dissolution and inadequacy.

Openness is also the process of stepping out of the individual and integrating into the organization. The atomization of society and the reintegration of individualized society are a basic tension and a key issue that innovative social governance aims to solve. First, the openness of closed communities helps alleviate the psychological distance caused by segregation among residents, easing the tension between the closure of social physical boundaries and the psychological distance segregation of residents, and facilitating the construction of a sense of belonging to the block from both physical space and psychological identity dimensions. Second, the continuous incubation and cultivation of social organizations can provide professional services that cross community boundaries, which will inevitably become an important governance subject in open blocks in the future. One construction standard is that the professional services of social organizations should highly satisfy residents' needs for safety, block belonging, and block culture, which is also an important opportunity and mission for the development of social organizations in the new era, and a crucial focus for alleviating the contradiction between people's growing needs for a better life and unbalanced and inadequate development.

References

Atkinson R, Flint J (2004) Fortress UK? Gated communities, the spatial revolt of the elities and time-space trajectories of segregation. Hous Stud 19(6):875–892

Asiedu AB, Arku G (2009) The rise of gated housing estates in Ghana: empirical insights from three communities in metropolitan Accra J Hous Built Environ 24(3):227–247

Blakely EJ, Snyder MG (1997) Fortress America: gated communities in the United States. Brookings Institution Press, Washington, DC

Coy M (2006) Gated communities and urban fragmentation in Latin America: the Brazilian experience. GeoJournal 66(1):121–132

Dou Y (2004) Returning to the city—some thoughts on the spatial form of residential areas. Archit J 4:8–10

Émile D (2000) The division of labor in society (trans: Qu D). SDX Joint Publishing Company, Beijing [French]

Feng D, Werner B, Zhu H (2011) Gate access communities and neighborhood relations in the context of suburbanization of residential areas: a case study of Guangzhou lijiang garden. Geogr Res 30(01):61–70

Goix RL (2005) Gated communities: sprawl and social segregation in Southern California. Hous Stud 20(2):323–343

Grant J, Katherine G, Kirstin M (2004) The planning and policy implication of gated communities. Can J Urban Res 13(1):70–88

Handel A (2014) Gated/gating community: the settlement complex in the West Bank. Trans Inst Br Geogr 39(4):504–517

He X (2016) Professional responses to grassroots community governance and social work. J Zhejiang Gongshang Univ (04):109–112

Helsley RW, Strange WC (1999) Gated communities and economic geography of crime. J Urban Econ 46(1):80–105

Huang X (2011) The "community nature" of community movements—a response and supplement to current community movement theories. Sociol Res 25(1):41–62, 243–244

Jacobs J (1961) The death and life of great American cities. Vintage, New York

Janoschka M (2002) The new model of the Latin American city: fragmentation and privatization. EURE: Revista Latinoamericana de Estudios Urbano Regionales 28(85):11–29

Jing Z, Zhang J (2006) Residential planning with continuous public space organization as the Main Line. Archit J 4:16–18

Lemanski C (2006) Spaces of exclusivity or connection? Linkages between a security village and its poorer neighbour in a Cape Town master plan development. Urban Stud 43(2):397–420
Madanipour A (2006) Roles and challenges of urban design. J Urban des 11(2):173–193
Manzi T, Smith-Bowers B (2005) Gated communities as club goods: segregation or social cohesion? Hous Stud 20(2):345–359
Merton RK (2001) Social theory and social structure (trans: Lin J). SDX Joint Publishing Company, Beijing [American]
Qin R, Yan X, Cao X (2008) Foreign urban gated communities and their governance. Econ Geogr (3):401–405, 429
Sanchez TW, Lang RE, Dhavale DM (2005) Security versus status? A first look at the Census's Gated Community Data. J Plan Educ Res 24(3):281–291
Song W (2010) Progress in research on gated communities. J Urban Plan 4:42–51
Song W, Zhu X (2009) Negative spatial responses to social differentiation in China's closed communities. Plann 25(11):82–86
Su Z, Lin B (2007) Urban residential space differentiation control: housing patterns and public policies. City Plan Rev (02):45–49
Sun L (2002) Analysis of practical sociology and market transition process. Soc Sci China (05):83–96
Sun K (2004) Research on neighborhood-style urban residential area models. Zhejiang University, Hangzhou
Sun B, Wu Y (2009) Advances and prospects in urban residential space differentiation research in China. Urban Planning 33(06):73–80
Thuillier G (2005) Gated communities in the metropolitan area of Buenos Aires, Argentina: a challenge for town planning. Hous Stud 20(2):255–271
Vesselinov E, Gazessus M, Falk W (2007) Gated communities and spatial inequality. J Urban Aff 29(2):109–127
Xu D, Song W, Zhu X et al. (2009) Formation mechanism and social space effects of closed communities. Urban Probl (07):2–6
Yu K, Zhang P, Zhang Z (2009) The mechanism and development trend of the privatization of urban community space—taking foreign gated communities as research objects. Urban Dev Res 16(6):94–101
Webster C (2001) Gated cities of tomorrow. Town Plan Rev 72(2):149–170
Wilson WJ (2000) The truly disadvantaged: the inner city, the underclass, and public policy. The University Press of Chicago, Chicago
Wu Q, Cui G (1999) Spatial differentiation patterns and formation mechanisms of residential spaces in Nanjing. City Plan Rev (12):23–26, 35–60
Xu M, Yang Z (2008) Controversies, misconceptions and gaps—a study on the current research status of closed residential areas from the perspective of urban design. Urban Plan Int (04):24–28
Zheng Y (2011) Reform and its enemies. Zhejiang People's Publishing House, Hangzhou
Zhong B (2003) Research on urban closed residential areas. Archit J 9:14–16

Chapter 8
Project-Based and Technical Governance: Grassroots Social Governance's Integration Challenges and Structural Dilemmas

8.1 Project-Based: Public Bidding Project-Based Practice and Its Dilemmas

The project system is a core mechanism in current grassroots social governance and an important institutional arrangement in the national governance system. It is an improvement and supplement to the government's bureaucratic system in the new era, a continuation and expansion of the national power construction in the new period in terms of system and mechanism (Jiao Changquan 2019). In 2019, the aim was "to break through the constraints of the original bureaucratic system represented by the unit system through means such as special transfer payments from the national treasury, to curb the differentiation effects caused by the market system, and to increase effective investment in livelihood projects and public services" (Qu Jingdong 2012).It is evident that "the project system is not only a system but also a mechanism that can make the system operate actively; at the same time, it is more of a mindset that determines how the state, social groups, and even individuals construct strategies and tactics for decision-making and action" (Qu Jingdong 2012).

Generally speaking, sociological research on the project system can be divided into two categories.

The first is the study of the project system as a system. Zhe Xiaoye and Chen Yingying (2011) conducted an early systematic analysis of the "project entering the village" phenomenon. They systematically discussed the "contracting mechanism" of higher-level governments, the "packaging mechanism" of local governments, and the "grabbing mechanism" of villages during the "project entering the village" process. Based on this, they presented the tension and game between the logic of centralized control at the higher level and the counter-control logic at the grassroots level. Qu Jingdong (2012) studied the project system from the perspective of the national governance system, considering it a "new dual-track system" in the reform process. Some scholars have studied the project system from the perspective of the public budget system, discovering that the core of the public budget system is

L. Hou, *The Integrated Service in Urban Community Governance*, Public Economy and Urban Governance in China, https://doi.org/10.1007/978-981-96-6775-8_8

the project system, and that the project system, in practice, constructs a comprehensive, vertically integrated project organization network. This network has shaped a new structural form and governance system within the government, growing into an overall governance mechanism that "pulls one hair and moves the whole body" in government operations (Jiao Changquan 2019).

The second is the practical research on the project system. This research direction is currently the mainstream in project system research, mainly analyzing the operational practice of the project system in specific governance fields, involving areas such as the provision of public goods, poverty alleviation, and grassroots social governance in government service procurement. This type of research often takes specific cases during the implementation of the project system as the object of analysis, focusing on the practical results of the project, that is, paying more attention to the "end" of project practice, while relatively suspending the operation mechanism and process of the project within the government (Xun Lili et al. 2007; Feng Meng 2009; Chen Jiajian 2013, 2015; Gui Hua 2014; Huang Zongzhi et al. 2014; Di Jinhua 2015; Fu Wei et al. 2015; Gong Weigang 2015; Li Zupai 2015; Shi Puyuan 2015; Jiao Changquan 2019). These studies have systematically analyzed the project system itself and its operational logic in real practice, providing important knowledge inspiration and experience accumulation for understanding the project system, and have significant value and meaning for understanding grassroots social governance mechanisms.

As an important exploration of local governance, since 2009, Pudong New Area in Shanghai has implemented public bidding projects, taking the lead in introducing the governance concept of the project system into the field of grassroots community governance and services. The aim is to transfer tasks that the government cannot do or do well to social forces by purchasing services from them. Over the past decade, this has gradually explored and formed a public service bidding operation mechanism and practice model. The practice of public bidding projects has significant implications for the transformation of grassroots government governance, the growth and development of social organizations, the optimization of community service systems, and the innovation of community governance mechanisms. Specifically, these achievements are mainly reflected in the following aspects: ① Demonstrating the significance of the system, leveraging the transformation of grassroots government governance; ② Improving resource integration capabilities, cultivating a number of large-scale social organizations; ③ Strengthening professional guidance, optimizing multi-field community service systems in grassroots governance; ④ Stimulating innovation in community governance mechanisms through multi-faceted interaction.

Despite the certain achievements in the practice of public bidding projects in Pudong New Area in recent years, the project-based practice of grassroots social governance still faces a series of structural dilemmas. These are mainly reflected in the following aspects: ① The project-based approach in service procurement may lead to the "suspension" of residents' needs, resulting in blurred governance goals and lost direction; ② Organizational suspension and superficial services, the homogeneous social organization ecosystem may lead to vicious competition and service homogenization, making it difficult to highlight the practical effectiveness of public bidding projects; ③ Fragmented services lack integration, and the advantages and limitations of different social organizations have not formed an integrated service model in urban community governance. to address these issues, a complementary mechanism for effective linkage is needed; ④ The rapid development of social organizations has led to a mix of good and bad, with prominent issues, particularly the governance risks inherent in the operation of unregulated community foundations; ⑤ A large number of endogenous social organizations (community social organizations) lack professional capabilities, and coupled with interest entanglements, may create serious institutional spaces for grassroots rent-seeking and corruption, urgently requiring strong intervention from relevant systems and regulations; ⑥ The depth of community work participation in community governance and the relative lack of professional functions have not been able to integratively stimulate social vitality in grassroots governance, and the formation of governance synergy still needs further exploration, among other issues.

These dilemmas are typically reflected in the following project evaluation. In 2015, the Shanghai RF organization undertook the H Street "Caring for the Elderly" project for disabled (mentally) elderly care services. During the mid-term evaluation, the evaluation agency made important rectification conclusions, mainly including the following issues.[1] First, the selection scope of service objects was too broad, and the project team did not yet understand the individual situations of the current service objects, mixing disabled and mentally disabled elderly during the project implementation, leading to a lack of targeted and effective services. Second, the coverage rate of service objects was too low, the overall project performance was low, covering only 120 service objects, accounting for only 30% of the demand population within the street. Third, various services were overall delayed or insufficient, and there were issues of non-standard operations. According to the expected goals and service content in the project proposal, the evaluation party found that the project implementer was seriously behind on multiple targets. Fourth, there was a certain gap between the knowledge and experience background of the main project staff and the project needs. The social workers at the project site had short working years, lacked project management experience, and insufficient service experience, while the project itself was highly professional, with close links between various services, requiring the handling of multiple social relationships, and the project service precision needed to be ensured, which the member could not handle well. Fifth, the financial compliance was poor. Although the project had independent accounting, it was difficult to reflect the characteristic of special funds for special purposes; the project detailed account summaries were filled in chaotically, unable to correspond with the project final accounts; some expense vouchers were incomplete, lacking detailed lists; some expense vouchers were non-standard; large expenditures did not have purchase agreements signed.

The practice of the Shanghai RF organization undertaking the H Street "Caring for the Elderly" project shows that external professional organizations have insufficient

[1] Cited from the "Mid-term Evaluation Report of the 'Caring for the Sunset Years' Incapacity (Intellectual) Elderly Care Service Project in H Street, Pudong New Area," internal material.

grasp of the needs of relevant groups within the H Street community. During the project implementation, there were issues such as unfocused service objects, weak targeting of service content, weak professionalism of service providers, and non-compliance in financial use. As far as the author knows, the project was "stopped midway" in that year's evaluation, meaning it was forced to stop due to a series of significant defects.

The above phenomena are basically consistent with the evaluation of the project-based practice of public welfare bidding by relevant personnel in H Street, that is, the self-service projects piloted and explored by the street starting in 2015, and the self-service projects continuously carried out in 2016 and 2017, were initially intended because the community public welfare bidding projects carried out in previous years had some obvious problems. For example, although it focused on cultivating social organizations, the entire orientation was centered on social organizations and higher-level governments, with projects as the main consideration, and the application and execution of projects were in a state of segmented operation. Essentially, it was "project-based," without considering the actual needs of grassroots people (this is consistent with the author's previous research findings on bidding). Therefore, the organizations undertaking public welfare bidding projects were not welcomed by the street and residential areas and their residents during specific implementation. As an alternative mechanism to the above services, the street has continuously carried out self-service projects for several years, aiming to actively cultivate community residents' autonomous teams and community backbone forces to carry out projects that meet actual needs, led by the party general branch of the residential area and guided by the neighborhood committee. It can be said that it is precisely because some external organizations entered H Street and failed to effectively land and respond to community needs, thus forming a suspended development logic, causing their governance practice and service functions to fail. In H Street, they prefer to explore more practical self-service projects themselves, with the street setting up special public financial funds, and the residential area autonomous teams applying for projects. From 2015 to 2016, there were 36 autonomous projects, and from 2016 to 2017, there were 36 projects. However, these autonomous fund projects also have problems. The core issue is the insufficient project-oriented thinking, where the packaging, initiation, and execution of projects are informal and non-standardized. Even some projects that did not pass the initiation review appear in later funding stages. This creates a clear tension and paradox, making it crucial to find a balance between technical governance in project operations and social governance in service provision.

In essence, the practice of public welfare bidding projects can be seen as a new governance system mechanism realized through project-based approaches. This practice reflects the application of technical governance in public welfare bidding, highlighting a project production system based on technical rationality. The problem is that technical governance, being efficiency-oriented, often leads to selective neglect of community residents' needs. Coupled with the inertia of bureaucratic systems and the dominance of management thinking, project-based approaches can easily become detached from the community, suspended in the community field. As Qu Jingdong et al. (2009) stated, "A major challenge faced by bureaucratic technical governance mechanisms is how to place a large administrative system above the specific experiences and problems of social and economic life, rather than losing affinity with grassroots society," which is also an issue that needs to be avoided in the process of community public welfare bidding. Research has found that due to the complexity of project contracting, packaging, and capturing, project contractors and capturers find it difficult to interact face-to-face sufficiently. Therefore, it is necessary to rely on third-party bidding agents as packagers to achieve full-process monitoring of project contracting, capturing, and management, reflecting a "dual contracting" project production logic. The fundamental reason for the above results is that the current public welfare bidding adheres to a governance logic based on technical rationality, overly emphasizing technical specifications and information management in practice. Through document control, it hopes to achieve overall regulation of project operations. However, the project-based practice of public welfare bidding is nested within the existing street system, where "standardized, procedural, and technical governance mechanisms often only provide a veneer of procedural legitimacy for the performance goals of the bureaucratic incentive system, while the public needs that the project system needs to respond to are often absorbed by the central work goals of the bureaucratic incentive system, causing a misalignment between the project system and public demand preferences" (Jiao Changquan 2019).

The emergence and existence of the aforementioned series of structural dilemmas actually stem from the tension between the optimization of community services and the rationality of technology. This necessitates further reflection on the practice process of project-based approaches and government service procurement, deeply reflecting on and adjusting the limits and boundaries of technical governance. Consequently, returning to community-based governance and service innovation, fundamentally concerned with the lives of residents (villagers), becomes an inherent part of the topic.

8.2 Suspended Development: Social Organization Participation Practical Dilemmas in Grassroots Governance Social Organizations

As an important dimension in the triadic structure of state, market, and society, are increasingly gaining an indispensable structural position. Over the past five years, social organizations have actively participated in social governance innovation and grassroots construction processes, gaining unprecedented development opportunities and space. The basic strategy of Pudong New Area's streets and towns involves two aspects: on one hand, introducing external professional social organizations to provide professional and supportive services within the jurisdiction; on the other hand, encouraging internal social forces to actively undertake private social service institutions. Additionally, actively cultivating community residents' self-governing teams to leverage their self-governing advantages and the organizational advantages of collaborative participation in community self-governance and co-governance. However, in-depth research has found that some streets and towns still face inherent dilemmas of suspended development in the construction of the entire social organization ecosystem and the exertion of governance functions.

8.2.1 Professional Function Limits of Community Endogenous Social Organizations

Currently, various types of resident teams, quasi-organizations, and community social organizations in grassroots community fields constitute a colorful community landscape and an important force in innovative social governance. In the grassroots community governance of H Street, residents' community public awareness is becoming increasingly strong, forming diverse community social organization systems such as interest-based self-governing teams oriented towards self-entertainment and cultural cultivation, homeowners' committees aimed at safeguarding their rights and interests, and volunteer teams concerned with public welfare issues such as community vulnerable groups and the community environment. According to incomplete statistics, H Street currently has about 210 community self-governing teams, with the vast majority active at the residential area level. During the research process, many community residents' teams... Autonomous teams are involved in the governance system of residential areas. For example, the LY Residents' Committee has more than 10 autonomous teams. These organizations are characterized by openness, interactivity, and cooperation.

Under the leadership of the Party General Branch of the residential area, they participate in multiple affairs such as elderly services, environmental sanitation maintenance, and neighborhood dispute mediation, becoming an important "extra force" in community governance. Under the guidance of social workers from the Residents' Committee, the autonomous teams in the residential area also play a service role for specific groups in the community by participating in the implementation of self-service projects. Combining the actual needs of the community, they have gradually developed a series of community autonomy projects with the H Street brand, such as the "Green Balcony" project, the "Mamma Mia" project, and the "Renhe Studio" project. These projects not only play a demonstrative and leading role in the governance process of the entire street community but also become representative governance cases in grassroots community governance in Pudong New Area.

However, upon in-depth analysis, it is found that most of the existing mass autonomous teams are of a self-entertainment nature, with a serious lack of social, public welfare, and professional attributes. They are more concerned with the needs of their small groups and lack attention to community, public welfare, and public needs outside their groups. This limits the effectiveness and role space of these mass autonomous groups in governance practice. Those groups that can participate in self-service projects promoted by the street have a certain degree of community and public welfare nature. The role played by these teams is more of a daily, basic self-help, and mutual aid service, which holds an important supplementary position for residents. However, an in-depth analysis of more than two years of self-service projects reveals that these autonomous teams still have significant room for breakthroughs in participating in some deep-level issues of community governance and responding to deep-level community needs, which are difficult to achieve in the short term through existing community autonomous teams.

In other words, solely relying on existing autonomous teams and projects, it is still difficult to effectively respond to some deep-level needs and structural problems within the community. This necessitates shifting the focus to other organizational forms.

8.2.2 The Entry Difficulties and Suspended Existence of Professional Social Service

Organizations In the context of government function transfer, social organizations have become an important professional force in the transfer of government functions. Through the mechanism of government purchasing services, on one hand, more organizational carriers have been cultivated for innovative social governance, and on the other hand, the growth of social organizations and the exertion of their professional advantages provide important guarantees for optimizing public services or improving the quality of social services. Based on the needs and motivations of innovative social governance, H Street has also introduced professional social organizations, including some social organizations introduced during the implementation of public welfare bidding projects coordinated by the city and district to provide related community public welfare services, as well as professional support-type social organizations introduced in the process of cultivating their own strength to participate in community autonomy and co-governance, and independent legal person social organizations that have grown and registered within the street itself. In terms of quantity, there are more than 10 social organizations with certain professional characteristics mentioned above.

However, overall, the role limits of external professional social organizations in the local governance field are very obvious, and there are multiple restrictions on the exertion of their professional roles, basically suspended in the community field space. For example, before 2015, some organizations implementing community public welfare bidding projects in H Street caused "additional burdens" on the work of residential areas because they did not adapt to the actual needs of the H Street community and often needed assistance from residential area personnel during project implementation. At the same time, third-party evaluations also found that their service effectiveness was minimal. This indicates that external professional social organizations need to possess a series of important qualities when entering local communities to provide services.

In addition, as a hub-type social organization, the street social service center also faces the issue of how to further de-administrate in practical practice, thereby playing its role in connection, linkage, and capacity building, which becomes a key point for the street social service center to consider next. Moreover, existing social organizations exhibit a high degree of homogeneity in service fields and operational structures. Even in service provision and role exertion, they face obvious convergence and the resulting homogeneous competition. In service provision, they show a logic of being absorbed by the existing system. These organizations also more or less exhibit phenomena such as external service administration, internal governance bureaucratization, and organizational development institutionalization during their operation, which is not conducive to the integration of society through these social organizations. The advantages in areas such as district resources, tapping into community vitality, promoting community trust, and cultivating community public spirit are not conducive to the development of community publicness, as well as the formation of community unity and shared community.

8.3 Identity Tension: Community Workers Unexpected Consequences of Career Advancement

The "1 + 6" document of the Shanghai Municipal Party Committee, specifically the "Shanghai Community Worker Management Measures (Trial)," points out the need to "categorize and standardize grassroots teams and establish a professional system." Among them, community workers refer to full-time employees of employment age who are directly engaged in community management and services in residential areas and streets, towns, and public affairs positions in the city, with all funding guaranteed and managed uniformly by streets and towns (excluding civil servant and public institution staffing). Currently, they mainly consist of full-time staff of community neighborhood committees of employment age, personnel hired by streets and towns, full-time community staff hired by streets and towns, and other personnel included with the approval of district and county party committees and governments. Full-time community staff dispatched by functional departments can be recognized in batches and gradually included. Based on comprehensive factors such as job characteristics, years of service, educational level, and relevant professional level, a job grade sequence for community workers is established. A salary system linked to job grades and performance evaluations is established, with reasonable salary standards set above the average wage level of city employees in the previous year, and dynamically adjusted according to the growth of the average wage of city employees. Channels for outstanding community workers to enter government agencies and public institutions are opened, with priority given under equal conditions. In the actual grassroots governance process, some outstanding neighborhood committee secretaries have gradually been transferred to relevant public institution or civil servant staffing, while community neighborhood committee directors have entered the staffing sequence, becoming true system insiders. This initiative can be said to be pioneering nationwide, attracting attention and imitation from many other provinces and cities across the country, including mega-cities like Shenzhen, which have learned from and emulated Shanghai's approach. However, this approach now appears to have produced significant unexpected consequences.

Firstly, the loss of flexibility after being included in the staffing, along with the accompanying identity transformation, can eliminate the initiative and enthusiasm of community workers in their work. Previously, grassroots community workers outside the system, when operating within the system, could have their work enthusiasm and initiative greatly stimulated and mobilized through the pressure-type system's layer-by-layer transmission by the streets. However, after the identity transformation of neighborhood committee workers, their identity within the system effectively satisfies their need for stability as a "halo," which leads to the elimination of mobility. The movement of community workers between different communities, especially between different neighborhoods (villages), becomes difficult, which is not conducive to the exchange and interaction of workers between neighborhoods (villages), nor to the exchange and introduction of urban community governance concepts and experiences into rural communities. In fact, the current significant gap in community governance between urban and rural areas in Pudong New Area can be narrowed through such a rotation and exchange form, but the channels for exchange between urban and rural areas for community workers after being included in the staffing are almost locked. At the same time, the thinking and working methods within the system also render traditional mobilization mechanisms ineffective, and with the shift of the service focus downward, the importance and flexibility requirements of grassroots work inevitably create a certain tension with the fixed nature of the system identity, which is not conducive to the full play of community workers' work enthusiasm and initiative.

Secondly, the identity difference between community cadres (secretaries and directors) and general community workers may create factors that are not conducive to the integration of community forces. In grassroots research, some community workers indeed reported: "The 'No. 1 Topic' of the Municipal Party Committee is a good thing for grassroots community self-governance and co-governance, but the current differentiated treatment of grassroots workers in the document may bring some negative consequences. For example, in the same residential area, only the (residential area) secretary can enjoy this (public institution staffing) treatment, while the deputy secretaries or neighborhood committee directors do not have this treatment, which may lead to psychological imbalance." Since the two identities coexist in the same community field, the identity difference between them is further amplified by the "zero-distance" vacuum effect, causing identity segregation between the two groups, which is not conducive to the formation of integrated community forces and the achievement of self-governance and co-governance.

Thirdly, the issue of professionalism among community workers exists in both groups, causing further segregation. In recent years, the state has vigorously promoted the professionalization and vocationalization of grassroots community workers nationwide, encouraging grassroots community workers to take the national social worker professional level examination and other forms."Certification for Employment" aims to enhance one's professionalism and work effectiveness. These initiatives are also being vigorously implemented in H Street. Among the 336 community workers in the street, 119 have passed the national social work professional level exams (including junior and intermediate levels), accounting for about 35.4% of the total number of community workers on the street. However, does passing the exam equate to professionalism? In fact, through surveys and interviews with grassroots community workers, it was found that over 90% of their time and energy is spent handling administrative tasks assigned by higher authorities, with very little professional practice that truly responds to residents' needs using professional methods. This creates a paradox: the state promotes the professionalization of grassroots community workers through mandatory institutional logic, using certification as the main means. However, in reality, community workers cannot change their long-standing administrative work content and model, leading to a clear tension between the professionalization process and grassroots governance practice.

This means that the research did not find a direct linear correlation between certification and professionalism. Instead, there is a clear division and conflict around professionalism among different entities in the community field. For example, community workers do not recognize the work of professional social organizations, and professional social organizations look down on community workers, considering them unprofessional. The previously analyzed lack of sociality in endogenous social organizations and the difficulty for professional social organizations to enter and establish themselves are somewhat related to this issue.

8.4 Dual Governance: The Gap of Imbalance and Insufficiency in Urban and Rural Community Development and Services Community

Governance and service innovation is a gradual process, resulting from the shift in governance focus at a certain stage of economic and social development. The different positions of urban and rural areas in the progression of economic and social development inevitably determine the gap in community governance and services. From the basic situation of the streets and towns in Pudong New Area, there is indeed an imbalance in development and governance in urban and rural community governance, presenting a clear "dual governance" landscape.

Firstly, there is a "hierarchical difference" in governance concepts. There is a "hierarchical difference" in governance concepts between urban and rural community governance, mainly manifested in the different states of existence of the "governance" concept in urban and rural areas. On one hand, there is a "consensus existence of governance" in urban communities, with governance and related concepts such as diversity, resident participation, consultation, autonomy, and "bottom-up" frequently appearing in official documents and policy texts. In street and urban community research, "governance" and related elements have deeply influenced the thinking and practices of leaders, community workers, and resident backbones, genuinely affecting their community actions. On the other hand, in rural communities, there is a "sporadic appearance of governance," with "management" and stability, as well as "top-down" thinking and vocabulary of cadres, frequently appearing in official summaries, reports, and opinion texts. Of course, this is indeed influenced by different problems and environmental factors faced by urban and rural areas. However, even from the perspective of leaders and workers responsible for community governance in towns, the dominant thinking is management rather than governance, administration rather than service. This "hierarchical difference" in concepts inevitably affects the practical reality of community governance.

Secondly, there is a "dual separation" in governance practice and effectiveness. Under the influence of the aforementioned "dual hierarchical difference" in governance concepts, urban and rural community governance in Pudong New Area has also formed a "dual separation" in practice advancement and effectiveness results. After the release of Shanghai's "Number One Project," Pudong New Area streets achieved significant breakthroughs in system reform. Firstly, there was a clear social shift in governance focus from the organizational structure. This is reflected in the transition from the original functional system to the new "6 + 2" organizational structure. Secondly, the "bottom-up" strategy of transferring government functions. The main approach was to cancel the original investment promotion function of the streets and instead strengthen their social service functions, returning to the public service, public management, and public safety attributes of the streets. Finally, community governance and service innovation were also included as important indicators in bureaucratic assessment incentives, which stimulated and mobilized the positivity of grassroots governance and service shifts, resulting in a plethora of community governance projects, cases, experiences, and practices in streets and communities. In contrast, the governance of towns' residential (village) areas did not see the simultaneous advancement of this series of systematic and systemic measures, creating a temporal, systemic, and institutional disparity between urban and rural areas, which is, of course, an unavoidable development progression and strategy. However, in reality, it has indeed caused an imbalance in urban and rural community governance. The insufficient development and asynchronous advancement of community governance and service innovation at the town level are evident. Therefore, how to further achieve urban–rural collaboration in community governance and services, how to selectively apply urban community governance concepts and experiences to rural communities, and how to achieve a "curve overtaking" in rural community governance in the new phase, especially preventing the widening gap in urban–rural community governance practices, are all directions that require further practical exploration and theoretical research.

In essence, grassroots community governance and service innovation in Pudong New Area also face a series of structural dilemmas. This dilemma is actually due to the asynchrony between the community as a "national governance unit" and the community as a "regional social community" in urban community governance. Community governance faces dual tensions between administration and autonomy, burden reduction and efficiency enhancement, and demand orientation and project-based approaches. The "new dual structure" in urban–rural community governance leads to inefficiency, lack of innovation, and difficulties in multi-stakeholder collaboration in urban community governance. As pointed out by Li Xiyuan (2018), "Although both the government and social work organizations highly value project performance, when the government strives to pursue technical governance methods, these methods tightly bind the social work teams undertaking the projects, making them busy coping with the government's technical governance process, weakening their investment in professional services, and gradually blurring the goal of local governments introducing social work professional services to achieve community governance. Community technical governance gradually becomes a 'myth' in the reform."

Overall, the experience of urban–rural community governance in Pudong New Area is more scattered, fragmented, and even isolated and closed, which to some extent causes community governance and service innovation to often fall into difficulties in terms of service effectiveness, governance innovation, and overall coordination. Therefore, it is necessary to construct a new model of community-based integrated social work services.

References

Chen J (2013) Project systems and grassroots government mobilization—a sociological examination of project–based social management. Soc Sci China (02):64–79, 205

Chen J (2015) Rethinking the structure of urban community governance in China—from the perspective of collaborative governance theory. J Wuhan Univ (Philos Soc Sci Ed) 68(1):71–76

Di J (2015) Policy burdens, information oversight, and reverse soft budget constraints—an explanation of local government organizational behavior in project operations. Sociol Stud 30(06):49–72, 243

Feng M (2009) Township governments' project packaging behavior in the post-agricultural tax era: a case study of northeast talahe town. Society 29(04):59–78, 225

Fu W, Jiao C (2015) "Coordinative" regime: township governments under project-based operations. Sociol Stud 30(02):98–123, 243–244

Gui H (2014) Analysis of project system and rural public goods supply system—taking agricultural land consolidation as an example. Politl Sci Res (04):50–62

Gong W (2015) Project-based governance and externalities in food production. Open Times (02):103–122, 5–6

Huang Z, Gong W, Gao Y (2014) Is the operational mechanism and effectiveness of "Project-Based" governance "Rationalization"? Open Times (05):143–159, 8

Jiao C (2019) From tax-sharing system to project system: institutional evolution and organizational mechanism. Society 39(6):121–148

Li Z (2015) The pragmatic dilemmas of project-based grassroots practices and their explanations—from the perspective of national autonomy. Polit Sci Res (05):111–122

Li X (2018) The myth of community technical governance: the dilemma of government project management and social work services. J Lanzhou Univ (Soc Sci Ed) 46(3):33–39
Qu J (2012) Project system: a new state governance system. Chin Soc Sci (5):113–130, 207
Qu J, Zhou F, Ying X (2009) From overall domination to technical governance—a sociological analysis based on 30 years of reform experience in China. Chin Soc Sci (6):104–127, 207
Shi P (2015) Bureaucracy as substance, projects as application: an organizational study of central project operations. Society 35(05):25–59
Xun L, Bao Z (2007) Government-Mobilized environmental policies and their local practices—a sociological analysis of ecological resettlement in inner Mongolia's S Banner. Soc Sci China (05):114–128, 207
Zhe X, Chen Y (2011) Project-based hierarchical operation mechanism and governance logic—a sociological analysis of the "Projects into Villages" case. Soc Sci China (04):126–148, 223

Chapter 9
Governance Community: Construction of Community-Based Integrated Service Model

The Fourth Plenary Session of the 19th Central Committee of the Communist Party of China proposed that "social governance is an important aspect of national governance. It is necessary to strengthen and innovate social governance, improve the social governance system led by the Party committee, with government responsibility, democratic consultation, social coordination, public participation, legal protection, and technological support, and build a social governance community where everyone has responsibilities, fulfills responsibilities, and enjoys benefits." Thus, the concept of community is linked to the academic field's research on "community" and the practical promotion of "community," attempting to integrate and unify the "community as a national governance unit" and the "community as a regional social life community." The exploration in practice also provides important inspiration and experience, especially since the release of the "No. 1 Project" by the Shanghai Municipal Party Committee, Shanghai's exploration in grassroots community governance has initially formed a model of grassroots social governance that features positive interaction between government governance, social regulation, and residents' autonomy, as well as community-based optimization of residents' (village) life.

However, as analyzed earlier, there are still some factors hindering the modernization of the social governance system and governance capacity in the current exploration of grassroots social governance, resulting in the "single soldier advance" style of reform not being effectively connected, and the synergy effect of governance innovation not yet appearing. Therefore, how to further deepen and advance grassroots social governance in the new era? How to construct and respond to the aforementioned obstructive factors and actively promote the construction of a community governance community, thereby achieving co-construction, co-governance, and sharing based on multi-party participation? In reality, the construction of a community governance community and the integrated service model based on it, as well as the exertion of governance functions in the community field, become the key to addressing the above issues, and subsequently, the key to promoting the modernization of grassroots social governance.

L. Hou, *The Integrated Service in Urban Community Governance*, Public Economy and Urban Governance in China, https://doi.org/10.1007/978-981-96-6775-8_9

9.1 The Real Dilemma of Grassroots Social Governance

Although the exploration of grassroots social governance in Shanghai in the new era has achieved relatively significant results, there are also obvious structural and institutional dilemmas. Firstly, the fragmentation and atomization of grassroots social governance are prominent, and there are institutional dilemmas in horizontal linkage and learning from each other. This is typically manifested in the production and reproduction of the "pairing competition" (Huang Xiaochun 2019) mechanism between different streets and towns, and different sectors, leading to the innovation achievements and experiences of grassroots social governance being locked in a "field lock" state, difficult to replicate and promote in different fields, with the social benefits of innovation achievements after multiple resource and policy inputs being significantly insufficient, and the cost of governance innovation remaining high, causing doubts about its sustainability. In grassroots society, there is a significant amount of "demonstrative governance," where innovation in practice fields shows a clear "goal substitution." This means that in grassroots social governance, there is a lot of innovation for the sake of innovation, with "innovation" itself becoming the goal of governance. The needs of community residents and their aspirations for a better life are suspended, ignored, or nested within "innovation," leading to numerous highlights and brands in grassroots social governance. However, the governance performance shows a "diminishing marginal effect," with no improvement in residents' satisfaction or sense of gain, forming an "innovation paradox." Thirdly, there is a risk of "ideologization" in technical governance within grassroots social governance, typically manifested as technocratic management thinking and technocratic authoritarianism, causing people to disappear from the governance space in grassroots fields. Governance in grassroots society thus evolves into a movement lacking subjectivity. With the strengthening of grid management and the support of big data and the internet as the governance focus shifts downward, "technology" is deified, becoming a "constant" in monitoring residents' daily lives in social governance, further reinforcing the governance mindset in grassroots society.

9.2 Community-Based Integrated Social Governance Services

The integrated advancement of the "Shanghai Model" requires further adherence to "cooperative co-governance" based on the "division of labor between government and society," deeply promoting and practicing the organic integration of party building and social governance, achieving mutual advancement and enhancement of institutional innovation and professional teams. This is also a "political logic led by party building, a service absorption logic with the governance focus shifting downward, and a life logic of selective participation" (Wu Xiaolin 2019), a composite governance logic that coexists simultaneously. It realizes people-centered development amid the continuous downward shift of the social governance focus and the strong cultivation of social organizations. Its typical feature is community-based and integrated services.

Community-based is a value concept, as well as a methodology and ontology in a holistic sense. Community-based means that "community" should become the basic unit and starting point of grassroots social governance and services, where different subjects engage in diverse interactions centered on public issues and public affairs of the community. The leading role of party building is crucial, especially in achieving the organic coupling of party building and social governance. In reality, with the continuous downward shift of the governance focus and the comprehensive strengthening of party leadership in the "community field," a new era of organic unity between party leadership and multi-subject governance has actually begun. Social governance must achieve the unity of party leadership, legal governance, and the participation and co-construction of diverse social subjects. Researchers are increasingly focusing on the role of party organizations in community or social governance and are striving to academicize this phenomenon. Indeed, party organizations are a unique organizational element in China's community system, and the party's organizational power and integration power are deeply meaningful concepts. In the community, party organizations "construct tasks," "promote systems," and "mobilize manpower," almost "omnipotent." This characteristic is a sample for understanding the characteristics of the Chinese system and has extremely important value and significance for creating a community life community, achieving the integration of various forces, and service linkage.

In fact, the community field provides the spatial background for the convergence and interaction of the party, state, and society. Xie Chuntao (2011) systematically sorted out the specific practices in the successful governance experience of the Communist Party. Based on this sorting, more academically strong analytical frameworks have been formed, such as the "party, state, and society" or "party-government-society" analytical frameworks. Lin Shangli (2001) studied the general relationship between the party, state, and society, while Jing Yuejin (2005) studied the manifestation of the relationship between the party, state, and society in rural governance practice. This means that compared to the party, state, and society framework, the "party-government-society" framework is more suitable for analyzing social governance issues. The research and practice of "community-based" have become a key driver for the gradual popularity of the "party-government-society" analytical framework. Especially now, it is necessary to maintain sufficient sensitivity and reflection on the overall state of "party-government integration," systematically study and sort out the process of integration and legitimacy reconstruction achieved through services, which is of great significance and should be an important research content under the "community-based" methodology.

In the perspective of integrated governance, grassroots community governance mainly refers to two dimensions. One is the construction of a community-based integrated service model. Based on different practical explorations in various places, it is necessary to integrate and connect the theoretical paradigm, practical advancement, methods and techniques, service foundation, and action strategies of community governance in terms of subjects, mechanisms, resources, methods, logic, and effects, achieving model integration.The unification of process integration and element integration. Secondly, the practical advancement of integrated services in community governance requires strengthening the Party's organizational power, integrating multiple theoretical paradigms, uniting various entities, adopting diverse methods, breaking professional boundaries, and reconstructing service processes to achieve effective integration and co-construction, co-governance, and shared governance of grassroots social governance by the Party.

Specifically, the proposal of integrated services for urban community governance is precisely based on correcting the previous phenomena of fragmentation, individualization, and atomization in community governance. However, it is not a simple amalgamation of multiple entities, strategic logic, and experiential practices within the community domain. Instead, it is a comprehensive framework based on a new service concept, logic foundation, and service process, changing previous service strategies and methods.[1] It is a reconstruction of governance that encompasses all elements, processes, and domains.

Urban community governance integrated services first focus on the localization of community governance, not services directed by the government or innovation, but community-based service integration oriented towards residents as a whole. Governance strategies and practical logic are embedded in the daily life habits of residents, flexibly unfolding as integrated services directly constrained by the specific scene structure and endowments within the community domain.

Urban community governance integrated services advocate for a partnership relationship, recognizing that although different entities in urban communities have different positions, they share a collaborative and cooperative relationship in terms of purpose and goals. Different entities jointly negotiate to solve the difficulties and problems faced by the community, achieving community development and community building.

Urban community governance integrated services aim to promote a strengths-based or community-based empowerment service. Adhering to an "internal community" perspective, it focuses on empowering community residents, comprehensively utilizing project-based and networked external systems and mechanisms to increase and activate the endogenous stock of community organization participation and resident mobilization. It designs targeted, specific integrated services based on the dynamic development and changes in community needs. The purpose of the service is not to help the community eliminate problems and return to a problem-free community life, but to assist the community and residents in finding methods and techniques to enhance their ability to cope with internal and external environmental challenges, emphasizing process goals and capacity building. Of course, this includes enhancing

[1] Tong Min (2016) summarized the experience of Western project services into four aspects: scene-based, cooperative relationships, capability-based, and teamwork. This analysis of integrated services for urban community governance draws on this line of thinking.

the ability to solve community problems and strengthening the ability to link and integrate resources.

Urban community governance integrated services uphold an integrated teamwork approach. Teamwork includes three basic connotations. (1) It is a team working method that emphasizes cross-professional collaboration, requiring the participation of professionals in social services such as social workers, as well as professionals from fields like law and journalism, and experts from practical fields. (2) It is a team working method that focuses on the collaboration between professionals and non-professionals. This includes professional social workers (community workers with social work certificates) and non-professional localized community workers, resident backbones, and volunteers. It also includes quasi-community social organizations (such as cultural and sports teams, interest groups) providing basic mutual and self-beneficial services, as well as community social organizations and professional social work service agencies providing refined, individualized professional services. Professional and non-professional organizations and individuals are jointly committed to constructing a governance community. (3) It is a team working method that emphasizes the joint participation of professionals and community residents. The identity and function of "experts" are limited to certain fields and aspects of community governance, with clear boundaries related directly to the expert's profession. What is particularly valued is the identity of community residents as local experts, which runs through all processes and aspects of community governance and services.

In summary, urban community governance integrated services start from the specific governance scenarios of the community, using an integrated teamwork approach to advocate for cooperative and strengths-based positive constructive service integration and reconstruction. This service model emphasizes the dynamic coupling and matching linkage of service supply, service integration, demand structure, and governance situation. It is also an integration of governance entities, strategies, and innovative elements serving the community in specific domains.

9.3 Strategies for Advancing and Developing Community Governance Integrated Services

From the perspective of the community of social governance, social governance faces difficulties in constructing a governance community, such as the imbalance of social policies, unequal distribution of benefits, and the lack of resident service demands. Therefore, it is necessary to achieve the equalization of public services and innovative holistic governance. It is essential to strengthen the organizational power of the Party, integrate multiple theoretical paradigms, unite various stakeholders, adopt multiple methods, break professional boundaries, and reconstruct service processes. The continuous advancement should focus on optimizing resident-centered services and integrating grassroots social governance services. In essence, the strategy for advancing integrated community governance services is a precise response and correction to the dilemmas and issues of new community governance innovation.The advancement strategy of integrated community governance services is essentially the specific practice and innovative advancement of the integrated service model of community governance.

9.3.1 Correcting the Value of Project-Based Technical Governance

The analysis in Chapter 8 shows that the project-based logic of public bidding and government service procurement may lead to the "suspension" of resident needs and a series of issues such as formalized and relational operations of service projects, resulting in blurred goals and lost direction in grassroots social governance. Therefore, community-based and resident-centered governance and service innovation should become important principles in grassroots governance to correct "project-based operations" and the technical governance based on it. Specifically, on one hand, the "community" in grassroots social governance is a "community of life" for residents, not just a "basic unit of grassroots governance." This means that the community is the basic space for residents to support each other and live daily, the basic source for nurturing resident needs, reconstructing social capital, and achieving a better life, and the field for the downward shift of social governance focus, as well as an important area for service delivery and community public development. On the other hand, it is necessary to clarify that the project system is the basic organizational mechanism for public service provision in current grassroots social governance, existing as a means rather than an end of governance. The design and operation of projects need to aim at meeting resident needs and optimizing their lives, setting up a people-centered system to achieve a dynamic and sustainable response to resident needs. This requires a conceptual reshaping, where the advancement of projects and grassroots social governance innovation should aim at optimizing the lives of residents.

9.3.2 Transition from Suspended Development to Embedded Governance

Social organizations, as an important force in promoting the disintegration of the unit system and social organization, have an indispensable function in participating in the social governance process. In advancing community governance, Shanghai highly values the role of social organizations, creating conditions to build an organizational system combining external professional social organizations, endogenous social organizations, and mass autonomous teams. However, the development of social organizations also presents a suspended dilemma of the limited professional functions of endogenous community social organizations and the entry difficulties of external professional social service organizations. Therefore, the awareness of "separation and cooperation between government and society" should be further strengthened. Based on sorting out the public management, public safety, and public service functions of the street, a series of list systems should be formed, including the necessary responsibilities list of the government, the list of functions that can be transferred out by the government, and the list of services purchased by the government from social forces. This clarifies the governance tasks within the street that require the participation of social organizations, as well as the necessary social organization categories, scale, service fields, and service advantages. In other words, under the guidance of the concept of "division and cooperation between government and society," the street can clarify its attributes through existing function sorting, then transfer functions that meet market principles to market operations, and services suitable for social organizations to social forces, forming a clear grassroots social governance pattern of "cooperation and orderly division of labor among grassroots government, enterprise organizations, and social organizations."

In reality, various complex factors may constrain the role and status of social organizations, which have not yet been emphasized and highlighted, and even the legitimacy of social organizations has not been effectively recognized, leading to unstable phenomena such as "up and down fluctuations" or "sometimes loose, sometimes tight" in national or local government policies related to social organizations. The author believes that under the premise of Xi Jinping's Thought on Socialism with Chinese Characteristics for a New Era established by the 19th National Congress of the Communist Party of China, grassroots governments should further consider the structural position of social organizations in the grassroots governance system in combination with their governance goals, innovate social organization-related institutional guarantees within their institutional space, and orderly advance the cultivation of social governance work, nurturing a diverse range of types and capable social organizations. A relatively strong and distinctive system of social organizations, particularly the construction of a social organization service system under the leadership of party building at the grassroots level, aims to form a closed loop of linkage and service.

A key measure in this regard is for the government to proactively strengthen and maintain the ecosystem of social organizations. The ecosystem indicators of organizations refer to the diversity of organization types in a region, the need for an organizational chain for development, and the complex yet orderly relationships between organizations. If the relationships are singular, it indicates that the development stage of social organizations in the region is still at a primary level. The capability of social organizations and their ecosystem become key indicators for assessing the development status of social organizations in a region, while the ecosystem of social organizations plays an important shaping role in the capability and function of social organizations.

Specifically, the street can further strengthen support and promote the following four types of organizations based on the existing foundation.

(1) Emphasis should be placed on the creation of hub-type social organizations. Currently, the street has established a street social organization service center to provide supervision and support services to relevant social organizations within the jurisdiction. However, according to the current operational logic of the city's street social organization service centers, they essentially remain government-run NGOs, whose specific operations must rely on strong administrative power, which inevitably leads to administrative logic. Therefore, it is not conducive to leading the development of other social organizations with characteristics such as professionalism, sociality, and public welfare. Combining the viewpoint of Ma Yili, former director of the Shanghai Civil Affairs Bureau, the current hub-type social organizations are merely "hubs" without the "link" function. If they cannot "de-administrate" and "de-power," it will be difficult to truly form hub-type organizations that are beneficial to the development of social organizations. Such organizations are also prone to becoming "second governments[2]". Therefore, the attribute positioning of hub-type social organizations should be "social" organizations, playing the "hub" function.
(2) Emphasis should be placed on the cultivation and development of professional social service organizations. Currently, H Street has two parts of such organizations: one part is external professional social organizations, including those related to public bidding and tendering by the street, as well as professional social work agencies entrusted by the street to carry out self-service project assistance plans and community worker empowerment plans; the other part is internal social service organizations, which have grown within the street's jurisdiction. From the perspective of organizational governance structure, these organizations currently lack formal, full-time professional teams and have not yet demonstrated strong professionalism. Moreover, some endogenous social organizations still receive annual funding allocations from the street. For internal social service organizations, there are some obvious drawbacks and risks in the actual operation process. Therefore, during interviews, they have consensually expressed the hope to shift their relationship with the street from "funding" to a contract system in the future, which is also to eliminate the path dependence and administrative consequences of these endogenous social organizations. In the future, further promotion of mutual communication and linkage between internal and external social organizations should be encouraged, creating more conditions for external social organizations to enter the jurisdiction and effectively land in the community, reducing the street's power subject's exclusion of external social organizations. At the same time, leveraging the professional advantages of external professional social organizations, forming an "internal–external linkage" organizational alliance to guide the capacity building and professional brand creation of endogenous social organizations. Only in this

[2] With reference to the special speech on "Social Organizations and Third-Party Evaluation" given by Ma Yili at the second third member meeting of the Pudong New Area Public Welfare Organization Project Cooperation Promotion Association held on September 27, 2017, the material is for internal use only.

way can the dilemma of "external organizations unable to land, internal organizations unable to do things well" be changed. The street should further create conditions to promote mutual empowerment and complementary advantages among social organizations, as professional social service organizations are the core entities truly undertaking the transfer of government functions. If this part of the entity cannot grow, it will seriously hinder the process of street social governance.

(3) Promote the transformation of mass autonomous teams into organizations with community, public welfare, and social characteristics. Among the existing 200 or so autonomous teams in H Street, some have already participated in affairs with community public welfare and autonomy, and to a certain extent, have played a role in responding to residents' needs, promoting resident participation, and enhancing community cohesion. However, overall, the current mass autonomous teams in the community generally face the following three dilemmas. One is the participation of personnel… The phenomenon of aging is severe. As volunteers and members of various community self-governing teams participate in some community public affairs, there are risks in terms of safety and other aspects. However, the current system has not yet established a good accidental insurance system for active elderly community members. Secondly, the existing community self-governing teams are highly homogeneous, making it sometimes difficult for them to assist with the complex and diverse community issues. Thirdly, due to the unclear legal positioning of community groups, they find it challenging to act effectively under the guidance of existing policy frameworks, especially lacking clear guidance on how self-governing teams can continuously participate in community self-governance and co-governance issues on the basis of self-entertainment, thereby forming an organizational system characterized by community, public welfare, and community public nature. Therefore, for the considerable number of existing community self-governing organizations, streets can further classify and guide them, strengthen the typological guidance and development of community social organizations, and focus on cultivating some self-governing teams that can address the needs of vulnerable groups in the community, such as families who have lost their only child, elderly people living alone, impoverished families, and families with disabled members. Such self-governing teams may initially be unable to provide appropriate services, which necessitates the introduction of external professional social organizations into street governance. Through "internal and external linkage" and the linkage of "formal and informal" social organizations, an organizational network system conducive to providing diversified community services can be formed. This organizational network system helps build community public spirit.

(4) Introduce third-party supportive social organizations in a timely manner to play their role in promoting construction through evaluation. In addition to the aforementioned types of organizational forms, supportive social organizations should also become an important component of the street social organization ecosystem. Currently, professional third-party evaluation agencies, which adhere to principles of fairness, objectivity, professionalism, and science, play

a more obvious role in providing professional support by independently evaluating services purchased by the government from social forces. For example, in recent years, H Street has strengthened the use of public finances to purchase social services, especially through the practice of self-service projects via the autonomy fund project, and has achieved some outstanding results. However, there are still some limitations when external professional support organizations guide H Street community self-governing organizations in carrying out projects: firstly, external professional social organizations have not deeply connected with the system and mechanism innovation of promoting community self-governance and co-governance in the street, thus playing more normative functions; secondly, due to the limitations of the nature of self-governing organizations themselves, their ability to participate in self-governance and co-governance practices is limited. Based on this, the function of third-party supportive social organizations should be strengthened. First, incorporate the community self-governing organizations, self-service projects, and other social organizations undertaking government functions within the street jurisdiction into the core governance agenda of the street, promoting their evolution in a direction conducive to modernizing the street governance system and governance capacity during the support and guidance process. Second, based on practice, form a network system that promotes the linkage development of professional social organizations and community self-governing organizations, further realizing the absorption of community self-governing organization members in the service provision of professional social organizations, providing resources for demand gatekeeping and relationship connection; at the same time, when self-governing teams carry out related self-governance projects, in addition to existing party-building instructors, members of professional social organizations can also be invited to serve as supervisors of self-governing teams or self-service projects, promoting the professionalization, standardization, and systematization of self-governing teams and self-governance projects. Third, in addition to playing the role of promoting construction through evaluation, supportive social organizations should also play a role in leading social innovation, that is, through the combination of research and evaluation, support, and supervision processes, reflect on problems in practice, extract experiences from practice, and bidirectionally promote the problems and experiences in practice to become important supports for guiding community governance innovation.

9.3.3 Resolution of Two Types of Identity Conflicts and Tensions in Grassroots Communities

This tension and potential conflict mainly stem from the systemic identity of the neighborhood committee secretary and director being different from the non-systemic identity of general community workers, essentially due to the disparity caused by different treatments and promotion spaces of the two identities. The development of the aforementioned social organizations as an increment and the emergence of the first grassroots mass self-governing organization with special legal person status nationwide, the neighborhood committee, provide a new opportunity for resolving the identity tension of neighborhood committee personnel. On one hand, based on professional development, further strengthen the professional capacity building and enhancement of grassroots governance teams. From a professional perspective, the further smoothening of the career advancement channel for community workers, the continuous strengthening of the status of social organizations, and their importance in grassroots community governance will largely bridge the gap of systemic identity. On the other hand, solidify the positioning of social organizations, further promoting the shift of the focus of social governance to the grassroots. The establishment of the status of the neighborhood committee as a special legal entity may bring new opportunities for its development. This requires neighborhood committee workers to actively respond and enhance their professional capabilities so that the neighborhood committee can play a greater role as an important contractor for government-purchased services in the process of shifting the focus of social governance downward. In this process, the identity of general community workers also facilitates playing a greater role, thereby addressing a series of issues that existed in the previous round of neighborhood committee reforms, especially the solidification effects brought about by systemic identity, which can be gradually resolved.

9.3.4 The Immense Tension Arising from the Juxtaposition of Diverse Governance Forms Needs to Be Dissipated

In the context of urban community governance, the enormous tension generated by the juxtaposition of diverse governance forms needs to be alleviated. The advancement of urban and rural community governance on different tracks also requires mutual learning and experience integration, which demands adherence to a brand-new concept of urban and rural community governance to achieve integrated development in the overall planning of urban and rural areas. Therefore, the simultaneous advancement of streets and towns needs to be strengthened. For example, due to the large number of streets and towns in Pudong New Area and the vast regional area, regional development is very uneven. Community governance and service innovation have achieved certain results at the street level, but the various towns in the near and far suburbs still need to advance simultaneously based on summarizing the street exploration experience. From the actual situation of the research, there is a significant gap between streets and towns in grassroots social governance and serving the masses. Some towns' social governance concepts are not yet fully in place and are still in the initial stage of social governance. This stage difference between streets and towns may provide important "latecomer advantages" and "opportunity spaces" for the leapfrog development of social governance in streets and towns.

Firstly, establish a linkage mechanism between streets and towns, advocating pairing and one-on-one assistance between streets and towns with similar conditions and a certain cooperative foundation, with particular emphasis on the "decisive participation" of street (village) level cadres in town (village) work, planning and guiding their community governance and innovation, and even implementing a concurrent or exchange work mechanism. Secondly, within the streets and towns themselves, an exchange and interaction mechanism can be first realized between communities (villages) at different development stages, making exchange a norm and an important reference for the assessment and promotion of community (village) cadres and street and town cadres. Thirdly, to fully diffuse the results of governance innovation and services, consider using the "Top Ten Innovation Cases" selection as a platform to host community forums on different themes, allowing governance experiences and service measures to achieve full dialogue and exchange, and on this basis, transform into specific actions for the practical work of street and town cadres and social workers. Fourthly, establish a community governance practice expert database. At the district level, through expert evaluations, resident representative discussions, and other forms, select a group of experts in the field of community governance practice around community governance practices, work ideas, methods, and effectiveness, forming a "think tank" for grassroots governance in Pudong New Area, which can be entrusted to a professional third-party think tank to operate, aiming to optimize and integrate intellectual resources and drive the coordinated advancement of urban and rural social grassroots governance.

Additionally, based on the particularity and stage of rural community governance, it is especially important to prevent: when the focus of governance shifts downward and resource services sink, some action subjects become interdependent, forming a profit-sharing order, excluding ordinary people, and leading to the involution of rural governance (Chen Feng 2015). It is crucial to prevent the continuous generation and reproduction of profit-sharing orders and grassroots governance involution in rural areas.

9.3.5 The Integration of Fragmented Grassroots Governance with Community-Based Services

(1) Strengthen the leadership and integration of party building, further guiding grassroots autonomy and community co-governance. The party's functions mainly focus on two aspects. One is integration, and the other is order, which is fundamental to constructing a governance community. The party in social governance is a unique cross-domain integrating force and is central. However, development cannot rely solely on this single element or force; otherwise, vitality will be insufficient. From the experiences across the country, it is evident that the

grassroots are very lively, and the community is bustling, with various forces and subjects having their space and venue within the community. But if the party's element is absent, the establishment of order, the direction of development, and other aspects may encounter certain problems, namely integration dilemmas. The party, whether from the perspective of order, integration, or development, has significant institutional advantages, which determine that it is inevitably the core and key to constructing an integrated service model for urban community governance.

From the innovative practices of the Shanghai model, it is suggested to establish a specialized regional Party-building committee to further leverage the guiding value and resource integration role of regional Party-building. By adhering to the combination of vertical and horizontal structures, with a focus on the latter, resources should be directed from vertical lines to regional clusters, accelerating the construction of a regional Party-building work system characterized by "Three Connections and Three Transformations" (multi-core linkage, multi-level interaction, multi-party alliance, networked organizational setup, mechanized resource integration, and normalized party member roles). It is essential to maintain and improve work carriers such as "visiting thousands, listening to tens of thousands" and public sentiment archives, striving to build a work system that connects and serves the masses. Encouragement and promotion of active exploration by various streets and towns in the co-discussion and co-governance of public affairs are necessary.

(2) Streamline the relationship between vertical and horizontal responsibilities, further innovate the operational mechanism of streets and towns. Further implement the reform of the street and town systems, effectively shifting the focus to social governance and serving the people. Develop a power operation map for district-level functional departments interfacing with streets and towns, further improving the vertical and horizontal operational mechanisms. Establish and improve work mechanisms to ensure the efficient operation of the new street and town systems, formulate specific and operable implementation methods, further optimize and perfect the preparations for the grassroots to undertake the shift of governance focus downward, and grant streets and towns the authority to assess personnel and obtain consent for the heads of district functional departments' dispatched agencies, enabling the grassroots to have both responsibility and authority, achieving the simultaneous downward shift of governance focus, service focus, and resource allocation.
(3) Focus on joint operations and interactions, further promote the integration role in service integration through big data and cloud platforms. It is necessary to fully develop and utilize information technology in grassroots social governance, with the understanding that technology is a means and approach to serve residents' needs, and its use should be embedded in the process of meeting the needs of residents (villagers). Accelerate platform construction to achieve dynamic collection and full coverage of community governance public opinion, improve

mechanism construction, and enhance problem discovery and handling capabilities. Promote the standardization and normalization of institution construction and operation. At the same time, be adept at using "Internet + " technology and thinking, integrating resources from various departments and lines, encouraging resident participation in development and interactive communication, improving the social development supervision mechanism, and achieving "no blind spots in information collection, no exceptions in resource sharing, and no barriers in interconnectivity."

(4) Optimization and reconstruction of systems and mechanisms in the construction of grassroots social governance communities. This is the key to achieving subject interaction and model integration, mainly referring to the horizontal and vertical dimensions of order linkage and coordination.[3]

Firstly, the horizontal order coordination mechanism. The horizontal order coordination mechanism is an open coordination mechanism based on multiple centers. The significant feature of this mechanism is that it is a consensus order based on multi-party "agreement" formed after equal consultation among different interest groups, organizations, and strata, resulting from democratic consultation. Of course, the operation of such a horizontal order coordination mechanism in the community also relies on some important conditions. Firstly, the basic premise of this mechanism is the existence of relatively independent multi-party subjects in community governance, which, due to the differentiation of interests, present as independent groups. Secondly, the coordination of these multi-party forces has relevant supporting systems and policies, and there are also positions and norms for different subjects in the community. Finally, the subjects participating in horizontal consultation should have rational expectations, understand other subjects, and possess the basic mental qualities for compromise, i.e., the mental ability for rational mutual gaming. From this perspective, these preconditions are not yet fully met in the current grassroots society, making it difficult to establish a horizontal order coordination mechanism, or even if established, it operates with very low efficiency, leading to insufficient social collaboration.

Specifically in the community, this horizontal order coordination mechanism refers to the process where diverse groups based on different interest demands, under certain self-positioning and normative constraints, mutually compromise and game to reach a "consensus." Based on this understanding, the focus of constructing a community governance community in the new era should be on the construction of two platforms. One is the platform for interest demands. This mainly refers to the institutionalization and regularization of the pathways and channels for expressing the interests of community participation subjects. For example, community Consultative councils, interaction and communication of residents' public opinion needs,

[3] Li Youmei (2012) analyzed the mechanism composition of social management from the two dimensions of horizontal order coordination and vertical order integration, which offers theoretical insights. This study primarily borrows Li Youmei's meso-level analysis approach to analyze the optimization and reconstruction of systems and mechanisms in the construction of grassroots social governance communities.

etc. This is the foundation and prerequisite for establishing a horizontal order coordination mechanism. Secondly, the construction of a public platform for interest games. In the reality of community governance, there are significant differences between various entities due to their different natures and positions. For example, groups such as street offices and community committees have strong organizational and gaming capabilities due to traditional governance inertia; in contrast, community non-governmental organizations and community residents are in a disadvantaged position and can only be passive in their games with the former, making the so-called horizontal order coordination mechanism merely formal. Therefore, it is necessary to establish a public platform for interest games to transform those "individualized voices" into "collective expressions," which is conducive to the establishment of a fair coordination mechanism and ultimately beneficial to community governance. This is the guarantee and key to establishing a horizontal order coordination mechanism.

Secondly, the vertical order integration mechanism. The vertical order integration mechanism is a top-down command coordination mechanism based on a unitary power foundation. Its significant feature is a hierarchical bureaucratic management structure and a relatively closed vertical command system, which is a "top-down" "bureaucratic consensus." Li Youmei's research points out that there are three important prerequisites for the operation of the vertical order integration mechanism in the community. First, there is a vertical, top-down resource allocation system. Wherever such resource allocation exists in the community, the strength of vertical integration will be greater, and the space for horizontal coordination will be smaller. Second, the main "uncertainties" in community development can be relatively accurately estimated and effectively controlled. Third, many demands in social life can be incorporated into a relatively standardized track. On this basis, the vertical order integration mechanism can more efficiently mobilize resources and meet the needs of the vast majority of social members.

The vertical order integration mechanism in the community mainly refers to the "top-down" power domain existing in the community. The relationship between different entities is more of a superior-subordinate administrative affiliation, and the consensus reached is merely a "collusion" formed by the orders of superior departments and the unconditional obedience of subordinates. Based on this understanding, the focus of constructing the vertical order of the community governance community should largely be on finding a rational path in practice to restrain the unlimited self-reinforcement of the vertical order integration mechanism and effectively connect the vertical order integration mechanism with the horizontal order coordination mechanism. It is necessary to continuously promote public participation and form effective social consultation, while stimulating social In the study of constructing an integrated service model in urban community governance, it is crucial to strengthen the legitimacy of vertical order integration while stimulating internal vitality and participation, achieving effective social integration, which is the key to the effective delivery of integrated services in grassroots society and the key to community construction. Essentially, this mainly refers to the reshaping of the relationship between the state and society. The state should act where necessary and refrain where not, while society actively develops and achieves coordination with the state. To this end, coordination and integration at three major levels must be achieved. First, the collaborative integration between government departments, including goal collaboration, work collaboration, and resource collaboration, integrating the powers and work of district-level government functional departments, street offices, and community committees into a government collaborative force that plays an important guiding and leading role in community construction; second, the collaborative integration between community units and between community residents, including the integration of residents' needs, community development goals, community construction projects, internal and external community resources, and interests, ultimately forming a community collaborative force from the independent unit, organizational collaborative force, and dispersed residents' collaborative force to play a leading and core role in community construction; finally, further connecting and integrating the government collaborative force after vertical integration and the community collaborative force after horizontal integration, achieving a constructive coordination network of crisscrossing in the community "field," ultimately forming a community construction dynamic mechanism and internal pattern of the community governance community characterized by "party leadership, government responsibility, democratic consultation, social collaboration, public participation, legal protection, and technological support" (Xia Xueluan 2002).

In summary, the construction of an integrated service model in urban communities is key to advancing the achievement of a social governance community. It is necessary to examine the needs of grassroots social governance within the context of national governance modernization. The construction of a community governance community is not a government action, nor is it purely a civil activity, but a process of joint participation and democratic consultation by various community entities and social forces. It is a process of forming a governance structure in the community field by different entities, elements, and links, requiring a series of vertical and horizontal constructions and linkages of systems and mechanisms to enable different entities in community governance to collaborate and form The synergy of community governance, thereby promoting the construction of a community governance community.

References

Chen F (2015) The order of profit distribution and the involution of grassroots governance: the logic of rural governance under the background of resource input. Society 35(3):95–120

Jing Y (2005) Party-state-society: three-dimensional relationships—characteristics of chinese politics from Grassroots practices. J Central China Normal Univ (Human Soc Sci Ed) (02):9–13, 29

Li Y (2012) Problems encountered in the new pattern of social management in China—a perspective based on mesoscopic mechanism analysis. Acad Mon 44(7):13–20

Lin S (2001) Leadership and governance: a political analysis of the transformation of party-state-society relations. Mao Zedong and Deng Xiaoping Theory Res (06):37–44

Tong M (2016) The professional logic of project services: the indigenous path of social work professionalization. Soc Work 3(25–32):124–125

Wu X (2019) Integration of governance power, service devolution, and selective participation: the "composite structure" of urban community governance in forty years of reform and opening-up. Chin Public Adm 7:54–61
Xia X (2002) Discussion on the theoretical framework of community construction in China. J Peking Univ (Philos Soc Sci Ed) 1:127–134
Xie C (2011) Why can those who have committed serious mistakes still gain the support of homo Sapiens?. Party Life (Heilongjiang) (07):52–55

Postscript

The practice of integrating community governance services is advancing in depth. This book, as a study and reflection on community governance practices at a certain stage, bears a distinct mark of the times. It is a realistic reflection and theoretical reflection on the process of shifting the focus of social governance in Shanghai to the grassroots, under the theme of "innovating social governance and strengthening grassroots construction." The construction of the integrated service model for community governance is also refined in practice. This book's theoretical reflection and critique of the internal logic of community governance have a clear constructive reflexivity, serving as a review, reflection, and summary of my long-term research on community studies. These are its characteristics, but also its limitations. The mutual construction of developing practices and constructing models in the community field presupposes a richer future for community governance research. Therefore, this book, as a record and witness of the times, hopes to enhance people's understanding and comprehension of community governance practices during this stage.

This book is based on the community governance practices in Shanghai, as indicated by its subtitle "Taking the New Round of Grassroots Governance Reform in Shanghai as an Example," especially since the "No. 1 Project" reform by the Municipal Party Committee, which has seen governance innovation practices in multiple neighborhoods in Shanghai. Therefore, I sincerely thank the civil affairs systems of various neighborhoods in Shanghai, the leaders of multiple streets and towns, and the predecessors and peers in the field of community governance research for their substantial assistance in the research and data collection process for this book. I also thank the community secretaries, directors, and community workers involved in the research for providing specific, vivid grassroots practice experiences and wisdom.

Thanks to many teachers and friends! Throughout the entire process of topic selection, discussion, writing, and completion of this book, I am especially grateful to Vice President Baijun Wu of East China University of Science and Technology for his repeated encouragement, support, and help; to Dean He Xuesong of the School of Social and Public Administration for his care and assistance during the writing of the manuscript; to Deputy Director Tang Youcai of the Humanities and Social Sciences Department for providing much help during the research in various districts and

L. Hou, *The Integrated Service in Urban Community Governance*, Public Economy and Urban Governance in China, https://doi.org/10.1007/978-981-96-6775-8

streets of Shanghai; and to Associate Professors Xu Xuanguo and Feng Meng for providing some empirical data support during the completion of the manuscript.

Thanks to East China University of Science and Technology Press and the editors for their diligent, responsible, and professional editorial work on the manuscript.

It is deeply regrettable that Professor Xu Yongxiang, my mentor, has passed away. The community development and social governance at our school is also an academic tradition initiated by my esteemed teacher Xu Yongxiang. Some chapters of this book are also the result of collaboration between my teacher and me. I still remember the scene when the teacher gifted me the book "Community Development Theory," with his earnest teachings still echoing in my ears. As a student, I am determined to continue to delve deeply and forge ahead along the academic tradition established by my teacher. In remembrance!

References

Asiedu AB, Arku G (2009) The rise of gated housing estates in Ghana: empirical insights from three communities in metropolitan Accra. J Hous Built Environ 24(3):227–247

Atkinson R, Flint J (2004) Fortress UK? Gated communities, the spatial revolt of the elities and time-space trajectories of segregation. Hous Stud 19(6):875–892

Bai Y, Zhang X, Zhang Y (1995) Investigation on strengthening the construction of neighborhood committees in Gudong street. China Civil Affairs (07):16–17

Blakely EJ, Snyder MG (1997) Fortress America : gated communities in the United States. Brookings Institution Press, Washington D. C

Blandy S, Parsons D, Sheffield (2013) Gated Communities in England: rules and rhetoric of urban planning. Geogr Helv 58(4):314–324

Breitung W (2012) Enclave urbanism in China: attitudes towards gated communities in Guangzhou. Urban Geogr 33(2):278–294

Brinkerhoff DW (1999) Exploring state-civil society collaboration : policy partnerships in developing countries. Nonprofit Volunt Sect Q 28(4):59–86

Bu W (2004) Is it moving towards community autonomy or establishing a community governance structure—reflections on the goal positioning of urban community construction in China. Theory Reform 6:58–61

Cai F (2016) Solving difficult issues in the field of people's livelihood with the "People-Centered Development Philosophy". Lab Econ Res 4(3):3–15

Cao H (2015) Research on urban grassroots community governance based on coupling theory. Exploration 6:93–97

Chen F (2015) The interest-dividing order and the involution of grassroots governance: the logic of rural governance under the background of resource input. Society 35(3):95–120

Chen G (2014) Research on the coupling of formal and informal politics in the process of local government innovation—taking public security microblogs as an example. J Public Adm 11(2): 60–69, 141–142

Chen J (2010) Corporatism and contemporary chinese society. Sociol Stud 25(02):30–43+243

Chen J (2013) Project systems and grassroots government mobilization—a sociological examination of project-based social management. Soc Sci China (02):64–79, 205

Chen J (2015) Rethinking the governance structure of urban communities in china—a theoretical perspective based on collaborative governance. J Wuhan Univ (Philos Soc Sci Ed) 68(1):71–76

Chen Y (2005) The boundary between administrative power and autonomous organization behavior urgently needs clarification. China Reform (05):35–36+71

Chen J, Lin D (2015) Practical exploration and theoretical reflection on the consultative governance model of urban communities—observation of community governance innovation in Nanshan District, Shenzhen "One Core, Multiple Elements." Soc Gov 1:84–92

L. Hou, *The Integrated Service in Urban Community Governance*, Public Economy and Urban Governance in China, https://doi.org/10.1007/978-981-96-6775-8

Chen J, Lu C (2009) General social capital and specific social capital—social capital and grassroots governance in Chinese cities. Sociol Stud 24(6):87–104, 244
Chen J, Zhang Q, Hu Y (2015) The evolution of inter-governmental power relations in project systems: mechanisms and impacts. Society 35(05):1–24
Chen W (2000) The Transformation of urban grassroots social management system: from unit management model to community governance model—A study on the target model, institutional innovation, and feasibility of community construction in Jianghan district, Wuhan. Theory Mon (12):39
Cheng X, Sun B (2017) Rethinking institutional design in community governance from the perspective of social capital. Chin Public Adm 4:53–58
Coy M (2006) Gated communities and urban fragmentation in Latin America: the Brazilian experience. Geo Journal 66(1):121–132
David E (1993) The political system—an inquiry into the state of political science (trans: Ma Q). Commercial Press, Beijing [American]
Deng Z (2008) The state and society: a study of chinese civil society. Peking University Press, Beijing
Di J (2015) Policy burdens, information oversight, and reverse soft budget constraints—an explanation of local government organizational behavior in project operations. Sociol Stud 30(06):49–72, 243
Ding H (2015) The application and limitations of the "State and Society" analytical framework—centered on research in sociological discourse. Sociol Rev 3(5):15–23
Ding Y (2013) The value significance and instrumental significance of the community—exploration of community construction and community governance. China Governance Review 2:24–41
Dou Y (2004) Returning to the city—reflections on the spatial morphology of residential areas. Archit J (4):8–10
Émile D (2000) The division of labor in society (trans: Qu D). SDX Joint Publishing Company, Beijing [French]
Erhard F (2008) Power and rules—the dynamics of organizational action (trans: Zhang Y). Gezhi Press, Shanghai People's Publishing House, Shanghai [French]
Evans PB, Rueschemeyer D, Skocpol T (1985) Bringing the state back in. Cambridge University Press, London
Fei X (1996) Academic self-reflection and reflection: collected works of Fei Xiaotong. SDX Joint Publishing Company, Beijing
Fei X (2009) Chinese gentry (trans: Zhao X, Qin Z). Life Reading New Knowledge Sanlian Bookstore, Beijing
Fei M (2001) Homeowners' committee and civil society in China. J East China Univ Sci Technol (Soc Sci Ed) (02):57–64
Feng M (2009) Township governments' project packaging behavior in the post-agricultural tax era: a case study of northeast talahe town. Society 29(04):59–78, 225
Feng D, Werner B, Zhu H (2011) Gate access communities and neighborhood relations in the context of suburbanization of residential areas: a case study of guangzhou lijiang garden. Geogr Res 30(01):61–70
Ferdinand T (1999) Community and society (trans: Lin R). Commercial Press, Beijing [German]
Fu W, Jiao C (2015) "Coordinative" regime: township Governments under project-based operations. Sociol Stud 30(02):98–123, 243–244
Gao B (2001) Folk rituals and the presence of the state. J Peking Univ (Philos Soc Sci Ed) 1:42–50
Ge T (2014) Community fragmentation and community governance. Tsinghua University, Beijing
Geng J, Yao H (2011) The production and reproduction of administrative power—a case study of the direct election process of the J neighborhood committee in Shanghai. Sociol Stud 26(3):153–178, 245
Gerry S, Hua F (1999) Governance as theory: five arguments. Int Soc Sci J (Chin Ed) (1):19–30
Goix RL, Vesselinov E (2015) Inequality shaping processes and gated communities in US western metropolitan areas. Urban Stud 52(4):619–638

Goix RL (2005) Gated communities : sprawl and social segregation in Southern Caliofrnia. Hous Stud 20(2):323–343
Gong W (2015) Project-based governance and externalities in food production. Open Times (02):103–122, 5–6
Gooblar A (2002) Outside the walls: urban gated communities and their regulation within the British planning system. Eur Plan Stud 10(3):321–334
Grant J (2005) Planning responses to gated communities in Canada. Hous Stud 20(2):273–285
Grant J, Katherine G, Kirstin M (2004) The planning and policy implication of gated communities. Canadian J Urban Res 13(1):70–88
Gu D (2016) The connotation interpretation and logical deduction of 'Three-Sector Linkage'. Academia Bimestris (03):104–110
Guan X (2017) Analysis of the objectives and overall welfare level of china's current social policies. Soc Sci China (06):91–101
Gui Y (2008) Neighborhood space: actions, organization, and interaction at the urban grassroots. Shanghai Bookstore Publishing House, Shanghai
Gui H (2014) Analysis of project system and rural public goods supply system—taking agricultural land consolidation as an example. Polit Sci Res (04):50–62
Gui Y (2007) Neighborhood politics: strategies for power operation at the urban grassroots and the adhesion model of state and society. Society (6): 102–126, 208
Han Z. Innovating social governance and strengthening grassroots construction is crucial to the overall reform and development of Shanghai [EB/OL] (2014 02 26) [2019 12 25]. http://shzw.eastday.com/shzw/G/20140226/u1ai124704.html
Han Z. Listens to the report on the "number one research topic" [EB/OL]. (2014 05 9) [2019 12 25]. http://sh.people.com.cn/n/2014/0509/c357908-21169655.html
Han Z. Continuously deepen innovation in grassroots social governance [EB/OL]. (2017 03 27) [2019 12 25]. http://sh.people.com.cn/n2/2017/0327/c134768-29925238.html
Handel A (2014) Gated/gating community: the settlement complex in the West Bank. Trans Inst Br Geogr 39(4):504–517
He H (2010) Harmonious community: report on the construction of harmonious communities in Shanghai. Xuelin Publishing House, Shanghai
He H (2006) Research on urban communities in china under the framework of the "State-Society" Paradigm. J Shanghai Adm Inst (4):96–106
He H (2003) The Evolution of urban grassroots social management systems in China: from the danwei system, street-residence system to the community system. Manag World (6):52–62
He X (2016) Professional responses to grassroots community governance and social work. J Zhejiang Gongshang Univ (04):109–112
He Y, Wei X (2016) Social governance collaborates with social work: the formation of governance techniques and art combining rigidity and flexibility. J Zhejiang Gongshang Univ (04):113–116
He Y, Cai H (2005) The "involution" of China's urban grassroots autonomous organizations and its causes. J Sun Yat-sen Univ (Soc Sci Ed), (5): 104–109, 128
Helsley RW, Strange WC (1999) Gated communities and economic geography of crime. J Urban Econ 46(1):80–105
Hua W (2000) The return from the Danwei system to the community system—50 years of changes in China's urban grassroots management system. Strategy Manag 1:87–100
Huang Z (2008) Simplified governance of centralization—China's semi-formal grassroots administration focused on quasi-officials and dispute resolution. Open times 2:10–29
Huang X (2011) The "community nature" of community movements—a response and supplement to current community movement theories. Sociol Stud 25(1):41-62, 243–244
Huang X, Zhou L (2019) "Pairing competition": a new mechanism for innovation in urban grassroots governance. Society 39 (5): 1–38
Huang Z, Gong W, Gao Y (2014) Is the operational mechanism and effectiveness of "project-based" governance "rationalization"? Open Times (05):143–159, 8

Huang D (2010) Multi-pronged governance strategies: a historical perspective on state building and grassroots governance changes. Public Adm Rev 3 (4): 111–140, 204–205

Huang X. Leading Shanghai's social governance innovation with party building [EB/OL]. (2019-06-04) [2019-08-05]. http://www.whb.cn/zhuzhan/xueren/20190604/267719.html

Huttman ED, Blauw W, Saltman J (1991) Urban housing segregation of minorities in Western Europe and the United States. Duke University Press, Durham

Jacobs J (1961) The death and life of Great American Cities. Vintage, New York

Janoschka M (2002) The new model of the Latin American city: fragmentation and privatization. EURE: Revista Latinoamericana de Estudios Urbano Regionales 28(85):11–29

Jiang X (2014) Innovation in social governance systems in the process of national governance modernization. Chin Public Adm (2):24–28

Jiang Z (2005) Community governance from the perspective of social capital. Henan Soc Sci (4): 30–33, 58

Jiao C (2019) From the tax-sharing system to the project system: institutional evolution and organizational mechanisms. Society 39(6):121–148

Jing Z, Zhang J (2006) Residential planning with continuous public space organization as the main line. Archit J 4:16–18

Jing Y, Liu C (2007) Direct election of neighborhood committees and urban grassroots governance—an analysis of the 2006 direct elections of neighborhood committees in shanghai. Fudan J (Soc Sci Ed) (1):132–140

Jing Y (2014) From purchasing services to collaborative governance—forms and development of government-social organization cooperation. Chin Public Adm (7):54–59

Jing Y (2005) Party-state-society: three-dimensional relationships —— characteristics of chinese politics from grassroots practices. J Central China Normal Univ (Human Soc Sci Ed) (02):9–13, 29

Jing Y (2003) Administrative democracy: significance and limitations—The enlightenment from Wenling's "Democratic Deliberation Meetings". Zhejiang Soc Sci(01):27–30

Jing Y (2005) The party, the state, and society: The relationship among the three dimensions—characteristics of chinese politics from the perspective of grassroots practices. J Central China Normal Univ (Human Soc Sci Ed)(02):9–13+29

Jing Y (2019) Bringing the party back in—reflection and reconstruction of the state-society relationship framework. Explor Free Views(08):85–100+198

Joel M (2013) The state in society: how states and society change and compose each other (trans: Li Y, Guo Y). Jiangsu People's Publishing House, NanJing[American]

Kang X (2005) Analysis of economic development issues in a harmonious society. Acad Exch (07):64–68

Kang X (2011) An analysis of brand building as the core competitiveness for the development of private enterprises—a case study of suning appliance. Econ Res Guide(20):49–51

Lemanski C (2006) Spaces of exclusivity or connection? Linkages between a security village and its poorer neighbour in a Cape Town master plan development. Urban Stud 43(2):397–420

Li X (2014) One core, multiple elements: Nanshan's exploration of rule of law at the grassroots level. Natl Gov 24:34–41

Li Q, Ge T (2013) Fragmentation of the community—an empirical study on community construction and urban social governance in Y city. Acad Circles (12):40–50, 306

Li H (2008) Village governance in North China—the state and rural society in the Late Qing and Republican Periods (trans: Sui Y, Wang S). Zhonghua Book Company, Beijing [American]

Li X (2018) The myth of community technology governance: dilemmas in government project management and social work services. J Lanzhou Univ (Soc Sci Ed) 46(3):33–39

Li Y (2007) Community governance: the micro-foundation of civil society. Society (2):159–169, 207

Li Y (2012) Issues encountered under the new pattern of social governance in china—a perspective based on meso-mechanism analysis. Acad Mon 44(7):13–20

Li Z (2015) The Pragmatic dilemmas of project-based grassroots practices and their explanations—from the perspective of national autonomy. Polit Sci Res (05):111–122
Li Y (2008) Promotion strategies for the professionalization of social work in china. Soc Sci Res (05):109–114
Li T (2001) Community development and resident participation. Hubei Soc Sci (12):69–70
Li Y (2014) Exploring effective pathways for social work to intervene in social governance innovation. Soc Work Manag 14(03):23–28+98
Li Y (2015) Reflections on Shanghai's new round of grassroots social governance reform. China Inst Reform Manag (08):28–29
Li Y (2017) New connotations and actions in China's social governance. Sociol Stud 32(06):27–34+242
Li J (2003) Community construction: Broussonetia papyrifera building China's civil society. J Hum (03):137–141
Li Y (2016) Analysis of grassroots social governance innovation in China's Megacities. J Party Sch Cent Comm C.P.C. (Chin Acad Gov) 20(02):5–12
Liang P, Yao Y (2004) Analysis of the development trends of administrative organizational models in the information age. Seeking Truth (S1):24–25
Lin S (2002) Community: the strategic space for China's political construction. Mao Zedong and Deng Xiaoping Theory Res 2:58–64
Lin S (2003) Community democracy and governance: case studies. Social Sciences Academic Press, Beijing
Lin S (2001) Leadership and governance: a political analysis of the transformation of party-state-society relations. Mao Zedong and Deng Xiaoping Theory Res (06):37–44
Liu X (2006) Comparison of urban community governance models and China's choice. Soc Res 2:59–61
Liu J (2008) The modern political party in social construction—new trends in the evolution of the social attributes of political parties and the resulting party-society relations. Learn Explor 6:103–106
Liu J (2014) The historical evolution of the Chinese communist party's view on social subjects since the founding of the People's Republic. J Wuhan Univ (Philos Soc Sci Ed) 67(5):45–52
Liu J (2016a) Community China: consolidating the foundation of national governance through communities. J Shanghai Univ (Soc Sci Ed) 33(6):73–85
Liu J (2016b) On the construction of new relations between the Chinese communist party and society in the new era. Soc Res 2:68–74
Liu J (2017) Social orientation: the logical premise for constructing new party-society relations. Theor Explor 1:110–116
Liu A (2015) A study on the state-society relationship in contemporary urban china and its theoretical reflections—an analysis from the perspective of political sociology. Sociol Rev 3(5):24–37
Liu X (2006) A comparison of urban community governance models and china's choice. Soc Stud (2):59–61
Liu Ye (2003) Public participation, community autonomy, and deliberative democracy: an analysis of public interaction behaviors in an urban community.Fudan J Soc Sci Ed(05):39–48
Liu Y, Lin M (2014) Formal and informal politics in the budget process: a case study of a special fund in province. A Public Adm Rev 7(4): 112–132, 185
Liwen H, Zhang B (2014) Grid management and separation of residence and station: logic, dilemmas, and reflections. Acad Forum 37(12):102–108
Liwen H (2016) "State and society" in grassroots social governance: changes, current situation, and reflections. J East China Univ Sci Technol (Soc Sci Ed) 31(4): 9–16, 24
Low SM (2008) Incorporation and gated communities in the Greater Metro-Los Angeles Region as a model of privatization of residential communities. Home Cult 5(1):85–108
Ma W, Gui Y, Luo T (2008) The state-society perspective in urban community studies: limitations, experiences, and developmental possibilities . Acad Res (11):62–67, 159
Ma Y (2008) Ritual interaction and the cohesive power of core values. Explor. Free Views (04):6–7

Ma Z (2001) Urban community autonomy is a growth point of socialist new democracy. J Beijing Admin Inst (01): 8–10
Ma L (2003) On institutional support for sustainable development. Theory J (04):117–118
Ma Q. What are the development ideas for social organizations in China during the 13th five-year plan? [EB/OL] (2015 05 11) [2019 12 25]. http://theory.people.com.cn/n/2015/0511/c40531-26980444.html
Madanipour A (2006) Roles and challenges of urban design. J Urban Des 11(2):173–193
Manzi T, Smith-Bowers B (2005) Gated communities as club goods: segregation or social cohesion? Hous Stud 20(2):345–359
Michel C, Erhard F (2007) Actors and systems—the politics of collective action (trans: Zhang Y). Shanghai People's Publishing House, Shanghai [French]
Michel C (2008) The bureaucratic phenomenon (trans: Zhang Y). Gezhi Press, Shanghai People's Publishing House, Shanghai [French]
Min X (2009a) The dual segmentation and evolution of community autonomy subjects. Sociol Stud 24(1):162–183, 245
Min X (2009b) Research on community power and prestige of residents' committees during the transition period. Society 29(6): 22–38, 222–223
Pierre C (2005) The broken democracy—a treatise on the revolution of governance (trans: Gao L). SDX Joint Publishing Company, Beijing [French]
Prasenjit D (2010) Culture, power, and the state: rural North China, 1900–1942 (trans: Wang F). Jiangsu People's Publishing House, Nanjing [American]
Pu X (1998) Reform trends in the management system of Megacity urban districts—also on the concept of "Two-Level Government, Three-Level Management". Polit Sci Res(03):53–58
Pudong Street and town social organization service centers achieve full coverage [EB/OL]. (2017 11 14) [2019 12 25]. http://mini.eastday.com/mobile/171114093552199.html
Qin R, Yan X, Cao X (2008) Foreign urban gated communities and their governance. Econ Geogr (3):401–405, 429
Qu J, Zhou F, Ying X (2009) From overall control to technical governance: a sociological analysis based on 30 years of china's reform experience. Soc Sci China (6):104–127, 207
Qu J (2012) The project system: a new national governance mechanism. Soc Sci China (5):113–130, 207
Robert King M (2001) Social research and social policy (trans: Lin J). SDX Joint Publishing Company, Beijing [American]
Robert Dale P (2001) Making democracy work (trans: Wang L, Lai H). Jiangxi People's Publishing House, Nanchang[England]
Sanchez TW , Lang RE , Dhavale DM (2005) Security versus Status? A first look at the Census' s Gated Community Data. J Plan Educ Res 24(3):281–291
Shanghai Municipal Party Committee conference on innovating social governance and strengthening grassroots construction held [EB/OL] (2016 02 17) [2019 12 25]. http://www.shanghai.gov.cn/nw2/nw2314/nw2315/nw4411/u21aw1105715.html
Shi F (2010) Homeowners' committee, quasi-faction politics and grassroots governance—a case study of a shanghai neighborhood . Sociol Stud 25(3): 136–158, 245
Shi P (2015) Bureaucracy as substance, projects as application: an organizational study of central project operations. Society 35(05):25–59
Skocpol T (2008) Bringing the state back in: retrospect and prospect The 2007 Johan Skytte Prize Lecture. Scand Polit Stud 31(2):109–124
Song D (2017) Community governance in transitional China: the cornerstone of national governance. Fudan J (Soc Sci Ed) 59(3):172–179
Song W (2010) Research progress on gated communities. Urban Plan Forum (4):42–51
Song W, Zhu X (2009) Negative spatial responses to social differentiation in china's closed communities. Plann 25(11):82–86
Su Z, Lin B (2007) Urban residential space differentiation control: housing patterns and public policies. City Plan Rev (02):45–49

Sun K (2004) Research on the neighborhood-style urban residential area model. Zhejiang University, Hangzhou

Sun L, Wang H, Wang S (1994) Social structure transformation in china since the reform. Soc Sci China (02):47–62

Sun L (2002) Analysis of practical sociology and market transition process. Soc Sci China (05):83–96

Sun B, Wu Y (2009) Advances and prospects in urban residential space differentiation research in china. City Plan Rev 33(06):73–80

Sun L (2002) Practical sociology and the analysis of market transition process. Soc Sci China (05):83–96

Sun L (2003) Stereotyping - excerpt from "New Trends in the Evolution of China's Social Structure Since the 1990s". South Rev (06):25

Tang R (2015) Innovation in community governance and the reconstruction of grassroots social governance models. Exploration 6:150–153

Tang H (2008) Returning to political buffer: a rational examination of the functional evolution of china's petition system in contemporary times. Wuhan Univ J (Philos Soc Sci) (04):573–579

Tang Y, Chen X (2003) Community autonomy: The return and promotion of grassroots democracy in urban society. Acad Circles (06):7–22

Thuillier G (2005) Gated communities in the metropolitan area of Buenos Aires, Argentina: a challenge for town planning. Hous Stud 20(2):255–271

Tian Y, Lü F (2009) The end of unit society and its social risks. J Soc Sci Jilin Univ 49(6):17–23

Tong M (2016) The professional logic of project services: the local path of social work specialization. Soc WorK (3):25–32, 124–125

Tong S (1997) The temporal characteristics of civilized communities. Society (09):26

Vesselinov E, Gazessus M, Falk W (2007) Gated communities and spatial inequality. J Urban Aff 29(2):109–127

Wang M (1997) Small places and big society—community observation of Chinese society. Sociol Stud (1):88–98

Wang Q (2015) Departmental game in administrative law enforcement: a typological analysis. Polit Sci Res 2:69–78

Wang J (2015) The construction of cooperative governance's broussonetia papyrifera: the formation mechanism of positive interaction between government and society . Polit Sci Res (4):98–105

Wang P (2014) The meanings and interrelationships of state governance, government governance, and social governance. J Chin Acad Gov 2014 (3):11–17

Wang M (2006) Social functions and classification of non-profit organizations. Acad Mon (09):8–11

Wang S, Ruan Z (2009) The development of social work in china under the background of harmonious society construction. Soc Sci China (05):128–140+207

Wang M, Le Y (2008) Analysis of the participation models of chinese civil organizations in public service procurement. J Party Sch CPC Zhejiang Prov Committee (04):5–13

Wang J (2015) The construction of cooperative governance in Broussonetia Papyrifera: The formation mechanism of positive interaction between government and society. Polit Sci Res (04):98–105

Wang S (2011) The embedded development of social work in China. Soc Sci Front (02):206–222

Wang S (2015) Social work mechanism broussonetia papyrifera in the networked service governance of social governance innovation. Academia Bimestris (03):47–52

Wang S (2016) The role of social work in building a co-construction and shared social governance pattern in broussonetia papyrifera. J Chin Acad Gov (01):43–47

Wang S (2014) The position and role of social work in the innovation of social governance system—A foundation- service oriented social governance. Soc Work (01):3–10+150

Wang M (2006) Experiences and insights from domestic and international NGO management. Society (02):23–26

Wang M, Jia X (2006) China non-profit organizations: definition, development and policy suggestions. 2006 Annual Report on China's Automobile and Motorcycle Parts and Supplies Industry 530–541
Webster C, Glasze G, Frantz K (2002) The global spread of gated communities. Environ Plan B Plan des 29(3):315–320
Webster C (2001) Gated cities of tomorrow. Town Plan Rev (72)2:149–170
Wei N (2003) Urban community construction and the development of community self-governance organizations. J Beijing Admin Inst (01):69–74
Wilson WJ (2000) The truly disadvantaged: the inner city, the underclass and public policy. The University Press of Chicago, Chicago
Wright Mills C (2016) The sociological imagination, 4th ed (trans: Chen Q, Zhang Y). SDX Joint Publishing Company, Beijing [American]
Wu W (2010) On the sinicization of sociology. The Commercial Press, Beijing
Wu X, Hao L (2015) Theoretical review of foreign community governance research since the "community revival movement." Polit Sci Res 1:47–58
Wu G, Yang L (2006) Community governance from the perspective of social capital. Urban Dev Res 4:25–29
Wu X (2019) Governance integration, service decentralization, and selective participation: the "composite structure of broussonetia papyrifera" in urban community governance over forty years of reform and opening-up. Chin Public Adm (7):54–61
Wu Q, Cui G (1999) Spatial differentiation patterns and formation mechanisms of residential spaces in nanjing. City Plan Rev (12):23–26, 35–60
Wu J (2012) Understanding corporatism—with a discussion on its applicability in the study of state-society relations in china. Sociol Stud 27(01):174–198+245–246
Wu X (2012) Review of research on urban community construction in China (2000–2010)—focusing on CSSCI indexed papers. J Public Adm 9(1):111–120, 128
Xi J. Earnestly unify thoughts with the spirit of the third plenary session of the 18th CPC Central Committee [EB/OL] (2013 12 31) [2019 12 25]. http://www.xinhuanet.com/politics/2013-12/31/c_118787463.htm
Xi J. Secure a decisive victory in building a moderately prosperous society in all respects and strive for the great success of socialism with Chinese characteristics for a new era—report at the 19th National Congress of the Communist Party of China [EB/OL] (2017 03 27) [2019 12 25]. http://www.xinhuanet.com/2017-10/27/c_1121867529.htm
Xia J (2010) Characteristics of governance theory and community governance research. Heilongjiang Soc Sci 2:125–130
Xia J (2012) Research on the governance structure of urban communities in China. China Renmin University Press, Beijing
Xia X (2002) Theoretical framework of community construction in china: an exploration of broussonetia papyrifera. J Peking Univ (Philos Soc Sci Ed) (1):127–134
Xiang D (2008) The development orientation and reflection of social work education in china. Soc Sci (05): 85–87.
Xiao L (2016) Community construction and reform of community governance system. Chin Inst Reform Manag 5:43–44
Xiao Y (2014) From "state and society" to "institutions and life": a perspective shift in the study of china's social transformation. Soc Sci China (9):88–104, 204–205
Xiao L (2011) "Community" research and "community research"—review of urban community research in China in recent years. Sociol Stud 26(4):185–208, 246
Xie X (2014) China's social structure and its implications—from the perspective of what kind of governance system China might establish. J Party Sch CPC Zhejiang Prov Committee 30(4):17–25
Xie C (2011) Why can those who have committed serious mistakes still gain the support of homo sapiens? Party Life (Heilongjiang) (07):52–55

Xie C, Fan X (2011) Historical enlightenment of the popularization of marxism. Seeking Truth (08):19–21

Xu X (2015b) Embedded governance: state, organization, and urban community construction—a case study of Z Street in Shenzhen City. East China University of Science and Technology, Shanghai

Xu X (2017) Organizational channels: functional positioning and action strategies of community social organizations. Soc Public Welf 2:88–89

Xu Y, Cao G (2016) Historical practice and conceptual analysis of "three-society linkage." J Yunnan Normal Univ (Philos Soc Sci Ed) 48(2):54–62

Xu X, Hou L, Xu Y (2017) Social rationality and the construction of a new social service system. Zhongzhou Acad J 1:58–64

Xu X, Huang L (2017) The socialization logic of grassroots party building—exploration and insights from Z street, Nanshan District. Shenzhen City. Leadersh Sci 20:19–21

Xu B, Li P (2012) State, society, spatial actors, power, and governance in community research—a review of recent literature on community research. J East China Univ Sci Technol (Soc Sci Ed) 27(5):36–47

Xu Y, Liwen H (2015) Grassroots construction and social governance: two propositions of current social construction in China. Hebei Acad J 35(4):110–115

Xu Y, Liwen H, Xu X (2015) New social organizations: connotations, characteristics, and development principles. Learn Pract 7:78–87

Xu X, Shen X (2008) Urban segregation of rich and poor and community stratification. J Central China Normal Univ (Hum Soc Sci Ed) 1:70–75

Xu X, Xu Y (2016) Three-society linkage" in grassroots social governance: connotation, mechanism, and practical logic—based on the exploration of Shenzhen City H Community. Soc Sci 7:87–96

Xu Y (2006) Division and cooperation between government and society: research on the reform and innovation of community construction system. Southeast Acad Res (6):51–57

Xu Y (2001) Community development theory East China University of Science and Technology Press, Shanghai

Xu M, Yang Z (2008) Controversies, misconceptions and gaps—a study on the current research status of closed residential areas from the perspective of urban design. Urban Plan Int (04):24–28

Xu D, Song W, Zhu X (2009) Formation mechanism and social space effects of closed communities. Urban Probl (07):2–6

Xu Y (1997) Governance: an interpretation of governance. Polit Sci Res(01):63–67

Xu X, Xu Y (2016) "The 'Tripartite Collaboration' in grassroots social governance: connotation, mechanism, and practical logic—based on the exploration of H community in Shenzhen." Soc Sci (07):87–96

Xu Y (2001) On resident autonomy in urban community construction. J Central China Normal Univ (Hum Soc Sci Ed) (03):5–13

Xu X (2015) Embedded governance: an analytical framework for innovation in urban community governance mechanisms—a critical reflection on the paradigm of state-society relations. Soc Work (5): 55–64, 126

Xu X (2016) Towards dual embedding: the evolution of government-society interaction mechanisms in urban community governance—an empirical study based on Shenzhen City H Community. Soc Dev Res 3 (1): 163–180, 244–245

Xun L, Bao Z (2007) Government-mobilized environmental policies and their local practices—a sociological analysis of ecological resettlement in inner mongolia's banner. Soc Sci China (05):114–128, 207

Yan J (2010) Community governance and social capital investment—theoretical explanation of innovation in Chinese community governance. Tianjin Soc Sci 3(3):59–64

Yan J (2013) Collaborative governance: the path to social management innovation—A theoretical reflection based on the state-society relationship. Chin Public Adm(02):58–61

Yang M (2016) State governance and grassroots governance from the perspective of "state-society" interconstructive relations—also discussing the historical changes and contemporary trends of governance techniques. J Guangxi Univ Natl (Philos Soc Sci Ed) 38(2):2–11
Yang M (2007) The community as a unit of national governance—a case study on residents' community participation and community cognition during the urban community construction movement. Sociol Stud (4):137–164, 245
Yang J, Ji X (2017) The historical and theoretical construction of changes in contemporary Chinese grassroots governance—based on the practice and reflection of urban grassroots governance. Mao Zedong and Deng Xiaoping Theory Res (2): 41–46, 108
Ye M (2016) Coordination of vertical and horizontal governance in urban grassroots governance: formal politics and informal politics—urban management experience from Shanghai. J Public Adm 13 (2): 128–140, 159
Ye N, Chen J (2010) Research on the mode selection and strategy of "Three-Society Linkage" in China. Nanjing J Soc Sci(12):75–80+87
Yu K (2000) Governance and good governance. Social Sciences Academic Press, Beijing
Yu K (2002) Introduction to global governance. Marx Real 1:20–32
Yu B (2007) The interactive relationship between state and society: a path for community and its organization research. Acad Res 5:91–95
Yu K, Zhang P, Zhang Z (2009) The mechanism and development trend of the privatization of urban community space—taking foreign gated communities as research objects. Urban Dev Res 16(6):94–101
Yu K (2001) Governance and good governance: a new political analysis framework. Nanjing J Soc Sci (9):40–44
Yu K (1999) Introduction to governance and good governance. Marx Real (5):37–41
Yu K (2006) Chinese civil society: concepts, classification, and institutional environment. Soc Sci China (01):109–122, 207–208
Yu J, Gao X (2012) The behavioral logic and institutional foundation of local development-oriented governments. Soc Sci China (05):95–112+206–207
Yu J, Ren Z (2012) Collaborative governance in contemporary chinese social construction: An analytical framework. Acad Mon 44(08):23–31
Zhang Y, Liu X (2015) The new normal of community governance in China since the 18th national congress. Soc Stud 5:103–109
Zhang X, Xu Y (2006) Discussion on the goals and approaches of social welfare socialization in China. Jiangsu Soc Sci 2:42–48
Zhang K (2006) The historical process towards cooperative governance. Soc Sci Hunan (4):31–36
Zhang J (1998) Political sociology and its main research directions. Sociol Stud(03):17–25
Zhang J (2001) State power construction and rural autonomous units: issues and review. Open times (09):5–13
Zhang Z (1997) The transformation of grassroots community organizations in china. Sociol Stud (04):15–25
Zhao C (2001) Urban community construction, civil society, and political development (Part Two). J Lanzhou Jiaotong Univ (05):11–15
Zhao M (2002) On organizational rationality. Sociol Stud (04):77–87
Zhe X, Chen Y (2011) Project-based hierarchical operation mechanism and governance logic—a sociological analysis of the "projects into villages" case. Soc Sci China (04):126–148, 223
Zheng H, Huang J (2012) New trends in social management and community governance in China. Gansu Soc Sci 6:1–8
Zheng H, Shao Z (2015) Applicability, localization, and internationalization of governance theory. Sociol Rev 3(2):34–46
Zheng S, Xu H, Wang H (2005) A review of grid and grid management. Syst Eng (3):17
Zheng Y (2011) Reform and Its enemies. Zhejiang People's Publishing House, Hangzhou
Zhong B (2003) Research on urban gated communities. Archit J (9):14–16

Zhou Q (2014) Grassroots governance: a discussion on modernity—a diachronic analysis of the modernization of grassroots government governance. J Central China Normal Univ (Human Soc Sci Ed) 53(5):19–28

Zhou X, Lian H (2012) The governance model of the Chinese government: a "control rights" theory. Sociol Res 27 (5): 69–93, 243

Zhou D (1993) On the urbanization of rural communities at the urban fringe—a study on urbanization in guangdong (Part 1). Sociol Stud (06):13–20.

Zhou Z, Jiang M (2013) Exploring interdepartmental coordination mechanisms of the chinese government: A narrative and diagnostic framework. Econ Res Guide 6(01):91–117+170

Zhu J (1997) Power transition in urban blocks: strong state and strong society model—an analysis of the power structure of a block. Strategy Manag 4:42–53

Zhu Y (2006) "Society and state" in modern China: a review and reflection. Jiangsu Soc Sci 4:176–185

Zhu J (2010) Between the state and the family: an ethnography of civic groups and community movements in Shanghai neighborhoods. Social Sciences Academic Press, Beijing

Zhu Q (2008) From new public management to holistic governance. Chin Public Adm (10):52–58

Zhu K (2003) On the institutional arrangement of community participation. J East China Univ Sci Technol (Soc Sci Ed) (01):13–17

MIX
Papier aus verantwortungsvollen Quellen
Paper from responsible sources
FSC® C105338

If you have any concerns about our products,
you can contact us on
ProductSafety@springernature.com

In case Publisher is established outside the EU,
the EU authorized representative is:
Springer Nature Customer Service Center GmbH
Europaplatz 3, 69115 Heidelberg, Germany

Printed by Libri Plureos GmbH
in Hamburg, Germany